Homeschooling

The Middle Years

SHARI HENRY

HOMESCHOOLING
The Middle Years

YOUR COMPLETE GUIDE TO
SUCCESSFULLY HOMESCHOOLING
THE 8- TO 12-YEAR OLD CHILD

PRIMA PUBLISHING

Library of Congress Cataloging-in-Publication Data

Henry, Shari

Homeschooling, the middle years: your complete guide to successfully homeschooling the 8- to 12-year-old child/ Shari Henry.

p. cm.

Includes bibliographical references and index.

ISBN 0-7615-2092-9

1. Home schooling. 2. Middle school education I. Title.

II. Title: Home schooling, the middle years.

LC40.H49 1999

371.042'2—dc21 99-38531

CIP

99 00 01 02 03 HH 10 9 8 7 6 5 4 3 2 1

Printed in the United States of America

HOW TO ORDER

Single copies may be ordered from Prima Publishing, P.O. Box 1260BK, Rocklin, CA 95677; telephone (916) 632-4400. Quantity discounts are also available. On your letterhead, include information concerning the intended use of the books and the number of books you wish to purchase.

Visit us online at www.primalifestyles.com

For Tim

. . .

Whose unrelenting belief that
I am better than I believe I am
encourages me to prove him right.

CONTENTS

ACKNOWLEDGMENTS

MANY THANKS to all the survey respondents, adults and children, for unselfishly giving their time and talents to help me present as fair a picture of homeschooling as possible. And special thanks to those among you who continued to answer my e-mail messages and phone calls when I needed even more information!

I'd like to thank the staff at Prima, most especially MaryBeth, for her consistent help. Thanks to Linda Dobson for asking me, "Wanna write a book?" and for everything else.

And a special thanks to the following people:

To Mom for being so persnickety about my grammar and to Dad for teaching me to defend my beliefs by poking holes in all my well-reasoned arguments

To Mark, Helen, Susannah, and the two Debbies for giving me so much editorial space over the years and encouraging me in my writing

To Maureen, a mentor, friend, and example

To Carol, Gail, and Jane for knowing me well enough to keep me humble and loving me anyway

To The Loop for telling me I can and reminding me why

To my husband and children for pulling double chore duty and keeping me grounded

And to God who makes all things possible

INTRODUCTION: THE HOMESCHOOL LEARNING JOURNEY

EVEN AS I enter my tenth year of homeschooling, I'm startled to occasionally hear others attach the word "veteran" to my name. I'm quick to think of those who went before me, the true pioneers in a movement not so long ago called "radical" or "reactionary" to the few onlookers who bothered to notice. I think of a mother who has raised eleven children to adulthood who found the time to help with my research for this book. I stand in awe of those who paved the way, long before homeschooling was a legal, much less accepted, way to educate our children.

When my children and I were out midday a decade ago, people asked, "Why aren't they in school?" I had an arsenal of quick, polite responses, and tried to avoid getting into grand discussions. I listened to the wonders of the local public school system (have you ever noticed that wherever people live is the very same place that boasts the best public schools?) as people not so subtly stated their disapproval.

Today is a different story. My fourteen-year-old enjoys the change, having been caught answering so many insipid and nosy questions over the years, including strangers quizzing him on his knowledge of math upon discovering our educational choice. Now when we're out midday, people are more likely to exclaim, "You must be homeschoolers! I wish I could do that." These people may provide a list of reasons why they can't homeschool their own children, and I'm never beyond dispelling their notions if they seem truly interested, but beyond that, their exclamation shows me that homeschooling has hit the mainstream as a valid educational option.

Parents who thought they were incapable of providing a high quality education for their children have, over time, seen a plethora of evidence to lead them to believe otherwise. Over the years homeschoolers have collectively scored an average of 20% higher than their schooled peers on standardized achievement tests. The most recent study, published by Lawrence Rudner at the University of Maryland, shows, once again, that homeschooled students typically score between 75% and 85% on standardized tests. Other studies have shown homeschoolers to be thriving socially as well, and that they are more civic-minded than their traditionally schooled peers. In fact, not a month passes when I'm not contacted via the Internet to participate in a graduate student's study of one aspect or another of homeschooling. By all accounts, homeschoolers are voracious readers, even the self-proclaimed weak ones reading more books per week than most of their non-homeschooling friends.

Homeschooling has become such a hot topic that an upper level staff member at *USA Today* wrote a glowing editorial on the subject, proudly claiming his status as a homeschool dad. My own mother researched how homeschoolers teach their children to read for her doctoral study in education.

No longer is homeschooling a journey into uncharted territory for only the most daring. Of course, some preparation and thought are in order before embarking on the trip. The more you prepare and research, the more comfort you will find in how many ways people have homeschooled successfully before you. There is no right or wrong way, only *your* way for *your* children.

In an effort to present you with the many options for homeschooling the middle years child—whether you're thinking about the trip, new to this journey, or have been traveling awhile now—I collected sixty-three lengthy questionnaires from homeschooling parents and thirty-two shorter ones from homeschooling children. Almost all of the data was collected via the Internet by either a simple request I posted on various parenting and homeschooling mailing lists or personal e-mail to a number of homeschooling friends and leaders around the country.

About one-fourth of the respondents have served as leaders in their local or state homeschooling organizations, yet they'd be quick to tell you they're not especially equipped for such a task. One of the best kept secrets of the homeschooling journey is the parents' personal growth and increased level of education as they come alongside their children to learn. As in all things, taking responsibility reaps great rewards, among them newfound interests and capabilities as you step into the delightful learning journey grounded within the safety net of your family.

Questionnaire respondents run the spectrum from those with graduate degrees to high school dropouts, from wealthy to those barely above the poverty line. They use a variety of methods and materials. Some are deeply committed to various causes within the homeschooling community (sometimes on opposing sides of one another), others simply want to educate their children in the most efficient way.

Part One of this book will introduce you to the respondents in more detail, while demonstrating the many ways homeschooling has worked for their families. You'll hear about their movement along the homeschooling continuum in eight areas: motivation, financial expenditure, approach, assessment, technology utilized, accommodations, parental involvement, and outside assistance. The continuum results will be referred to throughout the book, serving as a reminder of the many roads to a successful destination.

After meeting the families, Part One will go on to show you how to relish the joy of education while capitalizing on the special learning assets of the middle years child. Chapter Four will take you through a step-by-step checklist to get ready to homeschool, or to reevaluate what you're already doing.

Part Two moves into the nuts and bolts of curriculum choices. We'll cover the three R's in depth, and spend ample time discussing science, history and geography, foreign languages, physical education, and the fine and performing arts. In case covering these subjects sounds daunting and expensive, read on, and discover how a number of families overcome all sorts of challenges to give their children a well-rounded education. You can too.

Part Three helps you begin to put all this new information together. You may be surprised to realize how many great resources you already have on hand. If you come up short, don't worry. We have an "emergency starter kit" already packed.

Next, as travelers in this space age, we'll show you how homeschoolers incorporate the technological world into their homeschools, including computers, television, video cassette recorders, cameras, video cameras, and tape recorders. With the vast possibilities offered on the Internet, the world can truly be your child's learning oyster.

Then prepare for take-off for your trip to homeschoolers' top three destinations: the local library, your community, and homeschooling support groups.

If you think that caring for younger siblings and keeping house make homeschooling an insurmountable mountain climb, think again. Read about the gear other homeschoolers use to keep younger siblings happily occupied and included, and to keep houses from falling apart around them.

If you're impressed and intrigued but remain unable to permanently trek into homeschooling, consider trying shorter excursions. We'll show you how to complement your child's traditional schooling with part-time homeschooling.

Finally, read about how to find joy as you travel. As in all worthwhile pursuits, you will face some difficulties on your journey. Rest assured, so has everyone before you. Read about how and what homeschoolers have learned from their challenges, take note of the benefits, and then read what other parents who have completed their travels hold dear as memories of homeschooling the middle years child.

Clearly, there is no one right way to homeschool a child. Quite the contrary, once a child comes home with a committed and loving parent, there seems to be no wrong way. There are many roads to a successful homeschooling journey. So, climb aboard for the ride. You'll find lots of support and information and will reap tremendous benefits as you begin your travels. May this book help you prepare to embark on the ride of your life.

HOMESCHOOLING
The Middle Years

Part One

PREPARING FOR YOUR FAMILY'S LEARNING JOURNEY

1

THE HOMESCHOOL LEARNING JOURNEY

In This Chapter

- Where are they going?
- Why there are 1,000,001 ways to homeschool
- The amazing homeschool continuum
- It doesn't matter where you begin, just begin!
- Simple starting points
- Resources

AT THE HEART of parents' desire to homeschool their children are their goals both for their childhood and their future. It is natural to want to protect children's physical and emotional safety. Horrid stories of violence and drugs in schools used to be told from faraway cities in faraway lands. Now, most people hear such tales within miles of home—acid-laced cartoon "tattoos" being passed out on the playground, HIV-infected needles in vending machine receptacles, guns in the lockers.

Though the daily threat to eight- to thirteen-year-olds of a gundown or drug sale on the playground may still seem distant, it's naive to believe it's not a possibility. A more consistent and surreptitious threat, however, is that to the emotional well-being of your child.

The mantra of modern-day parents has become, "You teach your children what you can, then hope for the best."

> Homeschoolers have taken control, so they can do more than just hope for the best.

Homeschoolers have taken control, so they can do more than just hope for the best. Life may not offer any guarantees, but there are things we can do to work toward remedying the situation and to use these critical formative years to teach a higher standard.

Research has born out that teachers tend to choose favorite students as early as kindergarten. The favoritism continues through the years, magnified as labels are doled out. The slow learners are separated from the smart kids, each getting special attention. The majority of regular kids are lost in the vast wasteland of mediocrity, and who can't understand that?

Truth be told, almost everyone prefers to be around some people more than others. It's natural to have favorites. Most certainly, however, a person's own children qualify for such favored status. Parents tend to love even the most challenging of their children equally to the "perfect" ones, and having them home helps the parents gently bring what they see as inappropriate behavior under control in a safer emotional environment than an overly lit classroom of thirty peers. All children—be they labeled as learning disabled (LD), Attention Deficit Hyperactivity Disorder (ADHD), gifted and talented (GT), or average—are treated as unique individuals worthy of dignity within their own homes.

At home, children are loved consistently, safe from emotional distancing that comes when a teacher of thirty can't take care of one child's emotional needs while protecting another's. At home, children are protected from gun-downs, dangerous pranks, and playground bullies. At home, children can retain or regain a joyful, untroubled childhood all but lost to the rest of the fast-paced modern culture.

WHERE ARE THEY GOING?

AS YOU'LL SEE from the amazing homeschool continuum, most homeschoolers are most motivated by philosophy, religion, or politics. Conservative Christians are fed up with what they see as political correctness run amok, the purging of the impact of Christianity on our nation's founding in the history books, and science that excludes the possibility of God's creating the earth. Those who follow other faiths and practices of other cultures tire of what they see as a white Christian bias in schools, and want to help their children embrace their heritage uninhibited by the ridicule of peers who are unfamiliar with and ignorant about them. Feminists grow weary of watching little girls' math and science scores begin to drop in the sixth and seventh grades, claiming that, at home, it will remain honorable for daughters to continue to achieve high goals in those subjects. Those who cling to the importance of family decry the institutionalization of America, beginning with infants in day care at six weeks of age and continuing through thirteen years of schooling before the children reach adulthood. Homeschoolers want to reclaim that elusive thing called *childhood* for their offspring. They want timeto remember to acknowledge and celebrate life's many rites of passage. In a school culture that needs followers, they want their children to be leaders—well aware that society is crying out for more leaders of integrity.

> At home, children can retain or regain a joyful, untroubled childhood all but lost to the rest of the fast-paced modern culture.

Homeschoolers, even if not motivated primarily by academic achievement, enjoy the comparative success of their children to those in school. A dear friend of mine is raising five lovely children who consistently score exceptionally high on their yearly standardized tests. While she's quick to express her pride in them and explain that she's homeschooling for, in large part, just such academic results, she also has a fondness for exclaiming, "If I wanted to raise the best peach farmers in the South, then homeschooling would allow me to do so. That's just as honorable and important!"

Whatever your goals for your children, whatever their goals for themselves, you can give them the best possible chance of reaching those goals by bringing them home for school.

WHY THERE ARE 1,000,001 WAYS TO HOMESCHOOL

IT'S HARD TO stop people with a mission, especially when that mission involves their children. Whether motivated by fundamentalist religion or feminist ideology, the poor state of the public schools or the lack of creativity in the private ones, homeschoolers are people with a mission. Their children's academic success and exemplary character show homeschooling parents to be unstoppable.

Homeschoolers defy neat classifications. They are motivated by a variety of principles, they spend anywhere from a few dollars to thousands per year, they are spontaneous and highly regimented. Some don't own a television, others rely heavily on videos and educational programming for learning. Many use a number of outside teachers and coaches (in homeschool, private, or government-funded programs); others prefer a quieter, simpler life, rarely looking for outside assistance or activities. But they all love their children intensely and have decided to take a stand to defend a better way to educate them.

> It's hard to stop people with a mission, especially when that mission involves their children.

Everyone knows that providing one-on-one attention and capitalizing on a child's interests and abilities are two of the best teaching methods available. There's more. Parents with this level of commitment to their children will find ways to pass knowledge to them—because it's for *their* children. Parents committed at this level will find ways to revive lost family traditions and preserve them for the next generation—because it's for *their* children. Parents committed at this level will find ways to raise men and women of fine character and integrity—because it's for *their* children.

Read on to learn about the variety of means and methods homeschoolers use, knowing that each has a special story to tell, and that each child is being given the best shot at success imaginable. The most average parents care more deeply about their children than the most highly acclaimed teacher. Whether they raise the next Albert Einstein or the hardest-working peach farmer, you can be sure their children got the best they had to offer.

THE AMAZING HOMESCHOOL CONTINUUM

IN AN EFFORT to address the variety of ways people homeschool successfully, this book will provide potential travelers with more than anecdotal evidence. As you move through the pages of this book, you will read a number of real quotes from real homeschoolers, some beginners, some looking back on their trip, the majority somewhere between. You will read about the hows and whys of their excursion and perhaps find pieces of yourself in a strength here or weakness there. Gather the things that fit nicely into your luggage to pack for your own journey.

I graphed responses ranging from one to one hundred in eight categories, both for where the families are now, and where they were when they started homeschooling. I'll talk about the movement on the continuum line, that is, how homeschoolers change and adapt as they raise their children. One of the best pieces of advice I can offer prospective homeschoolers is, "Reserve the right to change your mind."

I do so almost yearly. For me, life with my children has not been static enough to permit me to remain unchanged in many of these eight categories. My family thrives just the same, as will yours.

Aside from their movement, you'll also read a lot about where the homeschoolers are today. If this survey is any indication, the statistics should encourage you that there are, indeed, 1,000,001 ways to homeschool successfully.

Meet the Respondents

Sixty-one homeschooling mothers and thirty-two homeschooling children provided us with information. They wrote from Alabama, Arizona, California, Florida, Georgia, Iowa, Michigan, Minnesota, Nevada, New Hampshire, New Jersey, Ohio, Oklahoma, Oregon, Pennsylvania, South Carolina, Tennessee, Texas, Virginia, and Washington—and British Columbia in Canada and Siberia in Russia. Three respondents did not specify where they lived.

Some homeschooling parents have only just begun their homeschooling journey, jumping in with a child between eight and thirteen years of age. Others who wrote have raised their children well into their twenties and thirties, having homeschooled for nearly two decades. Most of the respondents fall somewhere between. The number of years the respondents have been homeschooling is as follows:

One year	7	Ten Years	3
Three Years	4	Eleven Years	3
Four Years	4	Twelve Years	2
Five Years	3	Thirteen Years	3
Six Years	6	Fourteen Years	1
Seven Years	12	Over Fifteen Years	1
Eight Years	2	Unknown	3
Nine Years	7		

The number of children in each family:

One Child	10	Seven Children	1
Two Children	20	Eight Children	3
Three Children	15	Eleven Children	1
Four Children	3	Unknown	6
Five Children	2		

The ages of the respondents' children:

Some eight to thirteen, remaining children younger	21
Some eight to thirteen, remaining children older	7
All children eight to thirteen	17
Some under eight, some eight to thirteen, some older than thirteen	7
All children older than eight to thirteen	9

Six respondents said they hadn't moved along the continuum. Sometimes this was due to being a first-year homeschooler, yet one of these families had been homeschooling nine years. Furthermore, four new homeschoolers opted to only go through the continuum questions once, feeling they hadn't been homeschooling long enough to yet see any changes. One respondent did not fill out the continuum part of the questionnaire, so all figures offered in tracking movement are based on 56 total responses.

A majority of people moved in some categories but not others, and their movement was slight. In each category, however, there were a handful of homeschoolers who moved dramatically. Often these were those whose children had been pulled out of school after age eight or had undergone significant lifestyle changes that would affect their homeschooling (better-paying job, job loss, or in one case, a death of a parent).

For all the variables, a change of thirty points or more in either direction will qualify as a "significant change."

Motivation

0	100
Public school problems	*Matter of principle*

What motivates these travelers to take and continue their homeschooling learning journey?

Twenty-eight parents (50 percent) say their motivation for homeschooling has not changed, and nearly all of them began at 100 points, claiming a strong philosophical, religious, or political conviction to homeschool in the first place. As they homeschooled over the years, twenty-three (41 percent) said their philosophical reasons for doing so increased. Among those who began to homeschool due to public school problems, nearly all slid toward the right, beginning to develop philosophical reasons for doing so as well.

Five respondents (7 percent) said they moved closer to being motivated by public school problems, not necessarily relinquishing their philosophical reasons, but rather adding to them.

Twelve families (21 percent) indicated a significant change in their reason for homeschooling. All twelve moved toward stronger philosophical, political, or religious reasons for doing so.

When declaring where they were today on the continuum line, the vast majority of homeschoolers fall to the right of the midpoint on the graph (63 percent) rating philosophical, religious, or political reasons at 75 percent or higher; twenty-four families (43 percent) fall at the 100-point mark, saying those same reasons provide all the motivation to homeschool. Six families (10 percent) fall to the left of the midpoint, with three respondents (5 percent) falling at 75 percent or higher on the side of being motivated to homeschool by the problems with public schools. One mother was quick to point out that she pulled her daughter from a private school, not a public one, to homeschool her. She felt that school was a problem, whether private or public.

Financial Expenditures

0 — 100

Spend over $1500 per year — *Spend nothing*

Homeschool travelers were almost evenly divided in the amount of money they spend. Twenty (36 percent) spend the same as when they began their journey, eighteen (32 percent) spend more, and eighteen (32 percent) spend less. Of those, thirteen families (21 percent) have significantly changed the amount they spend, ten (18 percent) spending more and three (5 percent) spending less.

Today, these families are almost evenly split on what they spend as well. Twelve (20 percent) fall on the middle of the graph, spending approximately $750 per year, twenty-three (38 percent) on the right side, and twenty-five (42 percent) on the left. Fourteen families (23 percent) spend $375 or less, one traveler spending nothing at all, another "next to nothing." Twenty families (33 percent) spend $1,125 or more. The length of time of homeschooling seemed to have little impact on how much a family spends, though most veterans warn newcomers to choose carefully at first and admit to spending money on things they never used. Income level, spending habits, and general lifestyle were the more important factors in how much money a family spends on homeschooling.

Approach

0 — 100

Highly structured — *Unstructured*

Most homeschoolers move along the continuum in their approach to learning, though eleven families (20 percent) continue today with the same amount of structure they began their journey with years ago. Nine families (16 percent) became more structured in their approach over the years, often citing their core belief in the appropriateness of giving children more structured work as they got older. Two (4 percent) of these moved significantly. Thirty-six families (64 percent) moved to the right, becoming less structured in their approach, twenty-one (38 percent) of these moving significantly.

Today, eighteen of the families (32 percent) see themselves at the center of the continuum, somewhere between highly structured and unstructured. Twenty-four families (43 percent) are at 75 percent or higher on the unstructured side, nine (16 percent) see themselves at 75 percent or more structured.

Assessment

0	100
Formal testing	*Unconcerned about formal testing*

Twenty-six of the respondents (46 percent) moved to the right in assessing their children's learning, thirteen (23 percent) of them moving significantly toward not using formal testing as often, if at all. Ten families (18 percent) moved toward more regular, formal testing, four (7 percent) moving significantly. Twenty families (36 percent) did not change the way they assessed their children's learning.

Today, the families cover the spectrum. Seventeen (30 percent) of them fall on the midpoint between formal testing and not concerning themselves with such matters. Fifteen respondents (27 percent) use a substantial amount of testing, charting themselves within twenty-five points of the left side of the graph. Twenty-three (41 percent) fall within twenty-five points of the extreme right, not worrying about testing, and in many cases, being philosophically opposed to it.

Technology Utilized

0	100
No technology used	*All learning via computer and other technological means*

The amount of technology used in the homeschool environment saw more movement to the right (toward incorporating more technology into homeschooling) than any other area. While fourteen families (25 percent) have not increased or decreased their use of technology, an incredible thirty-eight (68 percent) use more technology in their homeschooling than when they started their journey. Sixteen of these respondents (29 percent) have increased the use of technology significantly, while only three of the four total who moved to the left did so significantly.

Today, however, few of these families are at the extreme right of the continuum, many using technology as enrichment or occasional lessons, and even then, only in some subject areas. Ten families (18 percent) sit at the midpoint on the graph, with only five (9 percent) to the extreme right, beyond 75 percent of their studies. Twenty-six families (46 percent) use the computer or television for 25 percent or less of their learning. Many families started their learning journeys without a computer, purchasing one after homeschooling one or more years. As children grew, so did the time they spent on the computer.

Space

0	100
A specific schoolroom set up	*No special accommodations for schoolwork*

Twenty-five homeschooling travelers (45 percent) have not changed the setup in their homes since beginning their journey. Twenty-two families (39 percent) have moved toward having no special accommodations, thirteen (23 percent) moving significantly. Eight families (14 percent) have moved to the left on the continuum, toward creating special accommodations for schoolwork, one (2 percent) moving significantly.

This continuum line of today's travelers is different from all the others in that people tend to fall within the twenty-fifth percentile of one side or another, with only a handful sprinkled on the middle ground. Fourteen (25 percent) say their homes are set up at 75 percent or more with specific accommodations for homeschooling, while thirty-four (60 percent) are at 75 percent or more with no special accommodations.

Parental Involvement

0	100
Mother; halfway point is equal involvement by both parents	*Father*

Of all the areas, parental involvement saw the least movement on the continuum. Thirty-three respondents (59 percent) claimed their situation had not changed since beginning to homeschool. Six (11 percent) moved toward the mother doing more of the teaching than when they started—none moving significantly. Seventeen (31 percent) moved to the right, with the father becoming more involved in the homeschooling, four of these (7 percent) moving significantly.

Today, three respondents (5 percent) characterize their homeschool as involving both parents equally, and 1 respondent (2 percent) said the father does 75 percent or more of the teaching. All other respondents fall on the left side of the midpoint, the vast majority, 45 families (80 percent) saying that the mother does 75 percent of the oversight of learning.

Outside Assistance

0	100
No outside help	*All learning is assisted*

Twenty (36 percent) travelers report no change in the amount of outside help they use in educating their children. Twenty-eight families (50 percent) have moved to the right over the years, including more assistance from outside sources, seven of these (13 percent) moving significantly. Eight families (14 percent) use less help than when they began their journey, one (2 percent) moving significantly in this direction.

Today, only three families (5 percent) fall at midpoint on the continuum, and five (9 percent) toward the right-hand side, finding most of their educational opportunities outside the home. The majority of respondents say the children are home for most of their learning.

Much as with technology use, it is probably fair to assume that as children grow, so will the need, desire, and willingness to find outside sources to contribute to their education.

Continuum Conclusions

> If you see yourself potentially lining up with a minority on a graph or two, don't feel alone.

People homeschool for various reasons and in various ways. If you see yourself potentially lining up with a minority on a graph or two, don't feel alone. First of all, homeschooling is perfect for individualists, so you'll fit right in. Second, to put even the one or two percentiles in perspective, multiply the survey results by the number of homeschoolers nationwide (estimated between several hundred thousand and over a million), even the tiniest percentage on this continuum of fifty-six homeschoolers finds many like minds. You may have to look a little harder, but you are not alone.

The Children's Questionnaire

Thirty-two children answered the following ten questions:

1. What is your favorite subject? Why?
2. What kinds of curriculum materials do you use to study your favorite subject?
3. What do you see yourself doing 15 years from now?
4. How do you see your homeschooling experience preparing you for that life 15 years from now?
5. What is your favorite activity outside of homeschooling? Do you like learning from other teachers/coaches? How is it different from learning at home?

6. Please list the five (5) favorite books you've read.
7. Do you like to spend time on the computer? What do you like best to do with your computer time?
8. What do you think of as your hobbies or areas of special interest?
9. What have been your favorite field trips (taken between ages 9–13)?
10. What do you like best about homeschooling?

I found the children's answers thoughtful and refreshing, and will refer to them often throughout the book. From their responses, I compiled a Top 20 Book List of no-fail titles to draw even the pickiest reader into the world of literature. Look for that in Chapter 5.

IT DOESN'T MATTER WHERE YOU BEGIN, JUST BEGIN!

EVERY TIME I SPEAK at a homeschooling fair, I can count on someone asking, "But if I'm not sure, wouldn't it be better to keep my children in school?"

Some would answer yes for a variety of reasons.

I answer an unequivocal no every time. Comparing what is going on in schools today with what is going on within homeschooling families, I think it would take a much larger degree of certainty or conviction to put my children on that big yellow bus than to keep them home with me.

At one point, today's homeschooling families were like you. Their children were like your children. The parents embarked on the journey called homeschooling with few answers as to what the future might hold. They began in different places, are in different places now, and will finish their excursion in various places still. It doesn't really matter where you are right now if you have a mission that involves the best education for your children. This book will show you how to prepare for a great trip.

> Comparing what is going on in schools today with what is going on within homeschooling families, I think it would take a much larger degree of certainty or conviction to put my children on that big yellow bus than to keep them home with me.

SIMPLE STARTING POINTS

✦ *Head for the local library or a nearby bookstore.*

Browse through some of the books listed in the Resources section at the end of this chapter. Bring home two or three that seem closest to fitting your goals, thoughts, and desires. Read the books, taking time to peruse their resource sections.

✦ *Compare the homeschooling magazines to see which is best for you.*

Send off for a sample of each of the magazines listed at the end of this chapter or check them out on the Web. Subscribe to one or two you find the most useful.

✦ *Take time going through the magazines.*

When the magazines arrive, be sure to study the ads as well as reading the articles. Resource sections of articles often mention great products as well. Begin to make a list of ideas and materials that intrigue you.

✦ *Send off for each of the catalogs.*

The catalog Web sites are helpful in getting to know the companies but I'm biased to the benefits of having a hard copy safely tucked in a big basket, marked up and tagged with Post-it notes. I grab these over and again as reference tools when my kids struggle with a certain subject or when other homeschoolers call for information. Catalogs are worth their weight in gold.

✦ *Check out various national support groups.*

Send off for introductory information or check out the Internet sites of the national support groups listed. Evaluate your needs for the information and support they offer. Consider joining as few or many as make sense for you.

✦ *Locate your state and local support groups.*

Write or call for information. Attend a meeting or two of your local groups to find the ones best suited to you.

✦ *Get information on homeschooling curriculum fairs.*

Find out when and where the state homeschooling fairs are held. Plan to attend, equipped with your list of intriguing resources. Not only will you be encouraged by the workshops but the vendor halls often boast the best selections of homeschool materials available, free of shipping charge! (If you're unsure about an item, wait. It's never worth saving nominal shipping fees for an item purchased on impulse that doesn't get used later.)

RESOURCES

Books

Here are some of the book titles mentioned most often on the questionnaires. Many will contain extensive resource sections of their own, so consider this list the first layer before digging deeper in the diamond mine of homeschooling. Look at the end of each chapter in this book for more titles specifically suited to that chapter's content.

Beechik, Ruth. *You Can Teach Your Child Successfully: Grades 4–8.* Arrow Press, 1992.

Clarkson, Clay and Sally. *Educating the Whole-Hearted Child.* For information, call 800-311-2146 or check out http://www.wholeheart.org.

Colfax, David and Micki. *Homeschooling for Excellence.* Warner Books, 1988.

Dobson, Linda. *Homeschooling Book of Answers.* Prima, 1998.

Farris, Michael, Esq. *The Future of Homeschooling.* Regnery, 1997.

Gatto, John Taylor. *Dumbing Us Down: The Hidden Curriculum of Compulsory Schooling.* New Society, 1991.

Graham, Gayle. *How to Homeschool: A Practical Approach.* Common Sense Press, 1992.

Griffith, Mary. *The Homeschooling Handbook.* Prima 1997. Also, *The Unschooling Handbook.*

Guterson, David. *Family Matters.* Harvest Books, 1993.

Harris, Gregg. *The Christian Home School.* Noble Books, 1994.

Hegener, Mark and Helen. *The Homeschool Reader: Collected Articles from Home Education Magazine 1984–1994.* Home Education Press, 1995.

Holt, John. *Learning All the Time.* Perseus Press, 1990. Also, *How Children Learn, How Children Fail,* and *Teach Your Own.*

Hood, Mary. *The Relaxed Homeschool.* Ambleside Educational Press, 1994. Also, *The Joyful Homeschool* and *The Home-Schooling Resource Guide and Directory of Organizations.*

Mackson, Rachel, and Wittmann, Maureen. *Catholic Homeschool Treasury.* Ignatius Press, 1999.

Macaulay, Susan Schaeffer. *For the Children's Sake.* Good News Publishing, 1984.

Moore, Raymond and Dorothy. *The Successful Homeschool Family Handbook: A Creative and Stress-Free Approach to Homeschooling.* Nelson, 1994. Also, *Better Late than Early, School Can Wait,* and others.

Strayer, Debbie. *Gaining Confidence to Teach.* Common Sense Press, 1997.

Swann, Alexandra. *No Regrets: How Homeschooling Earned Me a Master's Degree at Sixteen.* Cygnet Press, 1989.

Waring, Diana, and Duffy, Cathy. *Beyond Survival: A Guide to Abundant-Life Homeschooling.* Emerald Books, 1996.

Magazines

The following are the five favorite magazines of the questionnaire respondents, listed in alphabetical order. All are published bimonthly. For new homeschoolers, these magazines can be a wealth of information and philosophical encouragement. Perusing their advertisements will expose you to many helpful materials available for homeschoolers. Visit the magazine Web sites for sample articles, message boards, online chats, book reviews, resource sections, links to other homeschool sites, and listings of upcoming homeschooling conferences and seminars.

Also, be sure to ask for a copy of your local and state support group's newsletter. Over and again, questionnaire respondents said they counted on the local and state newsletters for important news and information. Check out the Resources sections in other chapters for magazines and periodicals geared to more specialized needs or interests.

Growing Without Schooling, 617-864-3100, or e-mail HoltGWS @aol.com. Sample issue $6, yearly subscription $25.

Home Education Magazine, 800-236-3278, http://www.home-ed-magazine.com, single issue $4.50, yearly subscription $24.

Homeschooling Today, 954-962-1930, http://www.homeschool today.com, single issue $5.95, introductory yearly subscription $9.99.

Practical Homeschooling, 314-343-7750, http://www.home-school .com, single issue $4.95, $10 for three issues, $19.95 a year.

The Teaching Home, 503-253-9633, http://www.TeachingHome .com, single issue $3.75, yearly subscription $15.

Homeschool Catalogs

Questionnaire respondents said these companies have been invaluable to them by providing a deluge of information, a wide array of high-quality products for all types of learners, and exemplary service. I have ordered materials from most of these companies, and have never been disappointed. Plus, the catalogs themselves are abundant sources of information too good to pass up. (Lifetime's catalog is 220 pages and Elijah Company's weighs in at just under the 200-page mark!) Send off for your copy today, but call first. Some companies charge a nominal fee. Also, keep your eyes open for the proprietors' workshops at local homeschooling fairs. They won't disappoint.

Bluestocking Press, 800-959-8586.

The Elijah Company, 888-2-ELIJAH; for curriculum counseling and questions call 931-707-1601, or visit their Web site at http://www.elijahco.com.

Greenleaf Press, 615-449-1617, http://www.greenleafpress.com.

Homeschool Supply House, 801-438-1254.

John Holt's Bookstore and Catalog, 617-864-3100, http://www.holtgws.com.

Lifetime Books and Gifts, 941-676-6311, http://www.lifetimeonline.com.

Rainbow Re-Source Center, 309-937-3385.

Sycamore Tree, 800-779-2650, http://www.sycamoretree.com.

Timberdoodle Company, 360-426-0672, http://www.timberdoodle.com.

Go online with favorite children's book publishers, too. Many of these books can be purchased at local bookstores, homeschooling conventions, and through homeschool catalogs. Check out these Web sites for up-to-date title listings.

Dorling Kindersley Family Library, http://www.dkfl.com.

Dover Publications, 31 East 2nd Street, Mineola, NY 11501.
Klutz Press, http://www.klutz.com.
Scholastic, http://www.scholastic.com/home.htm.
Usborne Books, http://www.usborne-usa.com.

Support Groups

A number of the books (*Homeschooling Book of Answers* being the most up-to-date) and magazines in this section offer extensive support group listings. The four magazines with Web pages previously mentioned all have listings or links to state, national, and foreign groups, or both. It's worth taking time to browse all of them. While much of the information overlaps, some does not. Consider the time spent a quick course in the completeness of support the homeschooling community offers.

Check out Karen Gibson's inventory of homeschooling e-mail lists, newsletters, and so on. Hands down, this is the most complete roster of e-mail lists I've seen anywhere. Whether you're looking for information or support about a specific curriculum, method, challenge, or religion, or about general state and national organizations, look here first: http://www.pipeline.com/~wdkmg/Karen/Lists.htm.

The following are some of the national groups respondents mentioned as most helpful. Each has a different focus, but all work diligently to promote the cause of homeschooling and to assist homeschoolers. You may find one—or all—to be useful. All have information about a number of other groups, and offer links to state or regional groups near you.

American Homeschool Association (AHA), 800-236-3278, http://www.home-ed-press.com/AHA/aha.html.
Home School Legal Defense Association (HSLDA), 540-882-3838, http://www.hslda.org (also, National Center for Home Education, fully funded by HSLDA, can be reached through this Web page).

National Home Education Research Institute (NHERI), 503-364-1490.

National Homeschool Association, 513-772-9580, http://www.n-h-a.org.

Moore Foundation, 360-835-2736, http://www.caslink.com/moorefoundation.

2

READY FOR SUCCESS: LEARNING ASSETS OF THE MIDDLE YEARS CHILD

In This Chapter

- Curiosity
- Independence and capability
- Perseverance
- Justice and fair play
- Compassion and kindness
- Simple starting points
- Resources

As children leave behind their early childhood years of unadulterated discovery and unparalleled energy, they enter a period most homeschoolers find equally delightful. From eight to thirteen children go through tremendous developmental changes, emotionally, psychologically, intellectually, and physically. According to questionnaire responses, the most important learning assets of the middle years child are curiosity, independence and capability, perseverance, a sense of justice and fair play, and kindness and compassion. Parents guide children who are becoming more capable, who yearn for more independence, who demand justice and fair play, who question logic and demand consistency, and who are incredibly compassionate. At the same time, the children maintain their rabid curiosity. They want to understand and to act on that understanding.

From eight to thirteen, children acquire a taste for the things of adulthood. They want more independence yet aren't quite ready to be let loose unsupervised. Volunteer and work opportunities are hard to come by (I'll explore options in Chapter 12). Middle years homeschoolers are ripe for more focused schoolwork, and for learning about good manners, hospitality and entertaining, and service to others, all to develop strong character along with strong minds. The questionnaires often mention a nineteenth-century British educator named Charlotte Mason. Her work, largely centered on instilling good habits in children during their formative years, serves as a philosophical foundation for many homeschoolers.

As children settle into their more capable minds and bodies, parents can use these years to draw out the best from their inherent learning assets. Eight- to thirteen-year-olds are ready to understand what it means to be curious without being nosy or careless, to be independent without losing an appreciation for the beauty of interdependence, to persevere while learning when it's OK to let go, to stand for compassion and justice while being compassionate and just to those who don't see things their way.

As children settle into their more capable minds and bodies, parents can use these years to draw out the best from their inherent learning assets.

These years are perfect for developing clearer communication skills. The middle years child is full of profound questions. What better way to learn good communication skills than to figure out how to find answers to big questions and then present the ideas so others might understand? The middle years child is eager to know about growing up. What a privilege it becomes helping these children harness the splendid inherent traits of their age, building their knowledge, strength, and character for a lifetime.

CURIOSITY

> *The whole art of teaching is only the art of awakening the natural curiosity of young minds for the purpose of satisfying it afterwards.*
> —ANATOLE FRANCE

AS LINDA DOBSON points out in *Homeschooling: The Early Years,* children are born curious. They want to explore. They ask endless questions. Parents of middle years children continue to list curiosity as the number one learning asset. For many subjects, children express an interest and parents need only point them to resources and provide materials. When homeschooling parents see a need for knowledge of less interest to children, they are ingenious at finding ways to awaken curiosity about those subjects as well. Most homeschooling parents view making a subject come alive for a reluctant learner as one of their highest callings. Once piqued, a child's curiosity will most often lead on to boundless discovery.

> Once piqued, a child's curiosity will most often lead on to boundless discovery.

Adults often talk about their own creativity or lack thereof, and speak with admiration or envy of those who are more creative than themselves. Homeschooling travelers report a different twist on Creative Road, however. Parents who once thought of themselves as having little or no creativity say they discover their own creativity again through homeschooling their children. They happily report helping their children rediscover creativity lost in school, and come to believe that school, by its very nature, worked to squelch that creativity.

Creativity is born from curious minds and free exploration, both of which need to be controlled in schools where curiosity and free exploration get in the way of expediency. A crowded classroom allows no quiet time for reflection or unmonitored musing. Survey responses point out that children at home aren't encumbered

> Parents who once thought of themselves as having little or no creativity say they discover their own creativity again through homeschooling their children.

by self-consciousness either. Worries don't exist about who may be watching and thinking them silly, or what onlookers might say. Children born in artistic homes talk about the vast amount of quiet time in their lives. Alone time allows children to draw on the creative depths of their minds. How can one write great stories, imagine magnificent drawings, ponder complex solutions to math problems, or envision that clever science fair project when every minute of every day is spoken for? Homeschooling provides this kind of time.

Children being pulled out of school may take some time to adjust to a slower pace. Often new homeschooling parents talk about a recovery period, an adjustment of sorts, upon removing their children from school. At the start, children may complain about being bored. Assure them boredom is a gift. While there are plenty of activities to fill homeschooling days, attempt to preserve that precious commodity of quiet time absent from the lives of their schooled peers.

If you have seen creativity wither, watch it grow as you water it and give it light at home. Sabrina, homeschooling mother of two in Texas, pulled her middle years children from school. She says, "I see the curiosity rebounding. In public school the curiosity got stifled because everything they needed was handed to them. Now they must think and choose which actions to follow through on."

Betty, homeschooling mother of an only child, agrees. She makes the following observation about creative thinking: "I think that imagination and creative thoughts can lead to linear and structured thinking but it rarely works in reverse."

Schools are concerned primarily with linear and structured thinking, which saps creativity from children. I'll discuss the academic benefits of art, music, and other creative endeavors in more detail in Chapter 8, but research shows artistic and creative endeavors enhance all other areas of learning, including the ability to think in structured ways. No evidence exists to suggest that linear thought enhances creative endeavors, though it may squelch them. You can have it both ways, but only if you allow for creativity. Your home is the perfect place to provide a better balance.

Creative homes present certain challenges, however. Phyllis, a homeschooling mother of two children in Alabama, tells of her daughter's curiosity about dead animals, "I can remember when we took her to a dissection. Her older brother and I were disgusted and decided to leave the room while she was busily digging her hands into a chicken. Another time, she begged her daddy to run down the road and get a deer's head that a hunter left behind. She hung it from a rope in our woods for weeks, observing it periodically."

> At the start, children may complain about being bored. Assure them boredom is a gift.

Phyllis tells another story that illustrates how these discoveries sometimes come up at home.

She says, "For a time, my son was so enthralled with fish that we had an aquarium in each room of the house. Gerbil tunnels graced every room as well. He could tell you more about gerbils and fish than anyone. One day, when his sister was young, she decided to see what would happen if she lightly tapped the aquarium with a hammer. Water began to pour onto the floor. My son grabbed wriggling goldfish and ran them to another aquarium, at the same time comforting his little sister saying, 'It will be OK. We can just move them to another tank and Mom will pick up the glass.' I have so many memories that I wouldn't have if they had been at school each day!"

Other mothers talk about science experiments in the kitchen or garage, mixing together simple ingredients from the cabinets and freezing them or watching them fizz. This can get dangerous! Lila, homeschooling mother of five in California, reports, "Once my son wanted to learn about combustion and nearly started a fire in the garage, not to mention leaving burnt spots in my bathroom

If you have seen creativity wither, watch it grow as you water it and give it light at home.

linoleum a few days later!" Nonetheless, it's worth the risk—it's better to teach and take reasonable precautions than to try to be perfectly safe, as the only way to do that is to do nothing at all.

Creativity grows where imagination is encouraged, or as Betty says, "Fantasy requires work."

Creative thinking shouldn't be interrupted by school bells summoning students to their next class. The same can be said for poking around in a dead chicken, building things in the garage, fooling around with magic tricks, or transporting goldfish from one tank to another. The brain is developed more fully, knowledge grasped more completely, by exploration.

Curiosity means more than allowing children access to those things that interest them. Middle years children are full of questions that are rarely possible to answer succinctly. Larissa, homeschooling mother of two in Texas, says, "They want to know everything—everything they don't already think they know, that is!"

Other homeschool travelers share similar sentiments, commenting on the fascinating and increasingly mature discussions middle years children instigate.

I remember thinking my son had a lot of questions at age three. I remember the relentless firing line of whys and what-ifs, often in the late afternoon, my most tired point in the day.

At thirteen, that same son now has much more grandiose whys and what-ifs that need to be answered, often at hours far later than my midafternoon slump. My ten-year-old daughter is following suit. Their days—filled with work, activities, and quiet exploration—are often spent on a more independent level than when they were young. By nightfall their minds slow down enough that the questions the day has posed bubble to the surface and are in need of answers.

Like the mother who was often tired in the late afternoon with toddlers' questions, I answer still. I remind myself it's a privilege to be the one being asked and I know that, like those days with little ones, these days with budding young adults will pass much too quickly.

The questions, whether about peer behavior, disturbing news items, a difficult math concept, or which book they should read next, are all part of the magical learning journey these young travelers are on.

INDEPENDENCE AND CAPABILITY

> *The great law of culture is: Let each become all that he was created capable of being.* —THOMAS CARLYLE

GRETCHEN HOMESCHOOLS four children in Tennessee. She says about her ten-year-old son, "He is so open and curious about everything. One day as he was asking his millionth question, he stopped and said, 'You know, I bet I could look that up and find out for myself!'"

They want to do it themselves. All of it. By the middle years, they often can. Middle years children can gather ingredients from high shelves, chop vegetables, set tables, arrange flowers, clean house, choose appropriate gifts for friends, mow yards, and do a number of other things they couldn't do when younger. Their newly established capability complements their desire to work more independently. The same holds true for their schoolwork.

> The brain is developed more fully, knowledge grasped more completely, by exploration.

Often, younger children resist schoolwork, not out of lack of interest or self-discipline, but out of a lack of capability. Teachers can mistake a child who doesn't want to read or write as obstinate when the child isn't developmentally ready to perform at the level expected. Their eyes may hurt if they try to focus too closely, their hands ache if they grasp a pencil too long. By the middle years, however, developmental maturity allows for more concentrated work.

Thinking of her own son and others she's observed, Renee—who homeschools one son in California—says, "They've often reached a basic physical skill for writing by this age, although many boys, especially, are still finding writing laborious."

Late readers begin to bloom in their middle years as well.

A homeschooling mother of one in South Carolina, Trudy says her daughter struggled with reading in school. She claims, "After coming home, the first time our daughter said her favorite subject was reading, we were so excited! We could not believe our ears."

Reading and writing flourish alongside the newly developed ability to think abstractly.

Kayla, homeschooling mother of two in Ohio, says, "This is the age where my children began to think abstractly. They understand cause and effect, which makes for interesting discussions about history and politics. They are physically able to engage in more intense study. My son goes camping now and really experiences the vagaries of nature. He has a basis of experience for making connections between seemingly unrelated topics. He can read a science fiction novel and relate it to Shakespeare or ancient mythology. This comes from both continued brain development and experience. It's fun to see these things come together."

Many mothers simply remark on their middle years children's willingness to learn, a willingness born from their maturity. Anna, who homeschools five children in South Carolina, says, "My daughter will take more initiative to do 'extras' without my prodding."

Unschoolers delight in watching this unhampered learning; more traditional homeschooling parents enjoy the lack of resistance to teaching. At this age, the children's cognitive development allows them to see the whys of certain subjects. Emily, homeschooling mother of two in Florida, points out, "They have developed a love of learning and are mature enough to see the benefits of knowledge."

The relentless demands of the early years child dissipate and travelers are quick to notice the relative ease of living with middle years children. Linda, who homeschools three children in Alabama, reminds us, "They are independent in their learning. It isn't necessary to hold their hand every step of the way." At this age, children read and follow through on instructions on their own, whether cooking, putting together model planes, or in one case, working with an ancient Rome kit.

People often ask how I divide my time between my ten-year-old and my thirteen-year-old. While we do a handful of projects together, they otherwise take charge of their work independently. They help choose from selected learning materials and we go over the kinds of things we think they should cover. They feel a sense of ownership over their learning and are eager to tackle the books and topics they've chosen.

Some homeschoolers exercise less control over their children's learning, some more. Regardless, the independence of this age and their increased capabilities are refreshing. Helen, homeschooling mother of two grown children from Alabama, looks back at this age, "They are so confident. They can conquer the world!"

Why not let them?

PERSEVERANCE

> *The necessity of the times, more than ever, calls for our utmost circumspection, deliberation, fortitude, and perseverance.*
>
> —SAMUEL ADAMS

CHILDREN IN SCHOOL have very little real work, even if those around them insist their schoolwork counts. Sometimes it does; mostly it's meaningless busywork. These same children have little time for real chores and real walks in the woods or real projects they conceive. They aren't learning perseverance. They're learning to tolerate and produce mediocrity.

At home, perseverance is not forced from the outside. Time on task is uninterrupted by bells signaling an end of one class and beginning of another. Homeschoolers can work a subject through to its logical stopping point or the point of mastery, however long it takes. Because homeschooling parents are on hand, children get help as they need it, not having to raise a hand or wait in line. Parents can step back if and when they believe the child needs to work something through without help, but watchful, compassionate eyes help keep frustration to a minimum while expressing expectation that the project will get finished.

Meaningless work is cut to a minimum at home, so children learn to persevere because their work is meaningful enough to persevere for. It matters to them.

TEN INDEPENDENT PROJECTS FOR KIDS

- Purchase and put together a butterfly kit or ant farm.
- Plan and plant a garden.
- Dip and decorate candles.
- Refinish a small piece of furniture.
- Plan a family meal, including writing the menu and grocery list, cooking, and serving.
- Build a bird house.
- Make paper.
- Sew a handmade quilt or natural fiber doll.
- Design and make a kite.
- Gather flowers, pine cones, or anything from your backyard or the woods and make a centerpiece for the dinner table.

Children surrounded by adults have plenty of opportunities to see models of perseverance. A lot of work worth doing includes aspects not necessarily fun to do. Middle years travelers are often crucial to running a family business or keeping a home running smoothly. They are privy to the nuances of adult conversations about work and relationships. Because homeschooling makes them part of day-to-day life, they closely watch parents work through difficult circumstances. Working through a paper or report, while not always easy, is understood as the natural course to follow.

> Homeschoolers can work a subject through to its logical stopping point or the point of mastery, however long it takes.

"At this age they have longer attention spans," Beckie, homeschooling mother of two from Washington, says. "My son is just starting to get over giving up hard things when he gets frustrated. His perseverance is starting to kick in."

Laura, who homeschools three children in Alabama, echoes Beckie's sentiments, "My children are able to spend many hours focused exclusively on a single pursuit. They have good memory skills and are able to memorize large and detailed blocks of information."

Often, an intense area of interest spills over into all subjects, serving as a useful springboard to facilitate the entire scope of their education. Mary Sue, homeschooling mother of three in South Carolina, says, "[My son's] interest in weather is the single most inspiring learning experience he has had. It has spurred interest in all areas of a traditional curriculum and has maintained intensity through the years."

Judy, who homeschools three children in Alabama, has seen the same thing in her home. She says, "Kids at this age have a desire to dig into something that interests them and become little experts." She continues, "Our son enjoyed dismantling things like old televisions and radios. We also have found them to be avid collectors of rocks, stamps, shells, leaves . . . you name it!"

Middle years children are fascinated with technological tinkering, and enjoy fixing things as well as creating them from scratch. They want to figure things out for themselves.

Like other homeschoolers, Deb, who preferred not to identify her home state, delights that her son is "able to satisfy his curiosities mostly on his own."

During these years, children may move from an hour or two of academic work to several hours a day, not always because parents perceive a need to do so, but because they want to. They leave these glorious middle years with a strong foundation in perseverance that will carry them through their final years of journeying as homeschooled students and beyond.

JUSTICE AND FAIR PLAY

Ius est ars boni aequi (Justice is the act of the good and the fair)

"I LOVE how this age is learning to question the rights and wrongs of the world," says Betty. "They are beginning to understand that the world is made up of many very different peoples and ideas. They are starting to shape their own ideals and values."

Many homeschoolers begin to dabble more in the great big world around them at this age. Parents may find sports, art classes, or a host of other group activities for a middle years child, all to bring forth talent or capitalize on an interest. Homeschool children are quick to notice the injustices of the group mind-set accompanying these activities. Rarely will a homeschooling parent punish all the children in the family for the wrongdoings of one child, yet punishing all for the misdeeds of one is common practice in many group activities and in classrooms across America.

It's not uncommon for a ball team to all run laps as retribution for the goofing off of a handful of players, for hockey players to skate "suicides" for the lack of attentiveness of one or two, or for a group of swimmers to swim an exceedingly difficult set because a small percentage didn't do the original set correctly.

My son and I were once told that the peer pressure of the kids who had unjustly endured the punishment helped the coaches enforce order. I thought the coaches shouldn't rely on children to do their jobs for them and resented my child being punished when he had done no wrong.

School parents complain less about this sort of thing because, by and large, it doesn't bother their children as much. The children are numbed to the inherent injustice of group punishment because it's standard practice as part of the classroom management they're subject to seven hours a day, five days a week.

These types of things *should* bother children at this age because they *are* unjust. Homeschools are great proving grounds for justice and fair play because they are free from such injustices and provide time for discussion and modeling to the contrary.

COMPASSION AND KINDNESS

No act of kindness, no matter how small, is ever wasted. —AESOP

MUCH AS CHILDREN are prone to lose their sense of justice if they are surrounded by constant injustices, they will just as likely lose their sense of compassion when surrounded by too much callousness. Kids get tough by learning life's lessons on the playgrounds, it's said. No one questions how much is too much or why people think toughness is a virtue to be developed for young children—until a few teens dubbed geeks blow away a library full of more popular kids on an otherwise ordinary April school day in Colorado.

Like a hothouse that gives plants a chance to grow strong before they have to stand against gale force winds and pounding hail, homeschooling gives children a chance to grow and develop in a safe environment. Homeschooled children grow strong in kindness and compassion before facing the sometimes brutal elements of human interaction later in life.

I've seen the need for this most plainly when middle years children are faced with the death of someone or something they love. Eight- to thirteen-year-olds suffer loss in a more profound way than younger children who don't quite grasp the permanency of death and in a less sophisticated way than older children who are more able to sort out their feelings. The middle years child will often need to erect elaborate memorials to dead gerbils and may take weeks to get over a death of a beloved family cat or dog.

My family's two Labrador retrievers recently died. My middle years children needed a unique-to-this-age-level chance to mourn. Homeschooling provided just that, and both are better off for it. They are better able to be good friends to those who go through similar things. They are better able to give themselves permission to be sad when life is sad, without being told to buck up or bounce back way before they feel like bucking or bouncing.

Homeschooled children grow strong in kindness and compassion before facing the sometimes brutal elements of human interaction later in life.

Homeschoolers tell charming stories about families helping and praying for others. A few parents wrote that their children automatically begin to pray if they see an ambulance pass by, for instance.

These children are learning compassion and kindness because they are living it. They are often eager to help others, and are ready to begin to serve the community at large as well. Jennie, homeschooling mother of two girls in Minnesota, sums up this age beautifully, "The middle years child is inquisitive, tenacious, refreshingly unjaded, hysterically funny, and extremely passionate about life!"

We can all learn from them.

SIMPLE STARTING POINTS

✦ *Visit your library or bookstore.*

Check out the resource section for books you'll find useful. If you're unfamiliar with the general capabilities of this age, you may want one of the basic child development books listed in the Resources section to have as a reference.

✦ *Encourage creativity and independence.*

Consider keeping some of the books with project ideas on hand. Order a Hearthsong catalog or visit their Web site. Have children make lists of items they need for projects of interest and help them locate those items.

✦ *Encourage children to work independently.*

Go through the independent project list in this chapter with your child, looking for ideas that spark an interest.

✦ *Continue to read aloud.*

Sometimes read-aloud time begins to fade at this age. Look into the character books listed in the Resources section for books made up of bite-sized readings. These portions are manageable enough for the family to share during a lunch break.

RESOURCES

Books

Child Development and Education

Ames, Louise Bates, and Ilg, Frances L., M.D. *Your Ten to Fourteen Year Old.* Delacorte Press, 1989. Also, *Your Eight Year Old: Lively and Outgoing,* and *Your Nine Year Old: Thoughtful and Mysterious.*

Elkind, David. *The Hurried Child: Growing Up Too Fast Too Soon.* Perseus Press, 1989.

Healy, Jane. *Your Child's Growing Mind: A Guide to Brain Development from Birth to Adolescence.* Main Street Books, 1994. Also, *Endangered Minds: Why Our Children Don't Think.*

Mason, Charlotte M. *The Original Home Schooling Series.* Tyndale House, 1989. (Originally published in 1935.)

Character Building: For Parents

Glaspey, Terry. *Children of a Greater God.* Harvest House, 1995.

Kilpatrick, William, and Wolfe, Gregory and Suzanne M. *Books That Build Character: A Guide to Teaching Your Child Moral Values Through Stories.* Touchstone, 1994.

Character Building: For Children

Bennett, William J. *The Book of Virtues for Young People.* Simon & Schuster, 1997.

Canfield, Jack, Hansen, Mark Victor, and Kirberger, Kimberly. *Chicken Soup for the Teenage Soul.* Health Communications, 1997. Also, *Chicken Soup for the Teenage Soul II.*

Canfield, Jack, Hansen, Mark Victor and Patty, and Dunlap, Irene. *Chicken Soup for the Kid's Soul.* Health Communications, 1998.

Project Ideas for the Middle Years Child

Beard, Daniel C. *The American Boy's Handy Book: What to Do and How to Do It.* Centennial edition. Godine, 1998.

Beard, Lina and Adelia. *The American Girls' Handy Book: How to Amuse Yourself and Others.* Godine, 1987. (Originally published in 1887.)

Burns, Marilyn. *I am Not a Short Adult: Getting Good at Being a Kid.* Little, Brown, 1977.

Child, Lydia Maria. *The Girl's Own Book.* Applewood Books, 1991. (Originally published in 1834.)

Clark, William. *The Boy's Own Book.* Applewood Books, 1996. (Originally published in 1829.)

Kids Shenanigans: Great Things to Do that Mom and Dad Will Barely Approve Of. Klutz Press, 1992.

Walker, Lester R. *Carpentry for Children.* Viking, 1985. Also, *Housebuilding for Children.*

Catalogs

One catalog appeared in so many surveys that it warrants being listed here by itself. The Hearthsong catalog has won The Parent's Choice Award for ten years and offers the widest array of fun and worthwhile toys and creative kits for children available.

Hearthsong, 800-325-2502, http://www.hearthsong.com.

3

THE JOY OF LEARNING WITH THE MIDDLE YEARS CHILD

In This Chapter

- Pathway to knowledge
- Pathway to social opportunity
- Pathway to strong families
- Pathway to safety
- Pathway to health
- Pathway from school to home
- Simple starting points
- Resources

MIDDLE YEARS CHILDREN are full of life and bursting with burgeoning capabilities. Travelers use the word "joy" again and again to describe homeschooling their eight- to twelve-year-old children. Challenges arise, however. Some children can sit and read or listen for hours. Others move incessantly. While they may share many of the same learning assets, each child has a unique way, or style, to best assimilate knowledge. Figuring out your child's learning style and teaching to it as much as possible will help keep the joy in your homeschool.

PATHWAY TO KNOWLEDGE

TAKING FULL RESPONSIBILITY for their children's education, homeschooling parents become quick experts in discerning learning styles. Working one on one, parents help children capitalize on their strengths and build up their weak areas. Most homeschool conferences offer workshops that help parents identify, then work with, their children's individual style.

Getting to know their children more intimately, parents can convey not only academic knowledge but also ideas about values, growing up, safety, and health. Middle years children are eager to explore.

A Trip That Fits Your Child's Learning Style

Homeschooling parents identify their children's learning style more clearly and can facilitate an education that fits more closely than any schoolteacher ever could. Living with our children, we watch them tackle projects and notice those things they can do with ease and staying power.

It's not uncommon for a wiggly child (kinesthetic learner) to be reprimanded in school for not being able to sit still. At home, this same child may play with Legos, work on models, or draw for hours on end. Parents take note of this ability to focus. Driven by their love for their child and unrestrained by the competing needs of large numbers of children in a classroom, parents are better positioned to bring out the best their children have to give.

There are times a wiggler needs to be still at home, but they are fewer and further between, and homeschooling parents can offer more breaks. The same holds true with other learning styles, for example: auditory learners can learn by listening to audiotapes or talking with their parents, visual learners can focus on a book or computer CD, children who learn best alone can do so, and children who thrive on group interaction can participate with siblings, parents, or other small groups of homeschoolers.

One of my children is a kinesthetic learner. It took me a few years to embrace the notion that movement helps her assimilate knowledge. With time, she's learned to be still when the situation calls for it (theater, church, ballets, and so on). Generally, though, she learns best while moving, so move she shall.

Begin to think about whether your child learns best by listening, looking (reading), doing, touching, or in groups or alone. If you lean toward unschooling, the child's learning style will direct the learning process and you can use the information to recommend materials that may be useful. If you use a formal curriculum, you'll want to know whether or not it's designed to meet the needs of your child. A little knowledge about learning styles will carry you a long way on the road of homeschooling.

> Driven by their love for their child and unrestrained by the competing needs of large numbers of children in a classroom, parents are better positioned to bring out the best their children have to give.

Sally homeschools two children in Nevada. She's thankful her children are "getting an education tailored to their learning styles and, to a certain degree, their interests."

Sally's daughter isn't interested in math, but has come to an understanding that she'll study it anyway. By meeting her daughter's needs and teaching to her learning style, Sally makes it easier for the child to buckle down for those subjects she doesn't particularly like.

Sally explains one way she's done this. "My daughter has learning difficulties and minor ADD," she says. "We go on hikes at a local conservation area. With the hands-on approach, she has learned so much that she is ready to give scientific names for many of the area plants."

Katrina, homeschooling mother of four in Oklahoma, has seen the same things. "Many times, my children see something in nature and want to find out more about the topic," she says. "We find bugs in the pasture. The children search and see who can fastest identify the bug. They also figure out which crops will come up first in our garden. When we began going to a local nursing home, the children were so confused about the process of life, they initiated a study about the human body and aging."

In an attempt to meet the variety of learning styles of children, schools must label and categorize. At home, you don't have to.

Renee pulled her son out of a private school to homeschool him. She says, "He's always been very bright and learned easily, but not in the way the schools require. With homeschooling, we could forget all those traditional ways learning is 'supposed' to be done and let him learn in his own way, or find ways to facilitate his learning. He's been like a sponge, because he is learning in his own way."

Catherine homeschools one of her two sons in Alabama. She says her eight-year-old does his independent work in a tent made of sheets. This suits his learning style and helps him focus, and would never be allowed in school.

It's hard to stop a homeschooled child from learning, whether on hikes, collecting bugs, or under a makeshift tent at home.

Building Up Strengths, Shoring Up Weaknesses

With the best will in the world, no hired teacher can care about any individual child as much as that child's parents can! So children who struggle in certain areas profit by getting more attention at home with a parent than they could possibly get at school. Few children are strong in all areas, and homeschooling parents often face the task of figuring out how to address specific problems. Support groups, conferences, and homeschooling publications offer encouragement from those who have walked the road before you, whether the problem is as minor as a resistance to writing or as major as a pronounced learning disability.

While Renee found her son blossoming at home, she couldn't deny he struggled with reading. She says, "When he was twelve, we found out he had vision skill deficiencies that made reading laborious for him. Once he went through vision training with a certified developmental optometrist, he became a voracious reader and went right into reading adult level, fine-print books. Before that, he didn't even care to read fourth- or fifth-grade level literature."

Vision therapy has helped a lot of homeschoolers. Others have tried different roads that have taken them to equal success. Homeschooling parents are tenacious in finding the right remedy for whatever ails their child's learning.

My son couldn't decode words until he was nine years old, and didn't read fluently until he was ten. I'm thankful he hadn't been labeled for years in school, but instead, could grow into his reading in much the same way other children grow in other areas.

Various problems require various kinds of help. I'll talk more about labels and how parents deal with learning difficulties in Chapter 9, but many parents find a good bit of success by teaching to the individual child, regardless of diagnosis or misdiagnosis.

While in school, Renee's son had been "mislabeled one thing or another." She says the family never "took the labels too seriously," rather, at home, "he was able to take his time and learn in his own style. Finding what learning methods worked well for him made all the difference. It was an ongoing process. I gathered books about things that interested him: magic tricks, science and nature, weird things, myths. He amassed an enormous body of knowledge during those years."

Homeschooling parents are tenacious in finding the right remedy for whatever ails their child's learning.

Labeled, mislabeled, or without labels at all, children benefit by having parents who know them well enough to know when to back off and when to encourage further work, not because the class is doing it, but because it's something the parent and child need to see worked through.

Missy homeschooled two boys through high school in California. She remembers the great benefit of knowing when to let one "work out problems on his own and not automatically give him the answers." She explains, "He developed a confidence about doing things on his own, which has stayed with him. To this day, he is very strong."

That kind of strength can be developed more fully at home, where children are safe from the emotional beating down common among peers at this age. As children move from eight to thirteen, they become increasingly brutal in school.

Sabrina says, "Middle school is a hard age. Everyone is developing so differently. Cliques are difficult for the most resilient of kids. Our son was not ready for the emotional trauma. We wanted to have time to develop strong coping skills and to learn to stand up to peer pressure. At home, his personal strengths develop and he can face his weaknesses without the constant critiquing of peers."

Children's maturity and development vary widely within this age group. It makes sense to give them room to mature at their own pace and to tackle learning in a way that suits them. They will be better off for the time spent being safely nurtured at home and having learning tailored to fit their minds and souls.

PATHWAY TO SOCIAL OPPORTUNITY

HOMESCHOOL TRAVELERS with children this age are frequently asked about the social opportunities their children are missing. Schools regularly host dances for younger and younger children. Fifth- and sixth-grade girls receive engraved jewelry from little boys across the room.

I've yet to meet a homeschooling parent who is disappointed about missing out on these pre-mating rituals, and questionnaires were filled with similar thoughts. Parents are also happy to be missing out on playground bullies, snobbish cliques, racism, ridicule of their children's faith, impersonal classroom learning, and barely edible school lunches.

Non-homeschoolers seem genuinely surprised when they discover that, despite these sentiments, homeschoolers aren't as isolationist as they might have suspected. (Though who can blame those who are?) Most middle years children are active in sports and music, theater and dance, and a host of other activities, often in large groups. The homeschooled children notice a difference between exclusively homeschool groups and others, though some seem to care less than others about those differences. My son's activities throw him with children from various schools in the area, but my daughter prefers an exclusively homeschooled horseback riding class to others she's tried. I'm thrilled I have choices to fit the needs of my unique children.

After pulling her two boys out of school, Missy felt the only compensation for social opportunities she had to make was "to keep them involved in sports activities. We live in a rural area and there were no neighbor children to play with. Sports provided physical exercise and friends, and taught them good sportsmanship."

Gail, homeschooling mother of two in Arizona, says, "We created our own social opportunities such as a homeschool Girl Scout troop, lunch dates with our homeschooling friends, field trips, and a junior high co-op."

Middle years children are ready to take on bigger things. Parents who are closely watching are there to help them find those things without letting go of the safety net of homeschooling.

Rose homeschools two daughters in Minnesota. She says, "It's difficult to find meaningful opportunities to interact in the 'real world' when the child isn't old enough to work or participate in many volunteer activities. Children in this age group are often ready to leave behind 'kid' clubs and classes and are eager to participate in the next step up but can't find a way to do so. My daughter with strong veterinary interests is too young to work at Animal Humane Society, a vet clinic, or a stable."

Despite being shut out of some opportunities, middle years children can learn to practice service, good manners, and hospitality at home (see "Service Ideas" sidebar in Chapter 12). They relish creating party invitations and thank you notes. They can help their mother as she readies the house for overnight guests or dinner company by creating a centerpiece or making part of the meal. They learn to interact with adults on a polite basis because they are treated as a respected part of the world around them.

My ten-year-old daughter, Bekah, desperately wanted to host a slumber party for her most recent birthday. She poured through party planners, cookbooks, and sale flyers. She planned the tiniest minutiae of the party, wrote a list of those things she needed, staying within the budget I'd given her. She wrote a menu for dinner, snacks, midnight munchies, and breakfast, and planned special games and crafts. The girls who attended were kept busy right up until they were ready to sleep, and awoke ready to finish any crafts they hadn't done. Two mothers later phoned to say their daughters wanted Bekah to help them plan their next parties.

I'm not sure Bekah could've pulled this off if she were in school. Her time would have been more limited, for one thing. Since she was old enough to hold a spoon and stir batter, she has had time to stand at the counter and help me prepare for guests. Now entertaining is second nature to her.

You can find social opportunities whenever and wherever you like. More important, you can teach excellence in behavior along the way, something sorely missing in our culture as a whole.

PATHWAY TO STRONG FAMILIES

HOMESCHOOLERS HAVE A vested interest in peaceful coexistence among family members. They're together constantly. Practice may not make perfect, but siblings learn to get along and grow deeply committed to one another. To make it to their final destination intact, homeschooling families learn the arts of caring, compromise, and communication. While veteran travelers have grown accustomed to this route, those newer to the journey remark enthusiastically about this closeness, the time together standing in stark contrast to when their children were in school.

> Homeschoolers have a vested interest in peaceful coexistence among family members. They're together constantly.

Homeschoolers cherish time. Time with family. Time to be together. Time to get to know one another. Time to travel to see grandparents. Time to stay in touch with those far away. Time to invest in siblings. No doubt, homeschooling builds strong families, both nuclear and extended. Families are able to stay more intact by sharing their values and passing them on to their children at home. Homeschool travelers unabashedly admit to feeling fortunate to, as one mother put it, "keep out the negative influence of peer pressure and the schools."

The middle years homeschoolers agree. They are thankful for being able to be home with their family each and every day.

Immediate Family

Janine, homeschooling mother of two in Georgia, voices sentiments similar to those of many on the homeschool journey. She says, "I love the family time. It is so easy for children this age to become dependent on peers for self-worth. I am proud of my son's handling of some tricky situations. I believe he was able to make wise decisions because he sees the adults in his life working through difficult decisions together." She continues, "Watching and living with adolescent mood swings can be hard, but it's better than if they had to go through this stage in school."

Larissa agrees, "Being with my son all day during those 'adolescent attitude periods' is good because we can work on them as they pop up."

Mothers of girls notice the same thing.

Rose says, "The greatest benefit has been managing to stay close to my daughter and remaining her confidante during a time many kids pull away. The mood swings can be difficult, but they pass with time. She told me all her heartaches. I don't think I would have had this privilege had she been in school with friends. I think the 'boy thing' and dating have been delayed dramatically. This is another way homeschooling allows them to grow more fully into who they are and not to follow the leader."

The preteens remain close to their siblings as well. They share science experiments and nature hikes in the woods, and vie for space near Mom when she reads aloud. They are so accustomed to being together that they don't consider separating in the same way that schooled children do. My six-year-old was a welcomed guest at her older sister's birthday party.

Homeschooled children value the quiet time together most. They enjoy clearing cupboards to come up with science experiment material, running out during a storm to get drenched in the rain, talking, reading, and playing with their siblings.

Larissa says, "I value the lifestyle. We have time to talk. When the boys experience something that excites them, they run to me to share."

Homeschooling parents appreciate the outward affection their middle years children display, at the same stage their schooled peers begin to separate from their parents. Kayla echoes many travelers when she says, "Best of all, he still gives his mom a hug and a kiss, says 'I love you,' and doesn't care who is listening."

Extended Family

The freedom of homeschooling allows families to visit grandparents and other relatives any time that suits them. Whether it's a fun-filled visit or an emergency excursion to help aging grandparents, homeschoolers can pick up and travel without the constraints of the school calendar.

> Whether it's a fun-filled visit or an emergency excursion to help aging grandparents, homeschoolers can pick up and travel without the constraints of the school calendar.

Emily says her children "help me care for their elderly grandparents, whom we moved into one of our rental houses across the street. My father is eighty-four and has Alzheimer's disease."

What more meaningful way could children spend their days?

Encourage grandparents to share family stories and traditions with their grandchildren. My mother-in-law visited last fall and taught the girls how to weave a Swedish pattern. The girls have always been interested in their Swedish ancestry and were thrilled to be able to learn an art form unique to their heritage.

Children today are losing their sense of family heritage. Homeschooling affords my family the opportunity to hold on to ours. My father gave my son a marine helmet from World War II. It had been my grandfather's. The simple, aging helmet piqued an interest. My son researched the years my grandfather had lived and wrote a lengthy report about his life and times.

We cook old family recipes and I share stories about my childhood memories of meals that included them. The children almost always ask for "one more story." They love to hear about ancestors—famous, infamous, and unknown. Studying their family heritage incorporates history, geography, reading, writing, researching, and other subject areas that may have interested the people they're studying.

Keeping memorabilia is a good way of preserving history for future generations. Children can learn to think in terms of world history by starting with their family's history and moving outward. Many homeschoolers share the hobby of scrapbooking. Children practice artistic skills, handwriting, and journaling while recording important events of their lives for future generations.

Whether enjoying the present or leaving a heritage for future generations, spending time with and learning about extended family is a worthwhile pursuit.

Values

Parents across America decry young people's lack of values. When children spend the better part of their lives being influenced by young peers, no one should be surprised that high standards taught at home wax and wane, and often don't survive. At home, the primary role models are parents and parents' friends. Children watch adults around them go through a number of difficult circumstances. They see behavior tempered by time and wisdom rather than impulse and immaturity. (I'll talk more about being your child's primary role model in Chapter 4.)

While some homeschooling parents use specific values or religious curriculum, most say they simply try to live out their beliefs and talk about why they believe and behave the way they do. Some families volunteer in their communities and hope that doing so conveys the importance of giving selflessly of their time to their children. Many attend religious services and activities, and about half say they use the Bible to teach values.

> When children spend the better part of their lives being influenced by young peers, no one should be surprised that high standards taught at home wax and wane, and often don't survive.

Rachel homeschools her daughter in Pennsylvania. She says, "We practice our religion and that shows our values. I model generosity and other moral and ethical values every day. We give *tsedaka* (roughly translated as charity, though it really means justice) every week. We are able to help others. We compare the importance of everyday things in our lives and we talk and share ideas."

"I deal with issues as they come up," says Kayla, "although I've used materials for some lessons. I hope my children learn by example as well. As my son has become involved with other teens, I've been pleased to see he thinks for himself. He's not impressed with gossip about pregnancies, dating, or drug use. Both of my children seem to have a good grasp of the Golden Rule, which is my main teaching tool. It takes time I don't think we'd have if they were in school all day."

Whether hearing siblings bicker over whose turn it is to get the front seat of the car, being handed too much change when purchasing candy at the theater, or watching a parent handle a rude salesperson, children will have lots of questions and time to observe. These teachable moments are priceless.

Janine says she and her husband have "been very clear about what we consider to be ethical conduct. Politeness, honesty, and family loyalty are mandatory. We insist they write thank-you notes for gifts."

Parents who sent their children to private schools they carefully chose share a distinct disappointment when they realize the schools are at odds with their family's values. Renee says, "It never occurred to me that school was going to be as bad for my son as what I had observed in schools as a teacher. I thought a private school that claimed to share our values would make a difference. It didn't. I got tired of teachers telling us how we should be raising our child or how he should be spending his time or how he should be learning."

The middle years are too crucial to allow too many outside influences that contradict the parents' values. "This is an age when kids seem to be forming their view of the world," says Judy. She continues, "They seem open and tenderhearted. I wouldn't trade anything for the opportunities I have had to influence and challenge my kids."

Homeschoolers realize the great privilege of allowing children to develop in their own way to fulfill their unique potential away from peers. Rose says, "I think the junior high years are particularly dangerous for girls. These are often the years when good reading, music, and wardrobe choices are set aside for whatever is popular with the reigning group in schools. I would rather give my daughters the opportunity, freedom, and environment to discover who they are and what their true interests are, uninfluenced by peers. I also think it's important to allow them to follow their individual rates of maturation and not be rushed to discard various elements of the younger years until they are ready to do so voluntarily."

Homeschooling allows them to do just that.

PATHWAY TO SAFETY

THE MORNING NEWS reports another horrific shooting in a public school. Children are getting into more and more troublesome situations at increasingly younger ages. They are expected to be prematurely sophisticated at ages we should be protecting their naïveté. Shortly after the shooting at Columbine High School in Littleton, Colorado, a major news network aired a feature on whether or not homeschooling would be an answer to the violence for some families. Homeschool groups across the country were reporting record numbers of phone calls coming in as people asked about homeschooling their children in reaction to the massacre.

Children are getting into more and more troublesome situations at increasingly younger ages.

The growth of school violence has become a legitimate reason to consider homeschooling. The major shootings we hear about on television are only the extreme tip of the iceberg. Guns are found in lockers, children get into fistfights on playgrounds and in school buses, and drug use and sexual activity are commonplace. We can't pretend that premature sexual activity is not a safety issue anymore, and driving under the influence of drugs and alcohol is a growing killer among teens.

Some people continue to accuse homeschoolers of isolating their children. My response: "Why aren't you isolating yours from such things?"

Homeschooled students are active in their community, excel academically, and have plenty of friends, without the modern-day risks of attending school.

PATHWAY TO HEALTH

AS CHILDREN ENTER their middle years, personal health and hygiene become increasingly important. Preteens become more private, more modest, and more diligent about wanting to look and feel good. I'll address physical education and exercise in Chapter 8. For now, think about the fifth- or sixth-grade health class, when children learn about their changing bodies.

Homeschooled students are active in their community, excel academically, and have plenty of friends, without the modern-day risks of attending school.

Only the boldest ask questions, though most girls and boys have plenty to ask. Whether classes are co-ed or with those of the same sex only, learning about sensitive issues in a group setting at such a formative age is awkward at best, cruel at worst.

Naturally, many homeschooling parents are not especially comfortable approaching the happenings of puberty with their children, though most look back and say it was a good thing to have done on their own. Some parents use specific materials or books (see Resources section), others have open discussions, and still others take their middle years children out for a special meal or celebration to mark the entry into a new stage in life.

Children this age are increasingly interested in maintaining good health. Parents comment that by bringing their children home, they see an increase in their physical health and stamina. The children are able to sleep when they need to, eat healthier foods, and accommodate outside activities more readily.

Janine says, "At this time of life when so many bodily changes are taking place, it's normal to need to eat and sleep whenever one needs to and my son has that option."

School districts around the nation have considered trying to implement later school starting times for middle years and teenaged students, but it's logistically difficult. It's not a big deal at home.

Perhaps most important, chubby preadolescents and lanky early teens can pass through these phases in the emotional safety of their home, without having the an entire school population watch and remark on it.

PATHWAY FROM SCHOOL TO HOME

I WAS SURPRISED by how many of the survey respondents had pulled children out of school during these middle years. There is an increasing awareness about the difficulties of this age and the critical nature of what the children are learning, both by direct teaching and osmosis. Parents and children may take a while to adjust, but all report great benefits.

Judy says, "There was an adjustment period for me having my son suddenly home all the time after being in school for more than two years. I could no longer do what I wanted while my preschoolers napped, and was uncomfortable about being out during school hours with an obviously school-aged child." She continues, "I became better at having conversations with him and thinking up ways to involve him around the house. Homeschooling oriented me more toward my home and made me want it to be the best place my kids could be."

The initial transitional period may be bumpy, but payoffs come quickly.

Within one year of homeschooling, Sabrina says, "[I saw] an overall reversal in the attitudes and behaviors of the boys. They had been exposed to so much that they forgot how to be polite and kind, especially to each other. This past Christmas was one of the best holidays we ever shared. There was an ease and calm we had not previously seen."

Beth agrees. "I'm so glad to always have them with me now. We are closer than ever before. When they were in school we didn't know each other as well because they were gone so much of the time."

It doesn't take long for homeschool travelers to see that they are more committed to their children's education than any school could ever be.

Sally says, "No one in the system cares as much about my children's education as I do, nor do they have the time and energy to dedicate to my children's education. My children, who formerly got lost in the crowd, are now standing up for themselves. My daughter used to think she was stupid because she didn't learn the same way as other children. We've been able to help her see her many strengths and how these can help her overcome any weaknesses."

Teaching to fit children's individual needs, helping them fill in gaps where needed, providing wholesome and meaningful social opportunities, building strong families and passing on unique family heritage, keeping them safe and healthy—these are the kinds of gifts you'll be giving to your children when you bring them home to school.

SIMPLE STARTING POINTS

✦ *Familiarize yourself with basics of learning styles.*

Read Armstrong's or Tobias' book or attend a workshop at a local homeschooling fair.

✦ *Make time for your children.*

Don't rush into too much school or too many activities when they first come home. Schedule tea parties, paint each other's nails, take hikes in the woods to collect bugs and leaves, build a fort.

✦ *Teach your children good manners.*

Practice manners at home. Children this age are usually wide open for learning the reasons for manners and how to put them into practice.

✦ *Come up with a game plan for how you will approach discussing puberty with your sons and daughters.*

Look through the materials listed. Choose ones you're most comfortable with and incorporate them into your homeschooling.

✦ *Teach your children their family heritage.*

Begin by having children write a short paper on a grandparent. Consider the hobby of scrapbooking.

RESOURCES

Books

Learning Styles and Parenting

Armstrong, Thomas, Ph.D. *In Their Own Way*. Tarcher, 1988. Also, *Seven Kinds of Smart* and *Awakening Your Child's Natural Genius.*

Elkind, David. *Ties that Stress: The New Imbalance*. Harvard University Press, 1995.

Markova, Dawna. *How Your Child is Smart: A Life-Changing Approach to Learning.* Conari Press, 1992.

Tobias, Cynthia. *The Way They Learn*. Focus on the Family Publishing, 1996. Also, *Every Child Can Succeed: Making the Most of Your Child's Learning Style, Bringing Out the Best in Your Child,* and *Do You Know What I Like About You?*

Manners and Etiquette

Barnes, Emilie. *A Little Book of Manners: Courtesy and Kindness for Young Ladies.* Harvest House, 1998.

Harris, Gregg and Joshua. *Uncommon Courtesy for Kids*. Noble Books, 1990.

Holyoke, Nancy, *Oops! The Manners Guide for Girls*. Pleasant Company, 1997.

Hoving, Walter. *Tiffany's Table Manners for Teenagers*. Random House, 1989.

Health and Personal Hygiene; Adolescence

Dobson, James. *Preparing for Adolescence.* Gospel Light Publications, 1980.

Gardner-Loulan, Joann. *Period* (with parent's guide). Volcano Press, 1991.

Haab, Sherri. *Nail Art.* Klutz Press, 1997.

Johnson, Anne Akers, and Stoneking, Robin. *Braids and Bows.* Klutz Press, 1992. Also, *Hair: A Book of Braiding and Style.*

Nursing Staff of Lucile Salter Packard Children's Hospital. *Family First Aid.* Klutz Press. Phone 800-558-8944.

Schaefer, Valorie. *The Care and Keeping of You: The Body Book for Girls.* Pleasant Company, 1998.

Family Heritage

Cardwell, Tammy Marshall. *Front Porch History.* Greenleaf Press, 1999.

Creative Memories. *Fast Formulas.* Creative Memories, 1998. Phone 800-468-9335, or check out http://www.creative-memories.com.

Crichton, Jennifer. *Family Reunion: Everything You Need to Know to Plan Unforgettable Get-Togethers.* Workman, 1998.

Hart, Cynthia. *Scrapbook Workshop: A Complete Guide to Preserving Memories in Archival, Heirloom-Quality Books.* Workman, 1998.

Lynam, Sandy. *Heirlooms from Loving Hands: Making Memories to Cherish Forever.* Harvest House, 1998.

Spence, Linda. *Legacy: A Step-by-Step Guide to Writing Personal History.* Ohio University Press, 1997.

Vanessa-Ann. *Making Scrapbooks: Complete Guide to Preserving Your Treasured Memories.* Sterling, 1998.

Periodicals

Time for Tea, Cindy Rushton. 256-381-2529, e-mail haroldr@getaway.net, single issue $2.50, $15 a year (12 issues) or $10 a year for e-mail version.

4

GETTING *YOU* READY FOR HOMESCHOOLING

In This Chapter

- Are you already homeschooling?
- Fear, doubt, and other internal stumbling blocks
- Life as your child's primary role model
- Legal issues: nothing you can't handle
- A beginner's checklist
- Simple starting points
- Resources

YOU'VE READ ABOUT the many ways people homeschool their children and their many reasons for doing so. You've become acquainted with the incredible learning assets you'll be able to capitalize upon as you teach your middle years child at home, and how to teach to individual learning styles so as to meet your child's unique needs. You've been encouraged about how homeschooling will build a stronger family life, and by the vast amount of social opportunities for homeschooled children.

Now it's time to get yourself ready. Sure, you can draw on others' experience, but you need to tailor the information to meet your particular needs. No child is a carbon copy of another, nor are their parents. Each family is its own unique tapestry woven by personalities, routines, and needs that can be accommodated by calculating out how homeschooling will complement the design already in progress.

You're probably homeschooling already, even if you don't call it that. If you're plagued by doubts about doing so full time, read on. Find out how to comply with your state law. Go through the Beginner's Checklist and set realistic, attainable goals.

Each family is its own unique tapestry woven by personalities, routines, and needs that can be accommodated by calculating out how homeschooling will complement the design already in progress.

You are up to the task. You don't have to be a master weaver, only willing to take hold of the loom. The pattern may become more intricate or more simple, but with time, it will be woven with abundant fibers of precious memories.

ARE YOU ALREADY HOMESCHOOLING?

CHANCES ARE, if you spend any time thinking of homeschooling, you're already quite involved in your child's education. Homeschooling tends to attract those who, for whatever reason, are very much in tune with their children's needs and desires. That doesn't mean those same parents have the most patience, most education, most money, the cleanest houses, or cook the best food. It only means that they, like you, want to spend more time with their children, and care about them enough to want the very best education available.

Think about how many ways you are homeschooling right now. How much time do you spend helping your children with homework? Many questionnaire respondents said they spent between two and four hours per night when their children were in school. Most homeschoolers spend no more than that. What kinds of things do you and your children talk about en route to various activities? Those same topics will likely serve as springboards for learning when you have more time. Do you enjoy watching educational programming and special documentaries? You'll be able to stay up later at night to watch more. Are you particular about the kinds of literature your children read? The best is available, for free, at your local library, and you get to help choose it. Educationally, homeschooling may not require much more from you than you're already doing, but it will give you more control over the kinds of things your children are exposed to.

FEAR, DOUBT, AND OTHER INTERNAL STUMBLING BLOCKS

FIFTY-FIVE OF THE sixty-three travelers say they had doubts when they began homeschooling. They forged ahead and saw success in spite of their worst fears. At times, the doubts spurred them on to working harder, evaluating more carefully, being better than they would've been otherwise.

Bea, a homeschooling mother of four from suburban Minnesota, says, "I cried and prayed and talked and talked to anyone who could help me."

Beth expresses similar emotions, saying, "I came down the stairs that first morning, wondering, 'What on earth have I gotten myself into?'"

Linda agrees, saying she remembers thinking, "What if I'm making a huge mistake?"

Then, Missy: "I was afraid I'd mess up my kids, that I hadn't a clue how this experiment would turn out, and that we all might get to the end and I'd find out it was a big, fat mistake!"

Even if time doesn't erase the doubts, they will dissipate. Bea credits an informative seminar with putting many of her doubts to rest. Beth said that looking at what the public school kids were learning and reminding herself of her own children's school experience helped her relax. Linda says time eased her fears, mostly because her children were so much happier at home. And Missy says her faith and husband provided a foundation of support. Missy's two sons are both earning impressive grade point averages in college now.

You don't have to be a master weaver, only willing to take hold of the loom.

Many travelers worried about whether or not they had enough patience. Others worried about their children's socialization. Some feared they would be lonely for adult companionship. Others forthrightly declared they didn't think they were "intelligent" or "smart" or "disciplined" enough. Their children proved important enough, and homeschooling right enough, that they worked to improve on their real shortcomings and realized other areas weren't as lacking as they'd thought. Patience grows with children underfoot all day. They fit more easily into the ebbs and flows of daily life.

Laura says, "Time and my children have proven me wrong. I used my doubts and fears as a list I needed to work on and have become a better mother by homeschooling them."

Catherine agrees, "I was determined to make homeschooling work for us, so I knew I had to learn to be patient and stay focused on teaching them."

Tap into the wisdom of homeschoolers who have been at it awhile.

Jennie says, "I found it comforting to talk with veteran homeschooling families, to hear that despite their occasional false starts and outright blunders, their kids exceeded each family's unique definition of 'success.'"

Homeschoolers talk about socialization as "the S word." It becomes an inside joke after time, but at first, most new homeschoolers are concerned about the effects of homeschooling on their children's socialization. No parent wants to raise socially inept children. It may be hard to believe at first, but homeschooling is the best thing you can do to raise a socially adept child. Jennie says, "Socialization wasn't the big deal I thought it would be."

Many realize it's not difficult to find social opportunities, and that controlling the social environment (and thus, keeping it more positive) is easy when homeschooling.

Doris, new to homeschooling this year in urban Alabama, says, "I was especially concerned that I could not satisfy my daughter's need for socializing. She is a very social person. Getting her involved in activities at our homeschool support school was one of the best things I could have done. She quickly made friends."

Some parents are reluctant about giving up their comfortable level of socializing with friends.

> At times, the doubts spurred them onto working harder, evaluating closer, being better than they would've been otherwise.

Mary Sue talks about her fears about her own loneliness, "I thought I was the only one in my area who homeschooled. I overcame my feelings of isolation by gaining Internet access. I found a whole community of like-minded folks."

A surprising number of new homeschoolers don't feel they're smart enough to educate their children at home. If you've completed the eighth grade, you should be able to teach your children well enough to get them to the point where they can learn independently.

Elementary and middle school teachers have degrees in elementary and middle school education. But what does that involve? They practice multiplying in order to teach fourth graders to multiply. They learn about the newest handwriting programs, how to choose the 'best' textbook, what makes for the liveliest bulletin board displays, and how to manage classrooms full of children, from record keeping to behavior problems. The most average high school graduate could produce average work in this not-so-challenging college major and teach children at any school in the nation. Up to 30 percent of schoolteachers have failed minimum competency tests in some states. The average parent need not feel intimidated!

However, many do.

"I was afraid I wasn't smart enough," says Annie, homeschooling mother of three in Georgia. She continues, "I realized that God gave me these boys to raise, and that He would equip me to educate them. I just take it one day at a time."

> "Our home has become the center of learning, a concept that has empowered our family."
>
> —Sharon, homeschooling mother of seven in British Columbia.

Resources abound for homeschoolers and curriculum companies are helpful. "There is a lot of curriculum out there to help," notes Heather, who homeschools three children in Iowa.

Homeschooling parents need not feel limited by what they know or don't know. Co-ops, Internet classes, and some school districts open their doors to homeschooled students.

Leigh, who homeschools the younger of her two daughters in Texas, says, "If it meant getting outside help for subjects I felt less competent in, we did so."

If parents choose not to use outside classes, they face and conquer their insecurities about their own intelligence. Sharon homeschools seven children in British Columbia. She says, "I didn't think I was intelligent enough, because I wasn't a teacher. Then I thought that surely I was at least as capable as the thousands of others homeschooling successfully. Our home has become the center of learning, a concept which has empowered our family."

Sometimes, answers aren't readily available. Long-term trust is needed instead.

Janine says, "I wasn't certain that I would always know the right approach to helping my children learn." She adds, "Guess what? I don't always know! But we figure it out together. I suppose I haven't really gotten over all my doubts so much as I've learned that they are common, and I can live with that."

Travelers learn to balance discipline and trusting in children's propensity to learn. Janice, homeschooling mother of three in Michigan, says, "I am not a tremendously disciplined person. I was afraid there would be days when I wouldn't feel like teaching. I have relaxed as I've seen how difficult it is for children to learn nothing. They're always learning in some way, shape, or form, even when we don't formally 'do' school."

LIFE AS YOUR CHILD'S PRIMARY ROLE MODEL

NEW HOMESCHOOLERS often worry about the enormous implications of being their child's primary role model. Some list this concern among their doubts and fears. These parents reflect on their weaknesses and use homeschooling as an opportunity for personal growth. As they teach their children about kindness, self-discipline, and integrity, they become more kind, self-disciplined, and develop more integrity for themselves.

> "Time spent with children is the most important thing. You don't get a second chance."
>
> —CAROL, MOTHER OF ELEVEN IN CALIFORNIA.

About half the respondents were unconcerned about being their child's primary role model.

"It's just part of being a parent," Janice says. Heather agrees, saying, "I know I'm putting far more into parenting than I would if they were in school every day."

Carol is the mother of eleven children in suburban California. She finds being a role model easy, adding, "When I began homeschooling, I had already raised seven children. I knew that time spent with children was the most important thing. You don't get a second chance."

Homeschooling parents live varied and interesting lives, and want to be the best role models for their children.

Linda says, "When we had children, my husband and I knew they were ours to raise. We assumed it was natural that we would be their main role models."

Renee agrees, "My son sees me do a lot of volunteer work. I create an interesting role model as far as participating in helping improve the world."

Travelers reflect on their shortcomings, and try to improve where possible. While Larissa isn't the worrying sort, she says, "I'm lazy and I know it, so I know I'm regularly modeling that one terrible attribute. For the most part, though, I try to be as good a role model as possible."

> "Homeschooling has taught me volumes about the complexities of forging a life well lived while navigating a road less traveled."
>
> —JENNIE, HOMESCHOOLING MOM.

The other half of respondents felt burdened by the responsibility of being a twenty-four-hour role model.

Anna says, "I am ever conscious of my behavior and attitudes. I'm proud to see my girls modeling my husband's and my good traits and I'm constantly reevaluating negative aspects of my personality and behavior."

Janine worries about being such a perfectionist, "I don't want my children feeling that way. I want them to strive to be their best, but I don't want them feeling they always fall short. The up side to this realization," she continues, "is that I'm learning to be less hard on myself. Also, they are spending so much time with us and seeing the things we find important being modeled. That's much easier than trying to wedge it in when you only get to see them a few hours a day."

Children will surprise you, both pleasantly and in ways not so pleasant. Esther homeschools three children in suburban Virginia.

She says, "When I started homeschooling I was ignorant about the practical side of child development. I did not count on my daughter wanting to spend day after day reading and arguing with me about how 'stupid' memorizing her multiplication tables was. I'm learning and growing all the time."

Jennie sums up the outlook of most veteran homeschoolers. She says, "Living with my daughters so intensely, and knowing they are observing me, is humbling, exhilarating, and enormously intimidating. I think homeschooling has inspired me to become a better person and a better mother. Homeschooling has taught me volumes about the complexities of forging a life well lived while navigating a road less traveled."

LEGAL ISSUES: NOTHING YOU CAN'T HANDLE

HOMESCHOOLING IS LEGAL in all fifty states, and because it's enjoying success and positive press, there is no reason to think it will ever be otherwise.

Occasionally problems crop up, mostly due to people either not fully complying with the law, or because of truancy laws that are sometimes used against homeschoolers by overzealous officials.

You may find people within your state have varying interpretations about the law's application. Go through the legal resources at the end of this chapter, contact appropriate groups, and read applicable books. Then decide how best to protect your family from legal strife.

Half of the questionnaire respondents belong to Home School Legal Defense Association, a national group that offers legal insurance to homeschoolers. The other half report that they do not feel such coverage is necessary.

Your peace of mind is important. Do whatever it takes to preserve that, and put your time and mental energy into homeschooling your children.

When in Rome . . . Know the Law of the Land

Know your state's law before you withdraw your child from school. State laws vary; some are much more restrictive and intimidating to the beginner than others. Get a copy of your state's law. Read it, talk to those in nearby support groups, and operate your homeschool in compliance with the law if you want to avoid any hassle from the authorities. In a number of states, you may be able to legally homeschool in a variety of ways. Be sure to look into each one and decide what's best for you. Also, don't be afraid to ask for exemptions if you think they apply. For example, states that require standardized testing may be required by their general education law to exempt children with learning disabilities, or at least provide a more appropriate method of assessment. If you know people in the public schools are enjoying such privileges, you will have a better legal leg to stand on.

Get a copy of your state's law. Read it, talk to those in nearby support groups, and operate your homeschool in compliance with the law if you want to avoid any hassle from the authorities.

Other things will vary from state to state as well. You may or may not have to meet with a supervising teacher, document your lesson plans, keep track of attendance, and so on. As you meet other homeschoolers, ask how they meet state requirements.

Only a small handful of travelers reported any legal problems on their questionnaires, and all were handled easily.

Janine says, "We almost had problems. We were a little misinformed about the law. We were threatened with truancy charges unless we put our son back in school. We did put him back in for a short time, while we learned the technicalities of the law. Then we withdrew him again properly."

Suzi, homeschooling mother of eight in rural California, says, "The principal threatened me, saying homeschooling was illegal. I enrolled my son in a through-the-mail cover school. The director was helpful and comforting." Doing this gave Suzi peace of mind, though homeschooling is perfectly legal in California.

Abby, homeschooling mother of eight in Tennessee, says, "I once spoke to the attendance officer for about an hour in my driveway and convinced him I was a relatively intelligent human being—and I called a lawyer when he left!"

The requirements of mandatory preschool screening statutes can almost always be avoided by homeschoolers.

"The school wanted to test my preschooler—mandatory in my state," says Bea. "I told them no, they insisted, so I contacted the state office of education and was backed up."

Avoiding standardized testing of school-aged children (if your state requires such) is trickier.

Betty also wanted to avoid the standardized testing requirement in her state. She says, "We are philosophically opposed to standardized testing. I tried to get the district to waive the requirement. I found information from professional journals and books, and researched the ill effects of testing. We have to be evaluated yearly here too, and my evaluator was supportive in addressing this with my district. In the end, my daughter was required to take the test. As expected, her scores were very low. I was called into a meeting with the homeschool supervisor and we talked about the situation. Since there is an inclusion in our homeschool law that test scores cannot solely be used to determine your program, our right to homeschool was never in question. I felt our privacy had been invaded, though."

Consider joining your state support group. There is power in numbers. Meet with different homeschoolers and ask questions. Also, plan to attend a conference where a workshop addresses your state's legal environment and requirements.

Record Keeping

Most states require some form of record keeping, though the amount and methods vary widely. As your children approach their teens, they may be studying subject matter that could legitimately count as high school credit. If you're homeschooling a twelve- or thirteen-year-old, be sure to find out if the requirements are different for high school than for the younger grades. For example, my son will be studying algebra and French at age thirteen. In my state, it will be important to document his work more closely to ensure he will get proper high school credit for his studies. We will also begin to track any volunteer work or athletic achievements, and plan to keep a portfolio of both his schoolwork and outside activities so he will have something concrete to present college admissions officers.

Record keeping may be as simple as notifying the school district or as complex as keeping daily lesson plans or a detailed portfolio of your child's work. Many homeschoolers keep records regardless of whether or not the law requires it. One mother files her children's work as it's completed. Others make elaborate scrapbooks filled with memorabilia, sample work, and writing about the activities. Like many homeschoolers, a friend of mine maps out her lesson plans on

RECORD KEEPING METHODS

- Journal
- Traditional lesson plan books (available at office or teacher supply stores)
- Attendance pages
- Calendar in three-ring binder
- Portfolio
- Simple lists of work completed and books read
- File of work samples and test results
- Attendance pages

her computer every Sunday evening. Others tend to write down work completed as children move through it.

Once you know your state's record keeping requirements, choose a method that will work for you. Many catalogs and curriculum companies offer record keeping resources. Don't hesitate to include your middle years child in record keeping. My son keeps track of his work and my daughter maintains a list of all the books she's read. Between ten and twelve, children can plan their work ahead of time, releasing you from the burden. Doing this also gives them a sense of ownership over the way they spend their time. For example, if my children want to go on a field trip or have a lighter load on a certain day, they plan to tackle extra work on the surrounding days that week.

A BEGINNER'S CHECKLIST

IN CHAPTER 1, you read where survey respondents fall on the homeschool continuum. Now it's time to think about where you see yourself in those same categories. Remember, you have the right to alter your course any time, but it's important to have a rough map drawn before you begin your journey, lest you get lost and give up. Move through the eight categories, one at a time, and begin to chart your course by answering the following questions.

Motivation

Why are you interested in homeschooling? Jot down any reasons that come to mind. Brainstorm about the kind of childhood you want your children to have, the kinds of memories you'd like them to take with them when they someday leave your care.

What kind of education is important to you? Do you think your children are headed for a vocational trade or the most prestigious university in the nation? How can you help them reach their goals?

How do you see your days flowing? Write down all your thoughts, then keep them on hand. You may want to return to these for an occasional reminder.

Financial Expenditures

Be realistic. If you're on a tight budget and don't see how you'll add homeschooling costs to your expenses, visit your library and peruse the shelves for useful resources. Talk to other homeschoolers to find out how they've done it. Look to see if there are items that can be cut from your budget to make room for things you may want to buy for homeschooling. Visit curriculum fairs. Pore over materials before purchasing. Prioritize. If need be, think of ways to earn extra money to pay for curriculum. A mother in Alabama breeds dogs to pay for hers. Others have annual garage sales that fund their homeschools.

If money isn't a problem, resist the temptation to buy too much anyway—you won't use it all. Be choosy and wise. Set a budget and stick to it, so you won't be caught off guard at year's end by staggering expenses incurred through homeschooling.

Approach

Where's your comfort zone? Let's face it, some parents are spontaneous and easy-going, others highly disciplined and routine minded. Some have an exceptionally high tolerance for noise and activity, others need more frequent breaks to regroup. Don't shame yourself. Be honest.

How important is it for you to stick to a basic, age-appropriate scope and sequence? How much structure do you think you'll stick to? How much relaxing would be too much for your personality? How much work do you need to see accomplished? Is your spouse supportive?

Many travelers are more comfortable beginning their journey with a traditional curriculum, others are determined to be hands-off. Some continue with complete curriculum packages, others branch out and try alternative approaches and materials. Unschoolers enjoy watching their children direct their own learning. Your way will be unique, whatever it is, and you can adapt along the way. All you need is a starting point, a compass, and a little courage.

> Your way will be unique, whatever it is, and you can adapt along the way. All you need is a starting point, a compass, and a little courage.

Assessment

First, know your state law. If you wish to be in compliance, follow the guidelines it gives for assessing your children's learning. Many travelers note they keep records above and beyond their state's legal requirements because they want to have a history of their child's work or to have records in case legal problems ever arise. Legal considerations aside, you may assess your child's learning by watching, observing, and talking, or you may want to administer more traditional tests.

Janine says, "I know what my son struggles with and what he has a good handle on. I assess by watching, listening, and knowing him." Do you think you could realistically assess your child's learning in this way? Many do. If not, use other methods.

You may find comfort in yearly standardized tests and more traditional periodic tests. You may assign book reports if you're unsure that your children are comprehending what they're reading. Think about how important testing is to you and how each child will respond to tests given at home.

Technology

Think about the kind of pace and feel you want for your homeschool. You may want a cozy, simple life full of late mornings and hot chocolate, snuggled under an afghan reading aloud to your children. Or you may see your family rising and shining, everyone tackling their work before facing busy afternoons filled with outside activities. You may like long leisurely nature walks, or you may prefer Web surfing for great Internet classes.

Of course, you may want a bit of both worlds. Decide how much television and computer use you think is appropriate for your homeschooling environment, and set realistic limits when you begin.

Physical Space

Where will your children be working? Do they have a place to call their own? Your kitchen table may work fine, or you may want to set up a corner with a desk and some shelves. Do plan to make room for learning materials, including books, paper and pencils, maps and globes, and craft items. Decide what areas of the house will work best and which items can be moved to suit your homeschooling.

Parental Involvement

How much can each parent contribute? In most cases, the mother does the majority of the teaching, but many fathers happily contribute. What is realistic to expect of someone after a long day at work? What kinds of things can the working parent bring to the homeschool? Assess your weak areas and encourage your spouse to pitch in on those.

Outside Assistance

Look at your budget again. Count the costs before you jump into too many outside activities. Measure the time and money spent against any benefits you hope to achieve. What kinds of things will enhance your homeschooling? What kinds of things will drain from it? If your children need quiet time and recovery from peer struggles in school, you may want to keep outside activities to a minimum at first. If, like some parents, you have a child who has been the center of attention in school, you may want to find plenty of activities right from the start. Think about which times of day you want to be out and try to find activities which work within your time frame. If possible, start slow. You can always add as you go along.

SIMPLE STARTING POINTS

✦ *Be honest about your doubts.*

Talk about them with veteran homeschoolers. Ask questions. If you live in an area where you can't find any like-minded homeschoolers, join an Internet group for encouragement.

✦ *Get a copy of your state's law.*

Find out how other homeschoolers comply with it. Decide how you'll cover the bases before questions arise.

✦ *Make a record keeping plan.*

Decide how best to keep records of your child's work. Purchase any tools you need to help in that regard.

✦ *Map out your thoughts and goals.*

Go through the Beginner's Checklist. Be realistic. Don't set yourself up for failure before you even begin!

✦ *Decide what kinds of learning materials you will want to use.*

Go through the list of resources and order more catalogs and call curriculum companies (or visit their Web sites) to get information. If you're unfamiliar with the various styles in which people homeschool (unschooling, eclectic, traditional, unit studies, classical, and so on), and not sure where you fit in, take time looking through catalogs for materials that fall into each category. Read a book listed in each section. It may seem like a lot, but spending time now will help you get off to a happier start.

RESOURCES

Legal Issues

Books

Kaseman, Larry and Susan. *Taking Charge Through Homeschooling: Personal and Political Empowerment.* Koshkonong Press, 1991.

Klicka, Christopher, Esq. *Home Schooling in the United States: A Legal Analysis.* Carolina Academic Press, 1998. Also, *The Right to Home School.*

Periodical

Court Report, 540-338-5600, http://www.hslda.org, bimonthly, free to Home School Legal Defense Association members, $15 per year to nonmembers.

Organization

Home School Legal Defense Association, see "Support Groups" in Chapter 1's Resources section for information.

Full Service Curriculum Companies

Abeka (Christian traditional), 800-874-2353, http://www.abeka.org.

Alpha Omega (Christian traditional), 800-622-3070, http://www.home-schooling.com.

Bridgestone Online Academy and Switched On Schoolhouse CD-ROM curriculum, http://www.switched-onschoolhouse.com.

AZ Home Academy (secular traditional), 888-235-1595, http://www.azhomeacademy.com.

Bob Jones University Press (Christian traditional), 800-845-5731, http://www.bjup.com.

Calvert School (secular traditional), 410-243-6030, http://www.calvertschool.org.

Christian Liberty Academy (Christian traditional), 800-348-0899, http://www.homeschools.org.

Christian Light Education (Christian traditional), 540-434-0750.

Clonlara School (secular eclectic), 734-769-4511, http://www.clonlara.org.

Covenant (eclectic classical), 800-578-2421, http://www.covenanthome.com.

Curious Kids (secular traditional), http://www.curiouskidshomeschool.com.

Eagle Christian School (Christian traditional), 888-324-5348, http://www.eaglechristian.org.

Home Study International (Christian traditional), 800-782-4769, http://www.hsi.com.

Kolbe Academy (Catholic traditional), 707-255-6499, http://www.kolbe.org.

KONOS (Christian unit study), 972-924-2712, http://www.konos.com.

Logos School (classical), 208-883-3199, http://www.logosschool.com.

Memoria Press (classical), 502-458-5001, http://www.memoriapress.com.

Northstar Academy (online Christian school), 888-464-6280, http://www.northstar-academy.org.

Oak Meadow School (Waldorf), 802-387-2021, http://www.oakmeadow.com.

Robinson Self-Teaching Curriculum (CD-ROM, Christian traditional), Oregon Institute of Science and Medicine, 2251 Dick George Road, Cave Junction, OR 97523.

School of Tomorrow (Christian traditional), 972-315-1776, http://www.schooloftomorrow.com.

Seton (Catholic traditional), 540-636-9990, http://www.setonhome.com.

Sonlight (Christian literature based), 303-730-6292, http://www.sonlight-curriculum.com.

Weaver Curriculum (Christian unit studies), 888-367-9871, http://www.weaverinc.com.

Willoway Cyber School (secular traditional, four "tracks"), 610-678-0214, http://www.willoway.com.

Diagnostic Assessment

Brigance Comprehensive Inventory of Basic Skills, Curriculum Associates, Inc., 800-225-0248, http://www.cahomeschool.com.

Scope and Sequence

Hirsch, E. D. *A First Dictionary of Cultural Literacy: What Our Children Need to Know.* Houghton Mifflin, 1996. Also, the Core Knowledge Series, published by Delta.

Lopez, Diane. *Teaching Children: A Curriculum Guide to What Children Need to Know at Each Level Through Eighth Grade.* Good News, 1998.

Each family finds the homeschooling method that works best for them, though often, homeschoolers draw from many. If you haven't subscribed to or ordered sample copies of the magazines listed in the resource section of Chapter 1, consider doing so now. Each has its own flavor and finding the one or two that fit closest with your methodology will mean receiving encouragement and resource ideas via mail every other month. Here's a list of books and curricula, broken into broad categories of methodology.

Catholic Education

Berquist, Laura. *Designing Your Own Classical Curriculum: A Guide to Catholic Home Education*. Ignatius, 1998.

Hahn, Kimberly, and Hasson, Mary. *Catholic Education: Homeward Bound*. Ignatius, 1996.

Charlotte Mason

Andreola, Karen. *A Charlotte Mason Companion: Personal Reflections on the Personal Art of Learning*. Charlotte Mason Research and Supply Company, 1998.

Levison, Catherine, and O'Brien, Deborah. *A Charlotte Mason Education: A How-To Manual*. Charlotte Mason Commniquetions, 1996.

Classical Education

Classical education Web site, including a classical education support online loop, http://www.classicalhomeschooling.com.

Teaching the Trivium: The Classical Approach to Christian Education Explained and Applied to Homeschooling, 309-537-3641, http://www.muscanet.com./~trivium.

Trivium Pursuit: Classical Excellence in Homeschooling, see *Teaching the Trivium*, the preceding entry.

Veritas Press, 800-922-5082.

Wilson, Douglas. *Classical Education and the Home School*. Canon Press, 1995.

Also see titles under "Catholic Education" as well.

Unit Studies

Bendt, Valerie. *Unit Study Idea Book* (Common Sense Press, 1997). Also, *How to Create Your Own Unit Study*.

Design-A-Study (curriculum), 302-998-3889, http://www.designastudy.com.

Homeschooling Today, see Chapter 1's Resources section for more information on this magazine.

The Prairie Primer (curriculum, grades 3–6), 505-534-1496, http://www.CadronCreek.com.

Unschooling

F.U.N. News (Family Unschoolers Network), 410-360-7330, http://www.unschooling.org. Single issue $3, $10 per year (four issues).

Griffith, Mary. *Unschooling Handbook: How to Use the Whole World as Your Classroom.* Prima, 1998.

Growing Without Schooling, see Chapter 1's Resources section for more information on this magazine.

Home Education Magazine, see Chapter 1's Resources section for more information on this magazine.

Leistico, Agnes. *I Learn Better by Teaching Myself* and *Still Teaching Ourselves.* Holt Associates, 1997.

Waldorf

Waldorf Education and Curriculum and Resource Guide, 916-961-8729.

More Catalogs

ATCO School Supply, 909-272-2926, http://www.atco1.com.

Bethlehem Books, 800-757-6831, http://www.bethlehembooks.com.

Great Source Education Group, 800-289-4490.

In His Steps, 800-583-1336.

Kudzu, http://www.kudzucompany.com.
Small Ventures, 972-681-1728.

Newsletters

Eclectic Homeschool, http://www.eho.org.
How to Homeschool, http://www.howtonews.com.

Part Two

A WORLD OF CURRICULUM CHOICES: HOW TO PROMOTE A LIFELONG LOVE OF LEARNING

5

DEVELOPING CLEAR COMMUNICATION SKILLS: LANGUAGE ARTS

In This Chapter

- Reading
- Writing
- Speaking and listening
- Simple starting points
- Resources

More than any other area, proficiency in language arts is crucial to a well-rounded education. Communication skills are learned from birth onward, as children want to speak to be heard, and later want to read to explore and write to communicate with others. There's no way to overstate the importance of clear communication in daily life, whether writing a convincing résumé, giving a corporate presentation, or listening to a friend who is in need. By eight to ten, most children have become competent readers and use this newly established skill as a springboard for all other subjects. They begin to take an interest in writing everything from extensive journal entries to brief grocery lists. Most homeschool

A FEW WORDS ABOUT CURRICULUM

Ahhh, curriculum and learning materials. The choices are staggering. I remember my first homeschool curriculum fair, the endless tables piled high with materials to teach every subject imaginable. I stood paralyzed by uncertainty of where to go first, and how to begin. By two o'clock in the afternoon, I was exhausted, my mind a jumbled-up mix of everything I'd seen and heard.

Most curriculum fairs are combined with workshops. By all means, attend workshops that interest you—and take notes. However, resist the temptation to head out of a workshop, dart to a vendor's table, and purchase that one item the speaker insisted would make or break your homeschool. Trust me on this—you will have ample opportunity to purchase that item again. There are very few things that will make or break your homeschool, none of which are offered at curriculum fairs.

Nonetheless, finding learning materials compatible with your goals for cultivating the homeschooling environment you want is important. Order catalogs and visit Web sites. Compare products and companies and prices before you purchase, whether at a fair or through the mail. When in doubt, ask. If you have reservations, wait. Your children can read and write and speak without curriculum at all. A simple, inexpensive math workbook should work fine and cover you legally even in the most restrictive states until you find that math curriculum you especially want. About everything else can be learned by good books. Again, you can add curriculum later. Remember, haste makes waste—so take your time.

Over time, you may purchase all sorts of materials to facilitate your children's learning. Look over the goals you wrote down for your homeschooling. Think about the learning assets of the middle years child and your child's particular learning style. How will the materials draw on the learning assets and meet the needs of that learning style? What is your budget? Once you've narrowed down your choices, don't be afraid to call the companies and ask questions if you're still not sure. Ask veteran homeschoolers if you can look through what they're using. To this day, a friend and I browse through each other's most recent curriculum orders to see if there's anything that might benefit our own children. New materials flood the market each year, some worthwhile, others not. Homeschooling e-mail lists (many run by curriculum companies) are a good way to stay on top of new items being released. I count on the recommendations of certain companies after years of success with their products, and pay less attention to catalogs from companies that, while good for other homeschoolers, haven't established a track record of being useful to my family. With each passing year, I inform myself a bit more fully and consider the needs of my children a bit more closely before writing that check or calling that 800 number to order.

Read on to find out how homeschool travelers approach teaching their children in various subject areas, and which products they find the most helpful along the road. Many Web sites listed in the Resources section offer samples of workbook pages, audio lessons, and so on. Including your children as you surf the Internet will help in meeting their needs and desires with whatever materials you find intriguing.

If you decide to purchase a full curriculum package, you may want to check out some of these materials and book lists as well. Many travelers who use curriculum packages find their children complete their work quickly and want to accelerate or enrich their learning with supplemental materials. Others add a unit study here or interesting project there to breathe more life into the textbook information, or to fill a gap in the curriculum. Sometimes a child's interest in a specific topic can't be sated by the curriculum only, so a few catalogs from supplemental companies may come in handy. (Don't forget the list in the Resources section of Chapter 1.)

children have very little trouble speaking and asking questions. To refine and develop language arts skills, travelers use a variety of methods and materials, which—although diverse—all seem to work equally well.

READING

HOMESCHOOLERS read voraciously. Whether the students use traditional reading curriculums or unschool, whether they count reading as their favorite subject or least favorite, books are abundant, and are read regularly, in homeschools.

Seven of the thirty-two middle years children who filled out questionnaires proclaimed reading as their favorite subject. Nine others listed reading as a hobby they enjoy. Many who dubbed other subjects favorites list a number of books in their preferred subject area as resources they enjoy using. Middle years homeschoolers have plenty of books at home and give library visits special status. Books satisfy children's desire for "real" knowledge but also take them to make-believe worlds, satisfying their desire to imagine things far from real.

> There's no way to overstate the importance of clear communication in daily life, whether writing a convincing résumé, giving a corporate presentation, or listening to a friend who is in need.

My own ten-year-old daughter says, "I love reading because I get to imagine I'm one of the people in the books."

As she reads, like other homeschoolers, she finds characters she can relate to and learn from. What a gift a love of reading is to the homeschooling parent and child.

It's not surprising that travelers vary in the books they allow and encourage their children to read, how they cover the wide variety of genres available, and how they assess reading ability and comprehension. Many travelers continue to read aloud to their middle years children. Bea echoes the sentiments of many when she says, "I love it when we cuddle up and read together."

Though most homeschoolers report reading strengths, some discuss the long road they took to fluent reading. Even in these cases, children are being nurtured to see value in and develop a love for reading, a skill that will serve them for years to come.

So Many Books, So Little Time

The majority of travelers are choosy when it comes to their children's reading material. Since there is only so much time and there are so many books, choosing carefully makes sense. Many travelers mentioned the book lists and reviews in the Sonlight (Chapter 4) and Chinaberry (Chapter 5) catalogs as especially helpful.

Doris is a new homeschooling mother of two middle years children in Alabama. To supplement her full curriculum she says, "I keep my shelves stocked with Sonlight's recommendations. These books are good literature and hold their interest."

In my family, we ban abridged books from our home, finding them lacking in style as well as substance. If a child isn't old enough to handle the original, we wait. Not so long ago, my daughter read an abridged version of a classic title (the abridgement had escaped our notice). She liked it okay. I was taken aback by her lack of enthusiasm for the material. Upon inspecting the book and realizing it was the shortened version, I went back to our shelves and discovered the original. She headed back to her room to read.

Within minutes, she exclaimed from down the hall, "Oh! Now I see what you mean! This *is* a great book!"

The experience was enlightening for her. She couldn't help running to share turns of phrase and details which had been missing from the abridgement. She kept repeating, "This makes so much more sense now."

We found something similar when my son was given a title from a popular contemporary series. He was old enough, in my opinion, to read the book and decide what he thought for himself, so read it he did. For about three chapters.

Then, disgusted, he threw the book in the garbage and said, "I see what you mean. The writing is boring and simple. I can predict what's going to happen. It's obvious. I don't want to waste any more time on this."

Because the children have been directed toward good literature, they are able to make wise choices about which books are worth their time now.

Some homeschoolers are less persnickety about their children's reading material, especially if the child was a late reader or if the material is a small part of the overall reading picture. Many homeschoolers let their children pick their own literature or exercise only little input over it.

Jennie writes, "The girls choose most of their reading materials. I assign some reading and make lots of book suggestions. Sometimes I'm more subtle and leave enticing books lying around for them to 'discover.' We still read aloud together, too."

Betty says, "I find that assigning something in particular is the kiss of death. But if I mention that I found it interesting and she might too, that's different."

Regardless of who does the choosing or what books are chosen, reading is a big part of the homeschooling picture for almost all of the travelers.

Covering Various Genres

By the middle years children have reached an age where they are ready to be exposed to a wider variety of styles and genres of writing. My children gravitate toward historical fiction, which isn't surprising with two history buffs as parents. We have encouraged them to branch out in their reading material. We stock our shelves and scour the library for fiction and nonfiction, fantasy and real-life adventures. The children also read newspapers and magazines. Over time, they'll branch out more. By the time they leave home, they should have a good grasp of the wide array of writing styles and genres so that they won't need to feel intimidated by any reading material presented them.

Do They Understand?

Children develop reading skills in vastly different ways. Some don't read well until they are old enough to read and understand high school material. Others read quickly, yet are much too young to grasp the hidden meanings in metaphorical writing. In general,

CHILDREN'S TOP 20 BOOK (OR AUTHOR) PICKS

- Little House series
- Boxcar Children series
- Marguerite Henry horse books (*Misty, Stormy, Sea Star, King of the Wind*, and so on)
- Chronicles of Narnia series
- Redwall series
- The Black Stallion series
- Gary Paulsen books (*Hatchet, Dogsong, Dunc & Amos series*)
- The Bible
- Encyclopedia Brown series
- Mandie series
- *Johnny Tremain*
- *Huckleberry Finn*
- *Where the Red Fern Grows*
- *The Scarlet Pimpernel*
- Left Behind series
- *The Hobbit*
- *The Lord of the Rings* trilogy
- The Time Trilogy (L'Engle's *A Wrinkle In Time*, and so on)
- Little Britches series
- *Julie of the Wolves*
- Hardy Boys series

PARENTS' TOP 10 CHILDREN'S BOOK PICKS

(All favorites were series rather than single books.)

Little House
The Chronicles of Narnia
The Boxcar Children
Hardy Boys
Encyclopedia Brown
Anne of Green Gables
The Coopers Kids
Annie Henry
Little Britches
Star Wars

travelers tend to let their children read a book regardless of whether or not the parent thinks it is too difficult or too easy. Beloved picture books are hard for many to say good-bye to. Others want to tackle Twain or Pyle or Dickens or Lewis well before they are able to grasp the symbolism or syntax. No harm's being done, but expectations for understanding should be adjusted accordingly.

Regardless of the method they use, most homeschooling parents are committed to assessing reading as painlessly as possible. They want to preserve their children's enthusiasm for spending time with books.

Reluctant Readers

Though most homeschooling parents consider reading central to a child's education, getting their children to read fluently isn't always a proverbial park walk.

Jennie writes, "My daughter didn't read fluently until around age nine. I wish I could say I was relaxed about it, but I remember fretting about it daily. She's reading just fine now, so I guess it doesn't matter."

Betty says, "We battled over reading time when my daughter was five or six. Finally I decided she wasn't ready and we just quit. We read aloud to her daily until one day when I didn't have time. The next day we went to the library, she brought home a pile of books, and approached me for help reading them."

Eileen, homeschooling mother of three in South Carolina, says, "My oldest son struggled and I worried he'd never read. He's in the seventh grade now and reads good books, but reads slowly."

Cassie, homeschooling mother of two boys in Pennsylvania, says, "I taught the oldest one to read at age five by teaching him a few phonics rules. The second child showed no signs of being ready for years. As it turned out, he ended up in vision therapy. Even now at age ten he can't read phonetically, but is learning to read by sight."

Judy taught two children to read by traditional methods using structured curriculum. Reading didn't come quite so easily for the third.

She says, "My thinking has changed as a result of dealing with my struggling reader and I am now using lots of great literature to encourage her."

HOW WE DID IT

Travelers report five basic ways they assess their child's reading ability and comprehension:

- Discussing books in a natural way
- Purposely asking questions about the books
- Assigning book reports
- Giving children worksheets or assignments for books read
- Giving tests

If you have a late-reading child, ask around for information and input from veteran homeschoolers. Chances are, your child will read fine by ten or so (without the labels that schools would issue), but if not, there are organizations and books that can help you find the help you need.

WRITING

NARY A DAY in adult life passes without putting the skill of writing to copious use. Because children see the adults around them writing, it doesn't take long for them to see the usefulness of learning to write. Little children scribble in imitation, but as they get older, they want to write so others can read their special cards, phone messages, or elaborate stories. Despite the varying ways parents find to help children in their writing journeys, all want them to be well equipped for future travels.

Handwriting

Most middle years children begin to learn cursive writing, though some parents find it laborious and useless. Preeminently, mothers of boys report that their sons resist writing in cursive, finding it a formidable task. Many adult males use block print for everyday use. Let's face it—learning beautiful cursive is not going to cost children college entrance or a future job. Because we live in times when children will be leaving for college and the workforce with laptop computers at their sides, many travelers make the sensible argument that there's no reason to take time away from other projects to teach cursive writing to a resistant child.

However, others feel equally strongly that learning beautiful script is a good discipline for children, a preservation of a soon-to-be lost art form. Also, children need to have a working knowledge of cursive writing to read the handwritten notes and letters they're bound to receive.

Some travelers purchase simple workbooks at a local teacher's supply store; others use the lessons included in their curriculum. Many parents teach handwriting as it comes up, asking the children to work on neater writing as they write letters to grandma or other everyday things. The two most popular handwriting programs among those answering the survey are *A Reason for Writing* and the Getty/Dubay *Italic Handwriting* series (see Resources section for information).

> If you have a late-reading child, ask around for information and input from veteran homeschoolers. Chances are, your child will read fine by ten or so (without the labels that schools would issue), but if not, there are organizations and books that can help you find the help you need.

Spelling

Homeschool travelers run the gamut in how they teach their children to spell. As with other areas, those who use full curriculum are supplied with spelling texts. Unschoolers see their children learn to spell by reading, and correct spelling only as it comes up naturally in the context of the children's writing or is otherwise relevant to their lives. Followers of Charlotte Mason tend to prefer copy work and dictation. (The parent dictates passages to the child and then corrects the work afterwards. This also works for editing and grammar as well.) Many homeschoolers assess the various programs available and use different programs for different children. Some use computer CD-ROMs as well.

Grammar, Punctuation, Capitalization, and Editing

Middle years children are ready to move beyond simply expressing themselves to start refining their writing. For most children, tools including grammar and punctuation rules help them become more adult in their writing.

As with handwriting and spelling, those who use a full curriculum turn to their ready-supplied books to teach grammar and editing. Unschoolers take a relaxed approach, correcting as it comes up, and often only when asked. Many unschoolers successfully use a number of the resources listed at the chapter's end, however, finding them helpful, creative, and meaningful enough to capture their children's interest.

There are a number of marvelous grammar and editing programs available. Some work on matter-of-fact memorization principles, others draw children into the complexities of the written word and force them to think critically about the words they are putting on paper.

Different children have different ways they approach writing. Too much correction too early can squelch a desire to write. However, children this age are capable of handling some fine-tuning. A program that fits your child can make all the difference. If it's user friendly, it will get more focused attention devoted to it. Though the majority of travelers say that they teach grammar and editing skills through overseeing their children's writing, the following programs were referred to frequently enough to warrant special mention. (Check the Resources section for ordering information. Be sure to check out the others mentioned, too. While some of the titles are lesser known, they are of impressive quality.)

- English for the Thoughtful Child
- Easy Grammar/Daily Grams
- Editor in Chief
- Great Editing Adventure
- Learning Language Arts Through Literature
- Simply Grammar
- Winston Grammar
- Writing Strands

Putting Pen to Paper

Your children are learning how to write or keyboard efficiently. They're brushing up on their spelling and grammar skills. Still, they must get practice, practice, and more practice in writing in various styles and genres. As much as drills help, the best way to become a good writer is to write. Check out the sidebars for writing project ideas. Many of the resources at the end of the chapter include great ideas for writing projects and how to develop children's writing more fully. As with reading, you will want your children to begin to write in various genres. Here are some to incorporate:

- *How-To Articles* acquaint children with thinking about details. Have your child write explicit instructions for someone to follow (how to bake chocolate chip cookies, mow the lawn, inflate a basketball, and so on). When the paper is finished, have another person try to follow the instructions exactly as written, to see if each detail was covered well.

JUST WRITE IT! (MEANINGFUL WRITING IDEAS)

Look for contests to enter
Write a letter to the editor of your local paper
Thank you notes
Invitations
E-mail friends and relatives
Menus and grocery lists
Keep a journal
Dictation practice
Poetry
Memory and copy work (famous quotes, Bible verses, Shakespearean lines, everyday phrases from Greek mythology, and so on)
Draw cartoons with captions

- *Essays* are great practice for describing opinions, observations, or events in an interesting manner.
- *Position Papers* teach children to clearly present and defend their point of view. Have the child pretend to be an op-ed writer for a large newspaper, choosing the topic to write about and defending the position clearly.
- *Stories* with dialogue, either real or imagined, familiarize children with the challenge of keeping story lines flowing while using quotations.
- *Proper Correspondence,* including letters, memos, holiday greeting cards, thank you notes, and responses to invitations, will put children at ease in social (and when they're older, business) situations.

Reluctant Writers

As with reading, writing comes hard for some children. It's heart-wrenching for a homeschooling parent to watch a child struggle with the written word. Rather than forging ahead and creating a grand distaste for the discipline and skill of writing, many parents have come up with creative ideas for nurturing a love for writing, developing capability along the way. Sometimes just a little waiting makes all the difference.

Wendy, homeschooling mother of two in California, says, "We took the writing program at our own pace. It was worth waiting to allow my son to comprehend and use the fine motor skills to learn to write and spell."

Katrina says, "We have made several books about things we are studying. For example, when studying children's authors, the children each wrote a short story. We then learned about making books, and the children illustrated and bound their books. We compile their writing into books like this and the children enjoy looking back and reading their old stories. It also shows them how much they have improved their writing and art skills."

Allowing children to dictate stories to the parent is another approach some parents use to encourage their reluctant writers. The parents write the story as dictated, then the child reads it aloud, hearing the mistakes and fixing them without too much frustration. Then the child rewrites the story from that copy—a much less overwhelming task for the reluctant writer than getting the initial story on paper from scratch. By age eleven or twelve, even the most reluctant writer usually moves beyond this need and is willing to tackle the projects listed in the sidebar.

SPEAKING AND LISTENING

TO GET ALONG WELL with others, children need to learn to speak clearly and politely and to listen with care. Learning when to speak and what is worth saying is a skill most adults could use a lesson or two in. Being a prolific speaker is no guarantee that someone is a good listener. We all know people who can articulate their ideas clearly and interestingly but quickly interrupt and browbeat others. It's a fine art to learn the proper balance of speaking and listening.

Everyday Speech as a Learning Opportunity

Though I've met a number of shy homeschooled children, very few have trouble articulating their ideas once you get to know them. Recently, a house guest said to me, "You sure don't have to worry about being solely responsible for conversing with guests in your home, do you?"

I'm thankful she meant the remark as a compliment!

Homeschooled students are at a distinct advantage over their schooled peers when it comes to speaking easily and with maturity. They are around plenty of adults who are genuinely interested in what they have to say—their ideas, thoughts, and questions. Unlike a classroom of students thrusting their hands in the air and grunting

MORE IDEAS

Write about your best (worst) day ever.

Interview a special relative, coach, instructor, and write up the interview. Keep it with memorabilia or photos of you with that person.

Write an essay about someone you admire.

Reports: write a book, science project, nation or culture of interest. . .

Write about a dream come true (The Day I Buy My First House, The Day I Win the Stanley Cup, and so on).

to gain the teacher's favor, homeschooled children are never rushed to put their ideas or questions forth. Over time and with the patience of a loving parent, even the most introverted who have trouble expressing themselves develop their speaking skills.

Encourage children to place phone calls, greet visitors, and accept package deliveries. These mundane tasks hone social skills while making this kind of chore much less intimidating as they grow older.

Finding Public Speaking Opportunities

Homeschooled children often participate in group activities where they can practice taking turns in talking and questioning, and occasionally have opportunities to speak in front of the group. Most support groups and covering schools offer geography bees and science fairs, where children give presentations and take advantage of a great chance for developing confidence and practicing clarity in their speech. Some offer public speaking classes or debate groups. My husband and I encourage our children to volunteer to make end-of-the-year presentations to coaches, knowing that standing up in front of their peers and their parents to say "thank you" and expressing their gratitude is a good way to practice genuine humility in an imposing situation. Children can plan special events, from Christmas programs to historical plays, to help them practice speaking in front of others.

As children get older, arrange a middle years panel as part of your local or state homeschooling fair. Give the children a chance to answer questions of others getting ready to launch into their homeschooling journey. Also, prepare your homeschooler for the possibility of being interviewed by local media, whether or not it's homeschooling related. My son was featured in a swimming article. We went over some potential questions prior to the interview, such as how to answer when asked about his grade point average. Handling an interview along these lines, answering the questions confidently but without offending those who don't homeschool, is a lesson in finesse.

Listening

Mothers often say, "Don't interrupt while I'm talking."

Yet children continue to interrupt. Perhaps they are modeling us more than we'd like to admit.

Take time to listen intently to your children, modeling empathetic and interested listening. Let them finish their thoughts before you interrupt with your own thoughts or grammatical corrections. Encourage them to do the same, teaching them to look in the eyes of the speaker, waiting their turn to talk, and thinking before they speak.

Have children repeat back to you things they've heard. Travelers who use dictation and narration say that such methods increase listening skills tremendously.

As children move through their middle years, their abilities and confidence in reading, writing, and speaking will grow by leaps and bounds. With their increased ability and the proper learning tools, their enjoyment of using the language arts will increase as well.

SIMPLE STARTING POINTS

✦ *Read at least one of the reading resource books listed.*

Take time to go through it, taking note of age-appropriate books that may interest your child. Make a reading list and then make a trip to the library!

✦ *Expose children to different genres of books.*

Encourage children to read in genres they find less appealing, even if it means one book a year outside their comfort zone. Over time, their exposure will add up.

✦ *Decide how best to assess reading in your home.*

If you have a late reader, talk to others and ask questions about what they found helpful.

✦ *Develop a game plan for writing.*

Be sure to cover handwriting (if it's important to you), keyboarding (see "Keyboarding" in Chapter 11 for teaching tools), spelling, grammar, and editing. Refer to the lists in this chapter for project ideas. Encourage children to respond to letters and e-mail, and to always write thank you notes upon receiving gifts.

✦ *Take time to smell the roses.*

Enjoy the slower pace of having children home. Take time to listen to them. Encourage them to listen as well.

RESOURCES

Books

Bendt, Valerie. *Creating Books with Children.* Common Sense Press, 1993.

Berquist, Laura. *The Harp and Laurel Wreath: Poetry and Dictation for the Classical Curriculum.* Ignatius, 1999.

Fry, Edward Bernard. *The Reading Teacher's Book of Lists.* Prentice Hall, 1997.

Fuller, Cheri. *Teaching Your Child to Write.* Berkley Books, 1997.

Graham, Gayle. *How to Teach Any Child to Spell.* Common Sense Press, 1995.

Heller, Ruth. *The World of Language* series. Paper Star, 1998.

Herzog, Joyce. *Developing Language Skills.* Simplified Learning Products, 800-745-8212.

Sebranek, Patrick. *Write Source 2000.* Great Source Educational Group, 1999.

Sheffer, Susannah. *Writing Because We Love To.* Heinemann, 1992.

Stillman, Peter. *Write Away: A Friendly Guide for Teenage Writers.* Boynton/Cook, 1995. Also, *Families Writing.*

Learning Materials

Handwriting

A Reason for Writing, 501-736-2244.

Italic Handwriting Series, 800-547-8887, ext. 4891.

Spelling, Grammar, and Writing

The Common Sense Spelling Book, 800-244-7196, http://www.rolnet.com/rpip/cssb.html.

Easy Grammar/Daily Grams, 602-502-9454.

Easy Writing, see Easy Grammar.

English for the Thoughtful Child, 615-449-1617, http://www.greenleafpress.com.

English from the Roots Up, 425-454-5830.

Explode the Code, Educators Publishing Service, 800-435-7728, http://www.epsbooks.com.

Great Editing Adventure, 352-475-5757.

The Latin Road to English Grammar, 530-275-2064.

Learning Language Arts Through Literature, see Great Editing Adventure.

Natural Speller, 302-998-3889, http://www.designastudy.com.

Rules of the Game, EPS, see Explode the Code.

Simply Grammar, Charlotte Mason Research and Supply Co., P.O. Box 172, Stanton, NJ 08885.

Spelling Power, 509-843-1484, http://www.castlemoyle.com.

Understanding Writing, Bradrick Family Enterprises, P.O. Box 2240, Port Orchard, WA 98366.

Vocabulary from Classical Roots, EPS, see Explode the Code.

Vocabulary from the Roots Up, see Explode the Code.

Wordsmith Apprentice, 352-475-5757.

Winston Grammar, see Explode the Code.

Wordly Wise, see Explode the Code.

Writing Strands, 800-688-5375, http://www.writingstrands.com.

Writing with a Point, EPS, see Explode the Code.

Audio

Boomerang! (children's audio magazine), 800-333-7858.

Grammar Songs, Audio Memory, 800-365-SING, http://www.audiomemory.com.

Growler Tapes audio adventures, 800-GROWLER, http://www.growler.com.

Jim Weiss tapes, Parent's Choice Award Winners, 800-477-6234, http://www.greathall.com.

Software

See "Language Arts" in Chapter 11's Resources section for software titles that help in this area.

Catalogs

Chinaberry Books, 800-776-2242.

Homeschooling Book Club, 248-685-8773.

Penny Royal Press, ronbrackin@msn.com, 3512 Fontaine Street, Plano, TX 75075.

6

THE IMPORTANCE OF MATH AND SCIENCE IN A TECHNOLOGICAL AGE

In This Chapter

- The study of math
- Science: exploring the natural world
- Simple starting points
- Resources

AS SOCIETY BECOMES more technologically oriented, the need for math and science skills increases dramatically. Where it used to be that only the most technologically minded found work in math- and science-related fields, the expanding computer world sounds the call for a growing number of students entering the twenty-first-century workforce. Universities have begun to add a fifth year to some technological degrees so as to make time for humanities as well as technological training. The third of the 3 R's no longer takes a back seat to the first two. It needs to be considered equally in order to establish a good foundation for a complex body of knowledge in a vast and ever-changing Space Age.

THE STUDY OF MATH

THE EDUCATIONAL WORLD that once barred calculators for tests now requires students to use $80 machines with specialized function keys in order to tackle the work before them. No doubt, a good grasp of numbers is crucial to getting along in the everyday world around us. When figuring dollar amounts at the grocery store, balancing one's checkbook, calculating how much wallpaper you'll need, or measuring the right amount of baking soda when tripling a recipe, a solid grasp of basic math is necessary. There's more. Strong math skills are required for most who want to enter the computer-laced job market. High school trigonometry and calculus classes once reserved for advanced math students are considered basics by many college admissions offices.

Eight of the thirty-two homeschooled respondents say math is their favorite subject. They especially like their supplemental math materials, such as board games, CD-ROMs, and manipulatives. Middle years children enjoy using their math skills in their everyday lives, practicing the concepts and drills they've been learning for years.

General Math

A good grasp of general math benefits children practically and carries them to higher math studies. From eight to thirteen, homeschoolers progress through general math, often ending up at algebra or geometry by twelve or thirteen. By eight or nine, most children have mastered addition and subtraction and are ready for multiplication, division, decimals, fractions, and percents—and use all of these in a number of ways. Most respondents try to balance teaching concepts with drill work; the latter being meaningless without the former, the former complemented and facilitated by the latter. As with writing, travelers find middle years children willing to undertake the mundane drill work because they see how it will help them solve their problems more efficiently. However, this is no time to abandon games, manipulatives, or other hands-on everyday practice, for these are the things that a love for and deep grasp of mathematics are made of.

Here are the five favorite math programs of the respondents, listed alphabetically:

- Jacobs Math (ten- to thirteen-year-olds)
- Key To series
- Making Math Meaningful
- Math-U-See
- Saxon

> This is no time to abandon games, manipulatives, or other hands-on everyday practice, for these are the things that a love for and deep grasp of mathematics are made of.

Travelers are loyal to their math programs and defend their choices with fervor. A number of respondents have used a combination of programs over the years, wanting to broaden their children's understanding and skill by doing so.

Students raised on Saxon have established a stellar track record on standardized tests, adding to its popularity. While the vast majority of travelers report great confidence in Saxon, some find it tedious and repetitive. And especially until age ten or so, many Saxon users add hands-on activities to their program studies to be sure the concepts are being grasped as well as the calculations.

Judy, who has intertwined Saxon with other texts in her home, says, "I have always used a math text, which sooner or later covers the basics. We spend about thirty minutes a day on math, and I am always looking for ways to tie in what we are doing in math with real-life activities such as cooking and shopping."

Bea, whose two older children used Saxon successfully, found the younger two had difficulty with it. She credits the more hands-on approach of Math-U-See with bringing both boys up to grade level.

Anna, homeschooling mother of five who now uses Math-U-See, says, "We used Saxon, but I found that teaching three lessons a day was too much work for me."

A close second to Saxon, respondents sing the praises of the Key To series. This series is broken down into five concepts (multiplication, fractions, decimals, percents, measurements), each made up of a series of workbooks dealing with that concept only. The program does not provide nearly as much drill work as Saxon and won't by itself make children fast at calculating unless they have a particular knack for it. We use the Key To series in our home, but have supplemented with drill work (Math-It) to cut the time it takes my children to work the problems and because we believe there's something to be said for being able to figure equations expediently. My son is ready to start algebra as an eighth grader, and has chosen both the Key To series and a more traditional Scott Foresman text.

Math-U-See and Making Math Meaningful are both strong in concept building as well. Programs by Harold Jacobs (*Elementary Math, Mathematics: A Human Endeavor*) involve the children in a way that removes the mystery and intimidation of math.

For my math-phobic child, none of the formal programs have held any appeal. Instead, she works with manipulatives, listens to audio tapes of math facts, plays computer games, and reads her way through Brown Paper School Books (*The I Hate Mathematics! Book* and *Math for Smarty Pants*), enthusiastically tackling every problem they toss her way. Interestingly, she can work problems at a much higher level when confronted with them in these books than when she sees them on a drill sheet.

Looking back at her son's middle years, Renee says, "We dabbled with *Mathematics: A Human Endeavor* just for fun and to give my son the confidence that he could handle higher level math."

Linda says, "My children mainly learn their math skills in their daily lives. They use some sort of math skill at least five times a week this way." She continues, "We don't have any formal math studies, but each child probably spends approximately three hours a week doing some sort of math."

Here are some other ways parents have approached exposing their children to various concepts, many of which you may be doing already:

Graphs and Tables

Mary Sue explains, "My son learned to graph by watching The Weather Channel and reading weather charts, graphs, and tables. He began at a very young age."

Katrina says, "We use graphs and tables in conjunction with our unit studies. We made a graph showing the changes in population during the 1800s, and compared it with the 1900s, for example."

Measurements

Many travelers say their children help out in the garage, and are learning measurement by building things such as tiny wooden sailboats, birdhouses, forts, or furniture.

Mary Sue says, "My son understands measuring from working with his father and grandfather in our shop."

Deb says, "My son weighs various things, such as rocks in his rock collection. He does these kinds of things as they happen, not as part of a planned activity."

Fractions

Whatever other materials they use, almost all the respondents say their children have cemented their understanding of fractions through cooking. My ten-year-old daughter—who could not grasp the notion of fractions, or why ¾ would be more than ⅔—took a long break from math around the holidays. I put her in charge of Christmas baking. I was nearby to help, but I stayed far enough away to let her work with the numbers on her own, especially when I'd said a recipe needed to be doubled or tripled. Perhaps because she had something to show for her work, perhaps because it was more clearly visible with delineated measuring cups, perhaps for reasons I'll never know, her understanding of fractions took hold that month. It was one of my greatest joys to watch the "Aha!" moments as she made the knowledge her own.

Linda's experience is similar. She says, "My son has learned about fractions by using them in recipes. Whenever we bake we double or triple the recipe. Sometimes I'll even write out a new recipe already doubled and then have the children cut it in half while making it."

Probability and Estimating

As with fractions, many homeschoolers come to understand probability and estimating by living with the concepts. There are a number of great board games that expose children to probability and estimating. Dice rolling and coin flipping are easy ways to explore the concepts as well.

Linda says, "We have learned probability and estimating through several different board games and cards, and by everyday experience. Estimating is a skill we work on all the time. When I go grocery shopping the children take turns estimating how much my total bill will come to or how much the sales tax will add to a purchase."

> Almost all the respondents say their children have cemented their understanding of fractions through cooking.

Word Problems

Days are filled with word problems. Allow children to figure out how much punch to make to have enough for a crowd of twenty, divide the candy among party bags for birthdays, and work within their allotted budget to get gifts for everyone on their Christmas list.

Mary Sue says, "We practice word problems all the time in our everyday living. I ask my son a question and he has to use his mathematical knowledge to figure it out."

Consumer and Practical Mathematics

These are the top six ways travelers report their children use their math skills in everyday life:

- Handling money
- Cooking

- Helping at the grocery store
- Measuring things around the house (decorating, models, sewing, and so on)
- Helping in a home workshop and building things
- Playing computer and board games

Homeschooling affords these children the time to be able to explore with numbers and apply their knowledge to the world around them. Katrina says, "We implement new math skills into daily life to help ingrain the concept of what they have just learned. Our children help with the cooking, grocery shopping, and work with Dad in his paint and body shop."

Mary Sue says her son "uses his skills every day in different ways —budgeting his money, helping me cook, and especially helping his father and grandfather with projects."

Most homeschool family businesses include children in the work. At any curriculum fair, you are just as likely to be helped (with every bit the knowledge of the adults) by a middle years child as by the owner of the business.

Lila says, "Sometimes I make up scenarios using family members and people they know. Sometimes we play games like 'The Budget Game' (a game I made up) with play money, where they have to make lifestyle choices and how to make their monthly income work for them."

By eleven or twelve, many children have begun to earn money on their own, babysitting, mowing lawns, or in other ways. Managing their money gives them real-life experience with a real life "budget game," as their parents expect them to pay for more extravagant items.

Our son plays hockey. We told him from the beginning what we would spend on equipment. To purchase anything more expensive than what we've budgeted for, he must earn money to pay for it himself. He baby-sits, does yard work, and works for the local semi-pro hockey team to earn money.

MONEY-MAKING IDEAS FOR THE MIDDLE YEARS CHILD

Be sure to check out the books listed in the Resources section for more ideas for money-making ventures for middle years capitalists.

- Baby-sitting: Spread the word, help in the church nursery, put notices in local and community newsletters. When people see how good you are with children, they'll call.
- Bread baking: Some homeschoolers have great success baking bread to sell to others. Start by baking on a day you're scheduled to run errands. Bring bread to the bank, post office, hairdresser, and so on. The fresh smell should sell for you. However, check local health codes first.
- House sitting: Let neighbors know you're available to pick up their newspapers and clear out their mailbox while they're gone. Keep everything in a box, organized neatly, for their return. Also, offer to water indoor plants.
- Lawn maintenance: One local homeschooler began a lawn care business to pay for college. His business grew to the point where he was able to hire enough employees to keep it running while he was gone. Others claim they've purchased their first cars, new road bikes, and other high-ticket items by mowing lawns.
- Cake decorating: Look for a local bakery or baker's supply shop that offers classes in cake decorating, or buy a well-illustrated book and teach yourself. Keep your ears open for birthdays, bridal and baby showers, and weddings. Check local health codes before starting.
- Pet care: Pet care is no longer limited to times when people go out of town. Many busy two-income families look for willing companions for their pets during daytime hours. Let them know you're home.

- Sewing: Many people (myself included!) prefer hiring others to make slight alterations or hem clothing. I manage to sew the little elastic strips on my daughter's ballet shoes but have paid for others to sew badges on my children's scouting vests, hem pants, and make recital costumes. Keep samples of your work available for those interested, and let people know you're available. If you live in my neighborhood, call me.
- Sports runner: There are a number of ways you can make money in local sports, especially if your area has college and semi-pro or pro teams. Find out how to become a bat boy (baseball) or stick boy (hockey). Learn to take stats and call the paper to see if they need someone to cover certain high school games. Organize a group of kids and offer to clean up the local stadium after games.
- Wash cars: Do this at your home or at the home of the owner. Gather soft cloths, cleaning solutions (for inside and out), sponges, a bucket, a hose, and a vacuum cleaner.
- Typing: If you've developed good keyboarding skills, post a note at a local high school or university offering your services for typing papers.
- Gift wrapping: Find busy families around the holidays and offer to wrap their Christmas gifts for them. Charge more if you supply the paper.
- Home business help: Look for people who run their businesses from home. Offer to help, whether it's cooking and cleaning while they work, doing simple filing or answering the phones, or other tasks they need done ASAP.
- Earn your keep: Ask to see how you can earn some of the money toward the cost of any classes you take. Most karate and dance studios, for example, have demonstrators who help the teacher. While they don't get paid, they get their classes for free. If you take riding lessons, ask if you can stay late to clean the stables or feed the horses to help pay for your next class.

Higher Mathematics: Now or Later?

Most travelers with middle years children have not approached algebra or geometry, though many keep it on the back burners of their mathematical agendas, expecting to study it down the road. Those who are college-bound gear up for higher math sooner rather than later; those who are less interested in mathematically oriented careers or who have no interest in college may dabble in the subjects for general knowledge but are in less hurry to get to them. Most travelers say it's harder to incorporate algebra into their daily lives than it has been with other math skills learned up to this point.

Be realistic about your children's abilities and needs. Look through various curricula and be open to farming out upper math studies, either to Internet or video courses or to local homeschool co-op classes.

Kayla says, "Up until algebra, my son used math skills in cooking, putting together models, using money, building forts, and playing games. Algebra isn't finding its way into our real lives as readily, but he's enjoying the challenge."

The curriculum they look to for studying algebra and geometry is affected by how they see math in their futures. My son uses Key To Algebra and Key To Geometry, but not for his full studies in those subjects. Because Key To's strength is setting conceptual groundwork, it is helpful to have those books on hand, but we don't see them preparing him for the kind of advanced algebra, trigonometry, analytic functions, and calculus he will face prior to college entrance. My daughter's goals, and thereby her needs, will be entirely different.

Be realistic about your children's abilities and needs. Look through various curricula and be open to farming out upper math studies, either to Internet or video courses or to local homeschool co-op classes. Some families have sent their children to local high schools or community colleges to pick up algebra and geometry.

Amy, homeschooling mother of two in South Carolina, says, "I am not good at algebra. There's a lady at church we paid to teach our daughter two times a week."

Linda says her daughter will "probably wish to use a textbook for algebra if she decides she needs to know it. I have been trying to decide which I think will suit her best."

About geometry, she says, "We have not done any formal geometry studies, but both children have picked up a lot of basic information by reading math books and by playing computer games. I have collected the Key To Geometry workbooks to use in the future."

Like the study of Shakespeare, the study of upper math can be demystified by talking about it with children as they move through the middle years, pointing out how they are using those subjects on certain levels already. Keep pattern blocks and thinking skills books on hand so children can play geometrically while building a framework for future studies.

SCIENCE: EXPLORING THE NATURAL WORLD

A WHOPPING ONE-THIRD of middle years children dubbed science their favorite subject. These children were often specific, narrowing down their field of interest to geology, chemistry, archaeology, or meteorology. To the outside world, they may seem obsessed with their intense interest, but homeschooling allows—even capitalizes on—this intensity.

The middle years are the prime years for unlimited exploration into the science world. Compared to the early years, children now have more freedom and capability to tackle complex experiments independently, not having to wait for an adult to oversee their work for safety reasons. Compared to the upper years, middle years children have more time to dive into a field. Because everything is so new and the books available for this age group are so much fun, their journey is one of unadulterated joy. This age group is old enough to journey into science camps or special science programs if their desires are that great—something most younger years children aren't ready for and something not as widely available for upper years children who are, by necessity, beginning to narrow down their areas of interest. Middle years children can handle archaeological tools to dig in their backyards for arrowheads, gather chemicals for making ad-hoc volcanoes in their kitchens, get under their car's hood to help with simple repairs, and spend hours with slides and a microscope. All the knowledge gained during their younger years begins to take form. It now makes sense to them when yeast begins to work or you take the dog for a yearly heartworm check. Regardless of whether or not they use a curriculum as the center of their science studies, travelers say there's no stopping children from foraging through the household supplies to put their new questions to the test.

Science in Your Backyard—Biology, Earth Science, Meteorology, Astronomy

Middle years children are collectors extraordinaire. Encourage the collection of rocks, fossils, butterflies, or whatever else strikes their fancy. Have them mount and label their findings.

Good field guides are a must (see "Science Titles" in Chapter 10's Resources section), as are a pair of binoculars, and eventually, a microscope. Check science catalogs for microscopes or attend a local school auction. Don't waste your money on the ones sold in toy stores. Children who are serious about studying science will quickly become frustrated with cheap instruments. For children who like to color or for those who get frustrated by the lack of realism in their drawings, you may consider purchasing one of the many science and nature coloring books now on the market. The pictures are sometimes accompanied by descriptions of the item shown on the page, enhancing learning.

> A whopping one-third of middle years children dubbed science their favorite subject.

Have children track weather for a while. Between the newspaper, the Weather Channel, and the Internet, they are able to keep up on pat-

HOW WE DID IT

Followers of Charlotte Mason get great mileage out of their nature journals, a trip any homeschooler can take. Buy a decent quality sketch pad and some good drawing pencils (Berol Prismacolor colored pencils are excellent and can be purchased at most art and craft supply stores) and go for a hike. Stop with the children when they see something of interest. They can draw the flower, bush, bird, or rippling brook. Have them write a little about what they've seen and date the drawing. My children especially like going back to the same spot, drawing it at different times of year and noting the changes.

terns developing in their neighborhood and around the world. Buy a good thermometer and mount it outside your window. Have children track the temperature for a period of days, then graph their findings. They can also chart humidity, wind, cloud formation, and so on. While outside in the evenings, point their eyes upward. Show them star formations. Read the myths about the various constellations. Reading a few books about astronomy will whet their appetite for learning more.

Children are eager to learn about human and animal anatomy and physiology. Inexpensive models can be purchased for children to put together and keep as a study tool. The middle years are a good time to teach basics of first aid, and for older children, if you think they are ready, CPR.

Chemistry in the Kitchen

Cooking special recipes, comparing cleaning fluids, or looking up prescription medicines in a medical guide, your budding chemist can spend many happy hours in your kitchen. My son has become a pro at mixing Borax with glue and a few other ingredients to come up with the perfect slime. He and the girls have been able to notice variations caused by slightly altering the ingredients.

> Middle years children can handle archaeological tools to dig in their backyards for arrowheads, gather chemicals for making ad-hoc volcanoes in their kitchens, get under their car's hoods to help with simple repairs, and spend hours with slides and a microscope.

Because they've all baked with me from the time they could peek over my shoulder from their backpacks, they are accustomed to asking questions and watching for certain chemical reactions in food, both from successes and failures. The yeast needs to bubble so much for good bread, but too much and the bread tastes more like yeast than anything else. They've seen the perfectly tempered chocolate, silky in appearance, which makes for splendidly creamy truffles. They've also seen overheating burn it or the tiniest drop of water coagulate the whole batch.

They know that vinegar cleans as well as more expensive cleaning solutions, that the right amount of bleach brightens their T-shirts but too much eats them, and that rubber stinks up the house if it slips out of its allotted space in the dishwasher and onto the heating coil.

Because we keep a number of science experiment books on hand, the children have only to be in the mood to play Chemist for a Day.

The Garage: Physics in the Toolbox

As with chemistry, most of us were raised to think of physics as a science studied by upper-level students only. Not so. Middle years children are ready to understand the laws of motion because they live them all the time. Get going too fast on inline skates on a steep hill, and falling hurts worse. Get a stick stuck in the spoke of your bicycle, and you'd better hold on for dear life. Drop an egg, it breaks; drop a feather, it floats. All these experiences and more can be explained on a deeper level now, as you begin to incorporate words like *gravity, motion, force, mass, energy,* and *resistance* into your vocabulary.

> Cooking special recipes, comparing cleaning fluids, or looking up prescription medicines in a medical guide, your budding chemist can spend many happy hours in your kitchen.

Building things and working on cars are two great ways to pick up the laws of physics. As children try to learn to hit a nail head into a piece of wood, they become frustrated by its bending. As they learn to hit straighter and with more force, their frustration subsides in direct proportion to the increase in understanding. Replacing fan belts, checking the wear and tear on car and bike tires, tuning up bicycle gears—all offer great opportunities to bring your children into the world of physical science.

There are some great toys and kits for budding physics enthusiasts. Look into advanced Lego, Erector, Fischerteknik, and Rokenbok sets for your middle years children. They will be challenged while having fun exploring the laws of physics without even knowing it!

Field Trips

I will cover field trips in greater detail in Chapter 12, but nearly half of the favorite field trips cited by homeschooled children were those related to science. The growing popularity of hands-on science museums is no wonder with these sorts of followers. En masse, they also enjoyed venturing to aquariums, special nature hikes, and tourist marinas such as Sea World and Marine Safari. Zoos are as popular with middle years children as they are with little ones. Don't ignore the educational value of science-oriented field trips. And many of these science museums are now online (see http://www.lam.mus.ca.us/webmuseums).

Nothing brings out the beauty of homeschooling's freedom of exploration as much as the field of science.

SIMPLE STARTING POINTS

✦ *Match math materials to your children.*

Once you've settled on your approach to teaching math, choose materials that will best suit your children. Include children in the math-oriented activities all around them. You'll appreciate their help as they learn to navigate grocery store aisles and cook meals!

✦ *Help children find paying work.*

Look over the sidebar on money-making ideas. Encourage your child to try one or more of the suggestions.

✦ *Demystify upper mathematics.*

Keep a few algebra and geometry materials around the house, dabbling with them here and there. Tackle these subjects in earnest when your child is ready.

✦ *Find good science experiment books and field guides.*

Check out a few field guides and children's science books from the library. *The Science for Every Kid* series is perfect for this age group. Go through experiment suggestions, helping your child list and gather necessary materials.

✦ *Consider starting a nature journal.*

Have children draw plants and animals and date their pictures so they can keep track of the life cycles of what they draw.

✦ *Look for nearby science field trip opportunities.*

If you're heading out of town for a vacation, call the Chamber of Commerce or Tourist Bureau in that town before you go. Plan an excursion to a local natural site that exhibits the flora and fauna of that area. Bring your nature journal along and note the differences from the backyard at home.

✦ *Find ways to play with math and science.*

Order games, toys, or kits you think would interest your child.

RESOURCES

Books

The following books are often referred to as Brown Paper School Books because when they were originally published, they had simple brown covers. That is no longer the case, but the books remain popular with middle years children, who love the hands-on approach. The following titles are appropriate for math and science studies; check out other resource sections for more Brown Paper School Books. All are published by Little, Brown.

Blood and Guts (1976)
Gee, Wiz! (1983)
Good for Me! (1978)
The I Hate Mathematics! Book (1976)
Making Cents: Every Kid's Guide to Money: How to Make It, What to Do with It (1989)
Math for Smarty Pants (1982)

More math and science titles:

Cobb, Vicki. *Science Experiments You Can Eat.* Harper Trophy, 1994.

Godfrey, Neale S. *Ultimate Kids' Money Book.* Simon & Schuster Books for Young Readers, 1998.

Hoffman, Jane. *Backyard Scientist.* Series of four. Backyard Scientist, 1987.

Jacobs, Harold R. *Mathematics: A Human Endeavor.* Freeman, 1994. Also, *Elementary Algebra* and *Geometry.*

Maybury, Richard. *Whatever Happened to Penny Candy?* Bluestocking Press, 1992.

Ransome, Arthur. *Swallows and Amazons.* Godine, 1986.

Sheffer, Susannah. *Earning Our Own Money: Homeschoolers 13 and Under Describe How They Have Earned Money.* Holt Associates, 1991.

Van Cleave, Janice. *Biology for Every Kid.* Wiley, 1990. Part of *Science for Every Kid* series, including books on astronomy, chemistry, constellations, dinosaurs, earth science, and ecology.

Wiese, Jim. *Detective Science: Forty Crime-Solving, Case Breaking, Crook Catching Activities for Kids.* Wiley, 1996.

Periodicals

Creation, 916-637-5568.

National Geographic, 800-647-5463, http://www.nationalgeographic.com., also, *National Geographic World* (for kids).

ZOOBOOKS, 800-992-5034.

Catalogs and Curriculum Companies

Activity Resources, 510-783-1300.

American Science and Surplus, 847-982-0874, http://www.sciplus.com.

Creative Publications, 5623 W. 115th Street, Worth, IL 60482-9931.

Dale Seymour Publications (Cuisenaire), 800-237-3142, http://www.cuisenaire-dsp.com.

Delta Education (catalog and monthly activities), 800-442-5444, http://www.delta-ed.com.

Edmund Scientific, 609-573-6250, http://www.edsci.com.

Home Training Tools, 800-860-6272.

Innovate Learning, 800-488-1175, http://www.innovative-learning.com.

Institute for Math Mania, 800-NUMERAL, http://members.aol.com/rmathmania/index.htm.

Key Curriculum Press, http://www.keypress.com.

Lawrence Hall of Science (University of California at Berkeley) teacher resources, 510-642-5132, http://www.lhs.berkeley.edu/.

Making Math Meaningful, 972-235-5149, http://www.cornerstone curriculum.com.

Math Essentials, 800-431-1579.

Mathematics for Everyday Living series, 800-695-9427, http:// home.meridiancg.org.

Math-It, Weimar Institute (available through various homeschool vendors).

Math Products Plus, 415-593-2839.

Math-U-See, 888-854-MATH, http://www.mathusee.com.

Mastery Publications, 828-684-0429, http://www.masterypublications .com.

The Rainbow, two-year science curriculum for junior high students, 800-831-3570.

Saxon Publishers, 800-284-7019, http://www.saxonpub.com.

Science-By-Mail, Boston Museum of Science, 800-722-5487, http: //www.mos.org.

Science Labs at Home, Castle Heights Press, 1610 W. Highland #228, Chicago, IL 60660 (order *Jr. Scientist's Field Journal*).

Science Projects, 267 Hickerson Street, Cedar Hill, TX 75104.

Science Projects and Newsletter, 972-291-3345.

Tobin's Lab, 800-522-4776, http://www.silverw.com/~tobin/.

TOPS Learning Systems, http://www.topscience.org.

Software

See Chapter 11 for more math and science software and Web sites.

7

UNDERSTANDING OUR LIFE AND TIMES: HISTORY, GEOGRAPHY, AND SOCIAL STUDIES

In This Chapter

- Essential items for your journey into the past and around the world
- History
- Geography
- Social studies
- Simple starting points
- Resources

THE CHOICES IN approach and materials for history, geography, and social studies are staggering. Large bookstore chains burst with history, geography, and social studies books. Homeschool vendors offer equally impressive—yet more selective—arrays of material and carry harder-to-find titles and study guides. It's easy to become overwhelmed, so take a deep breath before plunging in. Remember, there's no place like home to study history, geography, and social studies. You can begin right in your own backyard.

ESSENTIAL ITEMS FOR YOUR JOURNEY INTO THE PAST AND AROUND THE WORLD

TAKE OR LEAVE many of the learning materials you come across, but consider the ones listed in the following sections essential to your journeys in history, geography, and social studies.

Books

Great books are your children's closest allies in studying these subjects. Historical fiction is perfect for this age group. Wondering which events really happened and which didn't forces children to evaluate situations to figure which are the most realistic, to learn to separate truth from fiction.

Robert Lawson, author of the famous *Ben and Me,* employed talking animals to add flavor to his books—which is about as unrealistic as you can get. Yet these animals capture children's imagination, making them pay closer attention to the story line. I read Lawson's *Mr. Revere and I* to my son five years ago. The heavily accented British horse added to the merriment, making history an enjoyable venture. My son never questioned whether or not Paul Revere had a talking horse, but he asked a lot of questions about other, obviously more realistic events that occurred throughout the pages.

The *Childhood of Famous Americans* series shows readers what a major historical figure's life might have been like as a child. Since the characters in most of the books range around nine to twelve years of age, these books are perfect reading for the middle years child.

The D'Aulaires' books are more realistic and factual. It's refreshing to read award-winning children's books written sixty years ago, because they are less condescending to children's level of understanding. Children happily meet the challenge head on.

Landmark books remain as popular for children's history studies today as when we were growing up. Many great Landmark titles are out of print, however. Check used bookstores and used curriculum tables at fairs; also, check Chapter 9 for information about used book businesses operated by homeschoolers. Finally, check your parents' garage!

Recently, my son pulled out a Landmark book titled simply, *Alexander Hamilton and Aaron Burr.* Out slid a book report written by my brother twenty-five years ago. It made reading the book all the more important, and interesting.

The children's Top 25 List (Chapter 5) includes a number of historically flavored novels, any of which can spur further studies and additional activities.

A Basic History Text

A good history text or historical reference book is a must. Children may not be interested in reading books of this type cover to cover, but having at least one available on the shelves for quick and easy reference allows children to check facts and place them in a larger context.

Three of our favorites are *A Child's History of the World,* Kingfisher's *Illustrated History of the World,* and Joy Hakim's *History of US* (a ten-book series on the history of the United States).

Globe, World Map, and Atlas

These items are critical for studying history, geography, and social studies. Children like to locate where Laura Ingalls Wilder's family moved, how the Gold Rushers got to California, and the locations of battles, familiar and unfamiliar. Maps and atlases offer details, globes offer perspective.

Timelines

Every time I speak or host an online chat about history, geography, or social studies I am bombarded with questions about timelines. There

MONEY SAVER

Buy large rolls of newsprint from your local newspaper. It's inexpensive and the perfect size for creating detailed timelines.

are too many on the market to list them in the Resources section, but most homeschool vendors carry a variety for you to choose from. Look for one you will use—if you don't want to draw characters, look for a time-line kit that includes them. Some people like placing timelines in a prominent place in the house; others keep them bound in notebooks (less visual effect but still useful). Many buy rolled paper and have children draw their own, practicing math (scale) and art skills along the way.

Time-line books are invaluable. Regardless of what event, place, or figure you are studying, you can locate it in *The Timetables of History* and find out what was going on around the world at the same time in history and politics; literature and theater; religion, philosophy, and learning; visual arts; music; science, technology, and growth; and daily life. Genevieve Foster's books are wonderful tools for the same reason. Though they are written around a central historical figure, they take the reader around the world to visit other important people and ideas of the same period. Though most of her books are out of print (those still available are listed in the Resources section), they are well worth hunting down.

A Reliable Source for Materials

Read through the various catalogs with history materials listed at the end of this chapter or in the Resources sections of Chapters 1 and 4. Over time, you'll develop a special fondness for one or two. Which ones carry the kinds of materials that appeal to your children and are consistent with your ideas about and approach to history, geography, and social studies in general? I receive the Greenleaf Press e-mail lists, which provide me with reviews of new materials the company carries. I look forward to reading the pithy reviews, and trust the recommendation of the company. Having someone I know who thinks similarly doing the digging for me cuts down on my research time.

Order Dover's catalog directly or purchase their materials through other homeschool companies listed, but keep your eyes open for the publisher's name. They make very inexpensive paper dolls, models (New England Village, mummy, and many more), coloring books, and a number of other products which add a fun dimension to studying history, geography, and social studies.

A Method to Track Down Important Sites and Events

Get on the mailing list of a local historical society, purchase your local paper the day the weekly events calendar is printed, or surf the Internet, but find a way to keep on top of historical and cultural events near you. Many areas now boast living history farms, Civil War reenactments, restored homes of famous people, and so on. On top of regular tours, many host special events.

Encyclopedia

Purchase either a traditional encyclopedia set or a CD-ROM version. While there's something to be said for browsing through books at leisure, we like our CD-ROM encyclopedia. It doesn't take up any shelf space and does the searching for us. We don't use it much, but when we are getting started on a topic or need to check out a few specific facts, we're glad we have it. There are times my daughter will get caught up in a subject area and will study the topic for hours, until the information runs out. Then she either decides to be happy with the knowledge she's gained from the encyclopedia or she looks to other books and materials to help her find out more.

HISTORY

DIGGING UP THE PAST ought to be the most interesting topic there is. Nonetheless, perhaps no subject is worse taught in schools than history. People attribute "God helps those who help themselves" to the Bible though Ben Franklin said it. We freely use phrases such as "the truth will set you free," "opening a Pandora's Box" and "a tower of strength" without having a clue we are quoting the Bible, Greek mythology, and Shakespeare. With every inch that we become a more technologically capable people, we simultaneously become a people lacking discernment and sophistication. Teaching children sound history is a matter of utmost importance if they are to move forward with hopes of creating a better world.

Go through this list to evaluate the approach that will work best for you. None of the following need be mutually exclusive—they're presented merely to get you thinking about the possibilities.

Inward-Out or Outward-In

Begin with your child's life and those things that matter now and work outward—or begin with important world events and relate them back to things happening at home. Beginning with a child's life includes studying the home neighborhood, city, and state. You could also study the year the child was born. It's always fun to find magazines and newspapers published on or around your child's birthday (try used bookstores). Move through family history, including major events that ancestors were involved in. History will come alive to children studying their own family and relating it to the world around them.

With every inch that we become a more technologically capable people, we simultaneously become a people lacking discernment and sophistication.

Or, start with the world and come back to your own home, relating events as they happen, either contemporary or past. For example, if you decide to study the Civil War, talk about how the country would be different, then how your state would be different, and how your child's life would be different if the South had won.

Chronological or Great Events Centered

A child may become interested in a particular historical figure or great event and want to delve into the subject. One night while watching the news, an offhanded comment about the nastiness of modern-day politicians led to a remark about Aaron Burr shooting Alexander Hamilton. The statement captured my son's attention. He found a Landmark book on the dueling twosome and plunged in. He wrote a report and will most likely continue to study the lives and times of the two men.

My ten-year-old daughter, like many girls her age, is enraptured by pioneer days. She reads and rereads the *Little House* books, dresses up as Laura Ingalls Wilder, plays with the paper dolls, cooks from the accompanying cookbook, and likes to dip candles. The knowledge she is pulling from this one interest is astounding.

At some point children need to be able to place people like Aaron Burr, Alexander Hamilton, and Laura Ingalls Wilder in a historical context. Where did Hamilton draw his ideas from? What was life like for those who chose not to venture westward? What was going on around the world during these people's lives and how were they shaped by the events of their times?

Without placing events and people in the context of the chronology of the world, children run the risk of having a mixed-up image of history full of jumbled-up concepts and facts. Many homeschoolers, because of this, teach history chronologically, starting from the beginning of civilization and moving forward (or, if teaching American history, starting from our nation's beginning and working forward). Children are exposed to people and events in an order that makes sense, because it's the order in which the events happened.

Focus on American or World History

Many travelers teach American history during the middle years, moving to world history later. This is a manageable task since there is a plethora of great history literature geared to the middle years child. Family travels take homeschoolers to various sites where they further explore their country's heritage. Two hundred years may seem like a lot to a child, but it's much more manageable than starting with ancient Egypt thousands of years earlier.

It's impossible to form a deep understanding of world history by limiting its study to one or two years of high school Western Civilization classes.

On the other hand, many homeschooling parents begin with the logical beginning: the start of the world according to their worldview (biblical Creation or Evolution). By tracing human history from the start forward, children are able to put names, places, and events in sequence, helping them understand the big picture. Many people believe there's way too much emphasis on American history in schools, a history of merely two hundred years. It's impossible to form a deep understanding of world history by limiting its study to one or two years of high school Western Civilization classes. Therefore, using the middle years to teach world history gives your child a tremendous advantage over schooled peers in understanding the implications and contexts of current events and the world we live in.

Traditional Western Civilization or Multicultural Approach

Many travelers unapologetically follow the classical pattern for teaching history: focusing on great events and great men who have shaped Western Civilization, tracing ideas from ancient Egypt through biblical times and ancient Greece, and then to Rome, the Middle Ages, Renaissance, and Reformation and up through America's Founding

Fathers—who drew upon ideas from this path to shape our nation. Others believe that pattern of study focuses too much on white men and Eurocentric ideology, ignoring the contributions and ideas of many cultures outside the Western world. You may decide to combine a study of both, but you will notice certain philosophies inherent in books that adhere to one side or the other. Noticing these underlying assumptions can serve as great springboards for discussion to sharpen your children's critical thinking skills. Was Columbus an evil, greedy exploiter or a brave and brilliant explorer? Were the sixties a time of newfound freedom or the beginning of the downfall of America's moral fiber? Developing an awareness of the perspectives of various authors is an important skill to master.

Mix and match, throw in a unit study or unplanned excursion because of a field trip or great book that ignites interest. No harm done. As with other subjects, love and enthusiasm for history will carry children through their final years of homeschooling.

Making History Fun

Most of us remember history as being a dreadfully boring subject filled with unrelated dates and people that had little meaning to our lives. My children's schooled friends often whine about the tedium of history class. For tests, they frantically come up with tricks to memorize dates of battles, inaugurations, or other landmark events. Children need to have a context to help them place the facts they are learning—the knowledge needs to become their own. History, if taught right, should never be mundane nor should it throw anyone into a frenzy memorizing names and dates.

Nothing breathes life into history like seeing it in front of you. Children can play historical board games, trading in a colonial village or exploring America at large; they can cook from historical cookbooks, make old-fashioned crafts, visit historical sites, write reports to keep in family heritage scrapbooks, and watch television documentaries. My family has done all of the above and more, and my children don't understand how others couldn't love history as much as they do.

History- and military-related field trips ranked high on the children's homeschooling surveys. Visiting old battleships, air force exhibits, and historically prominent places and attending special history festivals rank high on their lists.

When my children studied our state history this year, the text served as reference only. Instead, we traveled the state, stopping at historical markers, visiting prominent sites (Helen Keller's house among them), and attended a Civil War encampment and an Indian Heritage Festival. We visited a local cemetery where five state governors are buried. I took some photos with the children in them; they took others. They wrote reports on what they learned in scrapbook pages, adding artwork to brighten the pages. They each have mementos from their year, a record of everything they learned, and something to pass on to future generations.

> History, if taught right, should never be mundane nor should it throw anyone into a frenzy memorizing names and dates.

A number of cookbooks include replicas of recipes from yesteryear. The *Little House* series and American Girls books have accompanying cookbooks. Dig into your mother's and grandmother's recipe files.

Unit studies are perfect for history—using the historical era being studied as the centerpiece for all other learning. The KONOS and Weaver curricula offer a variety of history-based units, as does *Homeschooling Today* magazine (see "Magazines" in Chapter 1's Resources section for contact information). My family has taken off on journeys through impromptu units on bread, pioneer life, Greek mythology, and a number of other topics, as a child becomes interested in such things. There's no mystery to unit studies; one thing leads to another. The child's questions will direct you to certain materials.

One caution about unit studies: they can be overdone. Most people who write units (myself included) don't really expect anyone to do everything listed. Instead, we research our articles and find things our children enjoy. To be sure we've covered the vast array of possibilities for what different children may learn from, we list every resource we come across and every idea that comes to mind. Some middle years children would rather have their braces tightened than make a feathered cap out of construction paper; others find it great fun. Expect to accomplish about one-third to one-half of the possibilities listed in most units. Your children will learn plenty and you won't burn yourself out. A self-proclaimed perfectionist friend once worked through a unit study on ancient Egypt with her children. By the time she'd finished it, she knew she never wanted to hear about ancient Egypt again. Anyone who has tried to do everything listed in most unit studies can relate to this sentiment.

One caution about unit studies: they can be overdone. Most people who write units (myself included) don't really expect anyone to do everything listed.

GEOGRAPHY

GEOGRAPHY naturally weaves itself into historical studies as you track the Westward Movement, chart Revolutionary battlegrounds, or look for Yugoslavia on a map. As with math facts, however, there comes a time when you may want to incorporate some drill work into your middle years student's geographical studies. Is it necessary to one's well-being that they recite the fifty state capitals? Probably not, but memorizing is a good mental exercise and knowing facts about other states, including their capitals, opens the world up a little wider to your child. Mostly, though, geographical studies should serve to enlighten children by giving them an appreciation for other people who, as different as they may be, are much like the children's own family.

Discovering the Big Wide World Around You

The more children understand the importance of differences in culture, religion, agriculture, and climate, the more they will come to better understand the differences between people.

Understanding the French Catholic roots of New Orleans, the Baptist roots of the Deep South, the free-spirited, independent roots of those who headed West, the diverse roots of New York, the shipping roots of the New England states, and the German and Scandinavian roots of Minnesota and Wisconsin sheds a light on why senators from those states vote the way they do and why people who live there think the way they do even today.

And that's just the tip of the iceberg. Looking into agriculture, whether in this country or around the world, it becomes clear to children why Asians eat so much rice, Midwesterners eat so much corn, and old Swedish cookbooks offer so few fresh fruits and vegetables. It's fun to explore why Northern cornbread recipes call for large amounts of sugar while their tea has none, and Southern cornbread isn't truly Southern with sugar but the tea is full of it! Maine lobster, Alabama catfish, New Orleans red beans and rice, Iowa pork, Texas and Carolina barbecue (nothing alike!), San Francisco sourdough, all have deep-seated cultural roots.

Various Ways to Learn Geography

Draw a map of the United States, and mark each state with important agricultural symbols, then look up the ethnic heritage of its settlers. Cooking meals or celebrating special events is a fun way to weave geography studies into your homeschool. Most libraries offer interlibrary loans; check out the Junior League or historical society cookbooks from various states to begin your journey. (The older ones are better for this as the new ones tend to be more trendy in their cuisine rather than true to the state's roots.)

The same can be done around the world. Library and bookstore shelves are filled with international cookbooks. Check some out and begin your international travels. Look for markets specifically geared to international cuisine. Ask the store employees about special events and, if those events are open to the public, plan to attend.

When you prepare your international meal, have children make place mats replicating that nation's flag. Each child can read a report written about their nation of choice after dinner. Look for Geography Bees in your homeschool community. Children progress through the ranks and compete with children from other states. Homeschoolers have performed well in the past.

Traveling is the best way to study geography. As with history, it's hard to miss what's right in front of you. Give each child a map and have them chart where they are. Track the mileage and your route on trips. Leave extra time to pull off the road for markers, note the differences from home (don't forget that nature notebook!), and by all means, stay out of chain restaurants. Look for local diners that serve local cuisine. These small mom-and-pop establishments are no more expensive than most fast food chains and will give your children great memories as well as a flavor for the area. Discuss local agriculture, take pictures of the children outside the restaurants, and then start a geography section in your scrapbook.

SOCIAL STUDIES

> Geographical studies should serve to enlighten children by giving them an appreciation for other people who, as different as they may be, are much like their own families.

IF HISTORY is mistaught in the schools by making it so boring, social studies is mistaught by making such a big deal out of it and still turning out an ignorant citizenry. Never has so much ado about nothing proven so fruitless as the teaching of social studies in the public schools.

Periodically, the news reports the shocking number of high school juniors and seniors who can't name the Vice President of the country or either of their two state senators, and who believe

> If history is mistaught in the schools by making it so boring, social studies is mistaught by making such a big deal out of it and still turning out an ignorant citizenry.

Africa is a nation. Yet year after year in elementary and middle schools, these students are supposedly learning such information in classes specifically designated to teach it.

Needless to say, a well-educated citizenry should have a working knowledge of their government and the legal system, world relations, and community life. It shouldn't be hard to acquire social studies knowledge—it should be the easiest of all subject areas to teach. How hard can it be to name the Vice President when he's always in the news or to name even one state senator when election time clutters the highways with signage boasting the name? How hard is it to understand that Africa is made up of over fifty nations if one looks at a decent map?

The Journey Begins Right Next Door: Learning from Your Neighborhood and Community

What do you know about your neighbors? People each have their own unique story to tell, each their own particular background and experiences. In a world whizzing by, take time to stop at the mailbox and get to know those living near you. What was life like for them when they grew up? Where did they live? What kinds of jobs have they had? What are their best memories? How do they feel about the current events being covered in the papers and on the television screen? These questions and more will begin to open up the world of social studies to your children.

The weekly calendar of your local paper contains information about special town days and festivals, ground-breaking ceremonies, and other events that provide good opportunities for your children to explore their community. Visit the local courthouse and downtown district. Watch a jury trial and observe the judicial process at work. Schedule a speaking engagement with a local police officer—police are often willing to talk to a group of homeschoolers about work in law enforcement. Plan a trip to the state capitol to observe the legislative process. Closer to home, pay attention to those issues that concern the City Council. Visit a meeting.

As you branch out of your neighborhood to the country and world, consider studying various cultures through holidays they celebrate. Compare Bastille Day with America's Independence Day. How are the celebrations alike? How are they different? What were the driving forces behind the two revolutions?

St. Patrick's Day, Mardi Gras, the Kentucky Derby, Cinco de Mayo, and St. Lucia Day are just a handful of grand events or celebrations your children can research and celebrate at home to learn about people around the country. The list goes on and on. Let the encyclopedia or world history book be your guide to get you started. The library, the grocery store, and your imagination will take you from there.

IMPORTANT REMINDERS

- Don't forget Dorling-Kindersley (888-899-0188), Eyewitness, and Kingfisher publishers when studying history! (See "Homeschool Catalogs" in Chapter 1's Resources section.)
- Check Chapter 1's Resources section for information on Bluestocking Press and Greenleaf Press catalogs. Both are especially rich in history materials.
- If you haven't ordered a Dover children's catalog by now, do so. Ask for the children's social study catalog. See Chapter 1's Resources section for information.
- Look for software titles related to history, geography, and social studies in Chapter 11's Resources section.

The News

At about age ten, children often begin to take an interest in the newspaper, television news, and weekly news magazines. By all means, censor those items you think are too weighty for children, but begin to include the children in discussions about the news of your state, the nation, and the world. Travel sections provide a great means to learn about other areas. The editorial pages are a wonderful way to hone reasoning skills and to read the whys behind different points of view. Many parents clip out objectionable or disturbing parts of a newspaper or magazine, then let the children read the rest. Also, depending upon your particular point of view, you should be able to find a weekly or monthly news or political magazine consistent with your beliefs. Many Christians read *World,* libertarians read *Reason,* moderate liberals read *New Republic,* and conservatives, *National Review,* to name a few. And many more are published by smaller publishing houses, often advertising in homeschooling magazines. Reading papers and magazines written in different countries offer a variety of points of view.

Assessing Learning

As you move through history, geography, and social studies with your children, you will most likely see gaps as they arise and be able to address them accordingly. Some curricula and materials include tests for those interested; many include worksheets and ideas for reports. Writing about various topics is a great way for children to solidify and present the knowledge they're gaining, and will give the homeschooling parent a record of what is being learned as well as a clear picture of their children's knowledge.

Sometimes homeschoolers give their children worksheets to fill out during field trips, a way to record what they're learning and for the parent to check the level of understanding. (See "Your Community: A Microcosm of Your World" in Chapter 12 for more on field trips.)

SIMPLE STARTING POINTS

✦ *Gather the essential items you already have in your home.*

Add those you need. Hang the world map, put the globe in an easy-to-reach place. Keep the history, geography, and social studies books near one another so children can find them readily.

✦ *Think about how you would most like to approach history.*

Your approach and philosophy will drive many of your material choices. Once you decide, then begin to look at various materials available.

✦ *Watch your children for ideas.*

Take any topic that interests your children and run with it—check out books from the library, go on a field trip, use your kitchen to cook a historical or international meal.

✦ *Attend special neighborhood or community events.*

How does each special event represent the uniqueness of your area? Teach children to look for clues and consider having them write reports or save newspaper clippings on such events.

✦ *Decide how to best assess historical knowledge.*

You can be flexible about choosing tests, reports, discussions, worksheets, or other methods of assessment. You may want to alternate the various methods.

RESOURCES

Books

Bell, Neill. *The Book of Where: Or How to Be Naturally Geographic.* Little, Brown, 1982.

D'Aulaire, Edgar Parin and Ingri. *George Washington.* Beautiful Feet Books, 1996. Also *Benjamin Franklin, Columbus, Pocahontas, Buffalo Bill,* and *Leif the Lucky.*

Foster, Genevieve. *Augustus Caesar's World.* Beautiful Feet Books, 1996. Also, *George Washington's World.*

Grun, Bernard. *Timetables of History.* Touchstone, 1991.

Hakim, Joy. *History of US.* Books 1–10, various publishing dates, Oxford University Press.

Harbison, Elizabeth M. *Loaves of Fun: A History of Bread with Recipes from Around the World.* Chicago Review Press, 1997.

Hillyer, V. M. *A Child's History of the World.* Calvert School, 1997.

Holling, Holling Clancy. *Minn of the Mississippi.* Houghton Mifflin, 1992. Also, *Seabird, Tree in the Trail, Pagoo,* and *Paddle-to-the-Sea.*

Kapit, Wynn. *The Geography Coloring Book.* Addison-Wesley, 1998.

Lawson, Robert. *Mr. Revere and I.* Little, Brown, 1988. Also, *Ben and Me.*

McKinney, Kevin. *Everyday Geography.* Contemporary Publishing, 1994.

Menzel, Peter. *Material World.* Random House, 1995.

Shearer, Cyndy. *The Greenleaf Guide to Ancient Egypt: History for the Thoughtful Child.* Greenleaf Press, 1989. Also, *Guides to Old Testament, Famous Men of Greece, Famous Men of Rome, Famous Men of the Middle Ages,* and *Famous Men of the Renaissance and Reformation.*

Various authors. *Childhood of Famous Americans* series. Aladdin.

Various authors. Landmark History books and biographies. Random House.

Zinn, Howard. *A People's History of the U.S.* Harper Perennial, 1995.

Other Learning Materials

Aristoplay Games (Made for Trade, By Jove, In the Land of Egypt, Where in the World?, Hail to the Chief, and more), 888-GR8-GAME, http://www.aristoplay.com.

Discover America (board game), 800-713-1105, http://www.discoveramer.com.

Lessons from History, Hillside Academy, 1804 Melody Lane, Burnsville, MN 55337. Also, The Art Part (companion to Lessons).

The Prairie Primer (unit study based on the Little House series), 505-534-1496, http://www.CadronCreek.com.

Runkle Geography (game for sixth through eighth graders), 877-GEO-TEXT.

Teaching American History Through Art, Visual Manna, http://www.rollanet.org/~arthis/index.html, 573-729-2100.

TRISMS (Time Related Integrated Studies for Middle School), 918-585-2778, http://www.trisms.com.

The Ultimate Geography and Timeline Guide, 800-426-4650.

Periodicals

Cobblestone, 800-821-0115, http://www.cobblestone.com.

God's World News, 800-951-5437.

Catalogs and Curriculum Materials

Beautiful Feet Books (*History Through Literature, Geography Through Literature,* and more), 800-889-1978, http://www.bfbooks.com.

The Drinking Gourd, 425-836-0336, http://www.thedrinkinggourd.com.

Hands-On History, 201 Constance Drive, New Lenox, IL 60451.

History Alive, 605-642-7583, http://www.dianawaring.com. (On-line newsletter also available.)

Jackdaw Publications (reproductions of primary sources), 914-962-6911.

8

FOREIGN LANGUAGES, THE ARTS, AND PHYSICAL EDUCATION: EXTRA OR ESSENTIAL?

In This Chapter

- Foreign languages
- Living an aesthetic life
- Participation in the art world
- Physical education
- Simple starting points
- Resources

EVEN WITH CHILDREN home all day, time sails by. Hours flow into days, days into weeks, weeks into years. And the hours and days and weeks and years are full. The thought of adding foreign languages, art, and physical education to an already busting-at-the-seams homeschooling life is overwhelming. How does anyone find the time?

Most colleges require foreign language credits, and the job market is wide open to those who speak a second language. Creative exploration and physical activity are both good for children—they enrich and enhance their studies. Meanwhile, studies of educational outcomes link listening to classical music with higher test scores;

performing and martial arts to more disciplined thinking; ballet, drawing, and playing an instrument to improved math skills. And medical studies show healthy bodies contribute to healthy minds. An astounding number of young children have high cholesterol and weight problems—no wonder they can't pay attention at school.

> Creative exploration and physical activity are good for children—they enrich and enhance their studies.

Homeschool travelers want to address these subjects and have come up with creative ways for finding the time to do so. Most travelers point out that they are learning right alongside their children, each family in its own unique way.

Phyllis says, "If I see a gap, I purchase a kit, play a game, watch a video, or show them an interesting book or Internet site. Generally this is enough to spark their interest to research the topic."

"For us," Deb says, "these subjects are all a part of life. We don't separate them." She goes on, "When we become interested in a topic, we check out materials, search the Internet, or visit places that will help us learn more about it."

Katrina says, "We try to incorporate as many subjects as possible into our unit studies so the children can see how things correlate."

Susan, homeschooling mother of four in Virginia, agrees. She says, "Unit studies are the best way to handle these subjects with a large family. I can include everyone at the same time and make adjustments for the younger children."

Heather takes a different tack, "We unschool. I let the kids learn what they want, when they want, how they want. I am merely a moderator, helping them find the resources they need to get answers they are seeking."

Grace, homeschooling mother of two in Washington, says reading covers most subjects and that "the most important thing is being open to the child's interests and willing to go with those."

For Rose, history was the unifying subject. She says, "Going through history chronologically and tying in literature, art, music, writing, science, and even math was very doable. I think history should be the core element of a curriculum."

You don't have to view incorporating these so-called extras into your homeschool as something beyond your grasp. One thing that really helps is to trade in the paradigm of school at home for one of creating a lifestyle of educational pursuit. There are ways to incorporate the study of these subjects into your daily life without allowing them to besiege you. Many of the travelers who responded to my survey have done just that, and reaped rewards by watching their homeschooled students pursue the learning of foreign languages, the arts, and physical education with vigor.

FOREIGN LANGUAGES

PLENTY OF AMERICANS live productive adult lives without speaking a second language. While some claim it's arrogant for Americans, in general, to care so little about learning another language, an equally compelling argument can be made that speaking another tongue is a skill most of us don't need. Yet foreign languages continue to rank as a requirement on college applications, a growing number of large cities are being proclaimed bilingual, and the resurgence of Latin is connected with more efficient learning in other subjects.

When deciding whether to study a foreign language and what language to learn, evaluate your child's interests, family heritage, future goals (from working for a high-power Japanese conglomerate to being a missionary in central Europe), and general educational philosophy. There's no time like the present to begin—middle years children are wide open to learning a foreign language and learn much more easily now than if they wait another five or six years. Also, studying a foreign language

When deciding whether to study a foreign language and what language to learn, evaluate your child's interests, family heritage, future goals, and general educational philosophy.

now will help them understand English better, and give them time to alter their course by changing the language they're studying or adding another after building experience with the first one.

Ancient Languages: Is Latin Dead?

A decreasing number of public high school students are learning Latin. It's virtually unheard of for elementary or middle years children to do so. Yet Latin was once memorized and recited by six- or seven-year-olds in classical schools. Today, thanks to the work of Douglas Wilson and others, classical education, and thus Latin, is enjoying a comeback. Proponents point to Latin's positive role in increasing thinking skills and mental discipline, and to the way it can serve as a foundation for a deeper understanding of the nuances of the English language. After all, English draws heavily upon Latin roots.

Students intrigued by the fields of science and medicine have all the more reason to study Latin. College-bound students benefit, as Latin studies markedly increase Standardized Achievement Test verbal scores. Time spent on Greek can complement the study of Latin. Biblical scholars need to have a grasp of Greek to study the New Testament, taking guesswork out of what may have been lost in the English translation. The same, of course, can be said for Hebrew and the Old Testament, a language young Jewish children have been learning for centuries.

Trivium Pursuit, a company run by homeschoolers (see "Classical Education" in Chapter 4's Resources section), offers a number of user-friendly resources for studying ancient languages. My children have enjoyed learning to write the Greek and Hebrew alphabets by following the simple instructions in two of their books.

Parlez-Vous Français?

The study of foreign languages is fundamental to European education, because of the proximity with which people who speak various tongues live. It's common for Western Europeans to know two or three or more languages; in fact, American tourists take Europeans' knowledge of English for granted. European children almost all begin to learn second and third languages in grade school.

Discuss your child's goals. Spanish is a relatively easy language to learn because of its consistent phonics and grammar rules, and because the Spanish alphabet is similar to the English one. With the increasing number of Spanish-speaking people in the United States, having the ability to communicate in Spanish is an asset to anyone now entering the job market.

A growing number of Americans are learning Japanese and Russian, due to our nation's business interests in both countries. German is also popular among homeschoolers, and materials to teach it are easy to find. Some parents teach their children a foreign language they grew up speaking, wanting to pass it on for practical and philosophical reasons. Grandparents take pride in their bilingual grandchildren and appreciate being able to communicate freely with them in their native tongue.

Esther says, "My daughter wants to learn Italian because I am Italian and she hears the language spoken. We use a CD-ROM. She has also begun to learn French with The Learnables tapes." She continues, "What motivates her, though, is that we promised to take her to the best French and Italian restaurants in town when she completes a series."

Regina, an American homeschooling mother of two in Siberia, Russia, helps her children cement their knowledge of Russian by having them "use Russian to study math and Russian literature."

Many homeschooling parents grew up speaking French and want to pass that onto their children, believing it to be a lovely and romantic language. Because I studied Spanish for seven years I felt comfortable teaching it to all three of my children who have learned a small amount by listening to The Learnables tapes. My son and I chose the Power Glide program for his French studies, and I purchased an extra workbook so I can learn along with him.

It doesn't matter so much what the impetus is for studying a language so long as the child is motivated to learn. A second language may come in handy for reasons you can't foresee, and the experience of learning one will make learning another easier if need be.

Talking with Your Hands: American Sign Language

Sign language is the only truly universal language. Some homeschoolers want to give their children the tools to communicate with the hearing impaired. Children who learn to sign learn a beautiful art form, a way to communicate with children who can't hear, and a highly marketable skill.

Children who learn to sign learn a beautiful art form, a way to communicate with children who can't hear, and a highly marketable skill.

Most children enjoy learning to sign the alphabet. Others become intrigued by using various signs, noticing how much they "look" like what they are communicating. Anyone who has seen a choral presentation with a signer off to the side appreciates the beauty of sign language.

My children enjoy reading and rereading *You Don't Need Words,* a book that discusses ways people have communicated through symbols and covers the basics of sign language. See the Resources section both here and in Chapter 9 for more information on sign language resources and special needs in general.

What Suits Your Learning Needs?

Most travelers say they tackle foreign languages from their home, either through videos, tapes, or the computer (CD-ROMs and Internet classes). Children need to hear a language in order to speak it, so unless you are comfortable using the language being learned, you will need some sort of audible help. Most programs on the market have accompanying audio tapes, even if they are book centered.

Some homeschool groups offer classes that give children opportunities to speak the language with others. Ask around and find a homeschooling parent who speaks another language fluently and will share that knowledge with others. Some travelers send their children to local high schools or community colleges for language learning. Doris says, "We are learning Spanish but will get some help from either a tutor or a community college in learning it further."

Opening your home to a foreign exchange student is another great way to learn a second language. You will hear the language from a native speaker, and you'll learn about another culture as well.

LIVING AN AESTHETIC LIFE

HOMESCHOOLERS have the opportunity to recapture the beauty being lost by our culture. The average school built today looks no different from the average jail. How dreadful to spend one's days in such a dreary place!

> As the pace of modern life strips a child's world of beauty, you can restore it in your homeschool.

Beauty does not have to be expensive. Reading a Wordsworth poem or listening to classical music played on the radio while sitting in a comfortable chair with an old quilt is a beautiful way to spend time. Pine cones with branches arranged neatly around them make beautiful fall centerpieces. As the pace of modern life strips a child's world of beauty, you can restore it in your homeschool. It doesn't have to be hard, just thought about—checking out a poetry book for your child's quiet time while at the library, turning on the radio to listen to your local classical station's midday selections, carrying a basket to gather pine cones or other free treasures while on a nature walk—they're all easy ways to incorporate beauty and art into your homeschool.

Here are some simple ideas to help you get started incorporating the arts into your life.

QUICK & EASY

Art Museums and Exhibits on the World Wide Web

Too busy to head out to your local art museum? Take a rainy afternoon, make hot cocoa, and see some of the finest art the world has to offer.

Cezanne Exhibit, http://www.cezanne.com.
Museum of Fine Arts, Boston, http://www.mfa.org/.
National Gallery of Art, Washington, D.C., http://www.nga.gov/.
Norman Rockwell Museum, http://www.nrm.org.
London's National Gallery, http://www.nationalgallery.org/uk/search/index.html.
The Louvre, http://mistral.culture.fr/louvre/.
Metropolitan Museum of Art, http://www.metmuseum.org.

Art Appreciation

Beauty begets beauty; creativity begets creativity. While writing, words seem to flow more smoothly if I sit in a lawn chair with a cup of tea by my side, sun beaming on my face, than if I stare at the computer screen commanding my mind to produce words. People tell me I need to enter the technological age. I think I'd rather smell the honeysuckle. It's not accidental that writing is easier among fresh air and fresh flowers. I think that's the way it's meant to be.

Painting and Sculpture

Order simple prints from one of the art companies listed in the Resources section. Frame your favorite larger ones. Cover your refrigerator or bulletin board with others. Or order selected back issues of *Homeschooling Today* magazine. Each issue of the magazine has a high-quality art reprint in the center, with an accompanying art history lesson (see "Magazines" in Chapter 1's Resources section). Have children look at the work of various artists, then talk about which works were produced during the same periods, and which ones were produced by the same artists. Use your time-line book to look up artists to see what was going on around the world that might have influenced their works.

Keep some good art history books around. My family likes *Sister Wendy's Story of Painting.* Occasionally, my children read a few pages, then want to look through our prints to find more work by the same artist.

Pay attention to local exhibits. Don't worry if you don't know anything about art. Ask a tour guide to help you. They appreciate an attentive audience and enjoy sharing knowledge about something they love! If you have Internet access, visit world-renowned museums on the Web.

Music

The least expensive way to expose your children to great music is to listen to the radio during the day. Research shows children who study to classical music score higher on exams than those who study to other types of music. My children concentrate for longer periods and produce better work when I remember to turn on National Public Radio—the most reliable source of classical music in my area.

Add to your personal classical music collection. The award-winning *Classical Kids* series takes children into famous musicians' lives, introducing both the musician and the music. We listen to *Mr. Beethoven Lives Upstairs* as often as we think of it.

Study the history of music by learning what people listened to before classical music arrived on the scene, and where music has gone since then. Include music with an international flair as well. Studying the folk music of various nations is a great way to learn about other cultures.

> The least expensive way to expose your children to great music is to listen to the radio during the day.

Reading through *Lives of the Musicians: Good Times, Bad Times, and What the Neighbors Thought* tickles my children's funny bones while teaching them about a number of famous composers.

Phyllis says, "For music and art, I have a variety of good music surrounding the children and good art books to browse through. We go to concerts and art museums, but it really isn't treated as a separate subject."

Grace says her children get out to explore the art world too, "We take the children to lectures, plays, and concerts."

Corinne homeschools two children in South Carolina. She says, "We play a lot of classical music and occasionally read about a musician."

Christina, homeschooling mother of three in New Hampshire, ties music and arts into other studies in her home. She says, "We casually study fine arts by displaying artwork around the house, looking closely at the pictures and narrating what we see. We briefly discuss the artist and when he worked."

Theater and Dance

The theater doesn't have to be imposing. Children take pleasure in going to plays and dance performances. Start with the well known and work your way to the more obscure—the *Nutcracker* and *Hamlet* are easier entry points than plunging in with more avant-garde works. Read the story behind the play or ballet before you attend. If they read ahead, children more easily follow the action and understand the meaning of what they see on the stage.

> Start with the well known and work your way to the more obscure. The *Nutcracker* and *Hamlet* are easier entry points than plunging in with more avant-garde works. Read the story behind the play or ballet before you attend.

Theater tickets can be costly. Look for matinees and free performances, or gather a group of homeschoolers and ask for group rates. Also, many towns offer "school" performances, a day where the performance is free for city school children. Call ahead to reserve your space.

Don't ignore community theater, church, and high school performances. Check the arts section of your paper for listings, and to stay abreast of which groups are establishing a reputation for producing high-quality work.

PARTICIPATION IN THE ART WORLD

Participating in the world of the arts goes hand in hand with art appreciation while also giving children specific skills. It's enlightening to observe mothers at the ballet studio watch their daughters' classes and become frustrated with their missteps. I wish those same mothers would display the courage to take an adult class. They'd learn how difficult ballet can be.

My younger daughter loves to dance. I imagine ballet will be a part of her life for years to come. My older daughter, however, pretty much despised it, but I encouraged her to finish a year of ballet so she could more fully appreciate the performances.

Learning how to create perspective and light in drawings, to play a scale in several different keys, to plié and relevé at the ballet barre, and to "throw" a voice to the audience all add to children's repertoire of cultural understanding while sharpening their academic and life skills. You can't progress too far in music or dance without using math. Conquering perspective incorporates high-level thinking skills, and standing in front of a crowd reciting memorized passages from a play builds confidence. Creativity makes children better students all the way around.

Painting and Drawing

Look through homeschool catalogs or your local art store to find a good how-to drawing program. Walter Foster's art books and *Draw Today* program are highly recommended by homeschool travelers. Invest in good drawing and watercolor paper, colored pencils, and watercolors. My children have spent hours with *Watercolor: For the Artistically Undiscovered* from Klutz Press.

If your children progress to the point where they need or want outside help, call your local art museum or art league for a list of classes taught by artists. Ask if they would be willing to teach homeschooling groups. Our local museum has designed weekday classes specifically for homeschoolers.

Or find other homeschooling parents who have artistic knowledge to share. Arrange private or group lessons. Consider trading your talents by teaching another small group. This can be done with music, theater, and dance as well.

Music

A number of travelers report that their children learn music at home with their parents' help or by teaching themselves. Klutz Press carries a few simple books with easy-to-follow instructions. Local music stores or homeschool vendors can help you choose a program to suit your needs.

Many homeschool children take private music lessons. Some also take lessons through their local homeschool groups or co-ops. Community choruses and church choirs are popular among travelers for exposing children to music basics.

Doris says, "My son plays the violin and piano, participates in the youth orchestra and children's community chorus, and plays hand bells at our church. My daughter plays the guitar, sings in the children's community chorus, and plays hand bells. Homeschooling gives us the flexibility to do these activities. Why should my children sit through elementary music class in school when they have nearly enough knowledge and experience to teach it?"

Theater and Dance

A large number of travelers' children take dance lessons. The majority take ballet, but they also list folk dancing, square dancing, Hebrew dancing, and sacred dancing on their surveys. Most take these classes at private or community dance studios, but as with music and art, many take classes with other homeschoolers through their local groups.

Most towns have community or children's theaters. A number of travelers arrange theater groups within their homeschool communities. Sometimes the children write their own plays; other times they perform more traditional ones. The American Girls Theater kits are ready-made and a perfect introduction to theater for middle years children.

Gail says, "Five years ago, the girls and I began acting in community theater plays. Then we put together our own play with a group of homeschoolers. A drama company grew from there. Currently, the whole family, including Dad, is cast in *A Midsummer Night's Dream.*"

PHYSICAL EDUCATION

Star athletes or clumsy, they are all happy to avoid school PE classes, another bastion of comparison and categorization among peers in a less-than-interesting environment.

PHYSICAL EDUCATION is important to most travelers, though they approach incorporating physical activity into their days in various ways. Whether they participate in competitive sports or take family walks, they are thankful homeschooling affords them the time to be active and teach their children a lifelong appreciation for living fit. Some make little fuss over including exercise into their days, others are sports aficionados, living and breathing for their next competition. Star athletes or clumsy, they are all happy to avoid school PE classes, another bastion of comparison and categorization among peers in a less-than-interesting environment.

To Compete or Not to Compete?

Twenty of the sixty-three travelers say their children participate in competitive sports. Among those who don't, some feel strongly that such activities are too prevalent in a society where the sports world runs amok; they also note the time such activities take away from family life. Others say their children simply aren't interested.

Those who have children heavily involved in competitive athletics appreciate the freedom homeschooling affords. One mother says her two highly competitive swimmers are able to participate more fully and are better rested and healthier than when they were in school.

Like most hockey players his age, my son doesn't get off the ice until late at night. I'm glad he sleeps as late as his growing body needs, and tackles his schoolwork when rested and ready.

Some homeschool groups have started their own competitive leagues and noncompetitive physical education days. A homeschool basketball team in Texas is taking the state by storm. Other groups prefer gathering at a local court, playground, or park and playing a more relaxed game of kick ball.

Living Fit

A large number of travelers say they enjoy being together too much to allow the rigors of an active sports-filled life to take up their time. Instead, they find things to do together. Among activities travelers list on their surveys are inline and roller skating, walking, hiking, biking, and swimming. Roller rinks and swimming pools will sometimes schedule special times for homeschoolers. We have arranged homeschool skating times at both the local roller and ice rinks.

Taking time to think about how these "extras" can fit into your homeschooling life will pay off. You'll see great benefits, and it's not quite as hard as you might think.

Renee says, "Once in a while I used to get carried away with trying to pack in these things. It was kind of silly though. It didn't take long to realize my son really didn't need to have such an orchestrated fuss over his education. He was learning plenty by reading, educational television, field trips, conversation, computer programs, and travel."

By combining good materials with a commitment to incorporate the subjects into your homeschool, foreign language, the arts, and physical education will begin to flow with the rest of your learning.

By combining good materials with a commitment to incorporate the subjects into your homeschool, foreign language, the arts, and physical education will begin to flow with the rest of your learning.

SIMPLE STARTING POINTS

✦ *Assess the importance of learning a foreign language.*

Decide whether or not learning a foreign language matters to you and your child. If so, discuss which language interests your child and choose a program or arrange for classes.

✦ *Think about learning at least a little sign language.*

Look over the various reasons people may want to learn to sign. If you decide sign language has a place in your homeschooling, visit Web sites and review materials to decide which suit you best.

✦ *Make room for art appreciation.*

To get started thinking about art appreciation, break down the larger picture into smaller ones of painting, music, theater, and dance. Peruse library shelves to find good books on the subjects. Consider purchasing one or two for references.

✦ *Contact NPR, PBS, and other local radio and TV stations for scheduling information.*

Make note of arts programming and include it into your homeschool days.

✦ *Look for classes in the arts.*

Check to see if your homeschool group offers classes in the arts. Ask to observe before signing up your child. Or check into some of the other options mentioned in this chapter.

✦ *Come up with a plan for physical activity.*

Evaluate your family's physical fitness and children's personalities. Are they interested in competitive sports or would they be happier with a smaller, more laid-back homeschool group, or biking with you? Whatever you decide, commit yourself and your children to daily exercise.

RESOURCES

Languages

A Greek Alphabetarion, The Alphabet for Biblical Hebrew, The Alphabet for Biblical Greek, 309-537-3641, http://www.muscanet.com/~trivium.

All-in-One Language Fun CD-ROM (Spanish, French, German, Japanese, and English all on one CD), 800-688-1937.

Artes Latinae, 847-526-4344, http://www.bolchazy.com.

BBC Language Course for Children, 888-248-0480, http://www.early-advantage.com.

Greek Tutor, 800-779-6000.

Language Adventure, 800-622-3574, http://www.LanguageQuest.com.

The Learnables, 800-237-1830, http://www.learnables.com.

Power Glide, 800-596-0910, http://www.power-glide.com.

Trivium Pursuit (see "Classical Education" in Chapter 4's Resources section).

Sign Language

Flodin, Mickey. *Signing for Kids.* Perigee, 1991.

Gross, Ruth Belov. *You Don't Need Words!* Scholastic, 1991.

Rankin, Laura. *The Handmade Alphabet.* Dial Books, 1991.

Sign Language Videos, 800-367-9661, http://www.signlanguagevideos.com.

Tiny Hands (2 tape video series), http://www.hiddencreekresources.com.

Teaching the Arts

Books

Arnosky, Jim. *Drawing from Nature.* Demco Media, 1987.

Beckett, Sister Wendy. *Sister Wendy's Story of Painting.* DK Publishing, 1994.

Brooks, Mona. *Drawing with Children.* Tarcher, 1996.

Card, Michael and Susan. *The Homeschool Journey: Windows into the Heart of a Learning Journey.* Harvest House, 1997.

Janson, H. W. *History of Art.* Abrams, 1997.

Krull, Kathleen. *Lives of the Artists: Masterpieces, Messes (and What the Neighbors Thought).* Harcourt Brace, 1995.

Libbey, Ted. *The NPR Guide to Building a Classical CD Collection.* Workman, 1994.

Muhlberger, Richard. *What Makes a Degas a Degas?* Metropolitan Museum of Art, 1994. Also, *What Makes a Leonardo a Leonardo?* and others in the series.

Peppin, Anthea. *The Usborne Story of Painting.* EDC, 1980.

Quine, David and Shirley. *Let Us Highly Resolve.* Cornerstone Curriculum Project, 1996.

Taylor, Judy, Whaley, Joyce, and Hobbs, Anne. *Beatrix Potter 1866–1943: The Artist and Her World.* Warne, 1996.

Thomas Nelson Publishing. *Rembrandt: The Old Testament.* Thomas Nelson, 1996.

Various authors. *Masters of Art series.* Peter Bedrick Books.

Venezia, Mike. *Getting to Know the World's Great Artists* (series). Children's Press.

Williams, Helen. *Stories in Art.* Millbrook Press, 1991.

Learning Materials

Adventures in Art, 972-235-5149, http://www.cornerstonecurriculum.com.

Draw Today and other Walter Foster art books, 800-552-DRAW.

How Great Thou Art, 800-982-DRAW.

Hurd, Thacher, and Casidy, John. *Watercolor for the Artistically Undiscovered.* Klutz Press, 1992.

Insight Technical Education, 877-640-2256, http://www.transport.com/~mpeterman (tapes and workbook).

Understanding the Arts, fine art centerfold in *Homeschooling Today* magazine, see "Magazines" in Chapter 1's Resources section.

The Young Masters Art Program, 800-210-1220 (video), http://www.newmaster.com.

See "Other Learning Materials" in Chapter 7's Resources section for History Through Art, Visual Manna, and other history materials that incorporate art.

Catalogs

A Child's Dream, 800-359-2906, fax for catalog—303-443-4923.

KidsArt, 800-959-5076.

National Gallery of Art (Publications Dept.), 6th & Constitution, NW, Washington, D.C. 20565.

University Prints Catalog, P.O. Box 485 Winchester, MA 01890.

Music

Books

Ganeri, Anita. *Young Person's Guide to the Orchestra.* With accompanying CD. Harcourt Brace, 1998.

Gindick, John. *Country Blues Harmonica for the Musically Hopeless.* With accompanying harmonica. Klutz Press, 1984. Also, *Country and Blues Guitar for the Musically Hopeless.*

Kavanaugh, Patrick. *Raising Musical Kids.* Vine Books, 1995.

Krull, Kathleen. *Lives of the Musicians: Good Times, Bad Times, and What the Neighbors Thought.* Harcourt Brace, 1993.

Smith, Jane Stuart, and Carlson, Betty. *The Gift of Music: Great Composers and Their Influence.* Crossway, 1995.

Tatchell, Judy. *Understanding Music.* Usborne, 1990.

Learning Materials

Artdeck game by Aristoplay, see "Other Learning Materials" in Chapter 7's Resources section for Artdeck contact information.

Christian Piano Course, Davidsons Music, 6727 Metcalf, Shawnee Mission, KS 66204.

Classical Kids Series of tapes, The Children's Group, BMG Music.

Music and Moments, 972-235-5149, http://www.cornerstonecurriculum.com.

Piano Discovery System, keyboard with computer software, check various homeschool vendors, music stores, and software companies.

Rue Publishing, Sacred Music Instruction, 800-721-2439, http://www.ourworld.compuserve.com/homepages/rue.pub.

Catalogs

Homespun Tapes, 800-338-2737

Theater and Dance—Learning Materials

American Girls Theater Kits, Pleasant Company.

Castle, Kate. *My Ballet Book.* DK Publishing, 1998.

Thomas, Annabel. *Ballet, an Usborne Guide.* EDC, 1986.

Our culture takes for granted the inherent goodness and importance of competition and athletic prowess. For a thought-provoking critique of competition, read *No Contest: The Case Against Competition* by Alfie Kohn (Houghton Mifflin, 1992).

Important Reminder: Check Chapter 11's Resources section for more on videos, software, and Internet teaching resources for foreign languages, the arts, and physical education.

9

TAILORING HOMESCHOOLING TO MEET YOUR FAMILY'S UNIQUE NEEDS

In This Chapter

- ✦ Too many bills and not enough money
- ✦ Single parents
- ✦ The gifted child
- ✦ The special needs and physically disabled child
- ✦ The academically labeled child
- ✦ Stay-at-home dads
- ✦ The only child
- ✦ Large families
- ✦ Other challenges
- ✦ Simple starting points
- ✦ Resources

HOMESCHOOLERS defy stereotyping. As discussed in earlier chapters, travelers bring their children home to school for various philosophical and religious reasons, and proceed using various methods and materials. And that's just scratching the surface of differences between homeschooling families.

Travelers come from all walks of life, and cross every conceivable demographic line. They are rich and poor, they have compliant children and difficult ones. Some have children with special needs, others, children who are gifted or learning disabled. For some, their lifestyles make homeschooling relatively easy; for others, great sacrifices and scheduling alterations are required.

If you think your situation is unique, you're right. If you think your situation prohibits you from homeschooling, think some more. You will find another family, somewhere, who shares some of the same challenges. They can offer insights to help you see homeschooling may be more possible than you might think. Hopefully, in the next few pages, you'll meet a few such families and find both philosophical and practical support from the road they've walked before you.

TOO MANY BILLS AND NOT ENOUGH MONEY

LACK OF MONEY is the number one difficulty travelers mention. Incurring the expenses of homeschooling while keeping one parent home full time is difficult.

The Simpler Life

All the travelers who listed money as a problem area say they've learned to appreciate the simpler life homeschooling affords them.

Lila is frank about her family's financial situation. She says, "Homeschooling is great for a poor family, because we don't have to worry about how our children dress or keep up with the current fashion trends. We're not running in different directions going to activities—because we can't afford to!"

> If you think your situation is unique, you're right. If you think your situation prohibits you from homeschooling, think some more.

Taking time to evaluate your needs will pay off. Most homeschoolers make some bad purchases along their journeys, so don't be surprised if you do, too. But keeping dud purchases to a minimum can save you a good deal of money.

Christina says, "A lot of what I've bought has turned out not to be useful. I now spend only a bit more than what I'd spend for hot lunches in public school. My advice is to learn a lot about anything before you buy."

Sometimes learning to be content is difficult. While many homeschoolers have computers, for example, some do not.

Corinne acknowledges she'd like to be able to afford a computer, but says, "I've accepted life as it is. We appreciate the catalogs that explain the materials carefully and use the library a lot."

The vast majority of homeschoolers get a lot of educational mileage from their libraries.

Esther says, "We get books from the library or share with friends, and once used a $12 workbook to cover about everything else."

Linda says her family has always been on a tight budget. "We have to weigh costs of each activity," she says. "I guess the most important thing is not to dwell on it or it can really drag me down. Our children understand our limitations. We try to find cheaper alternatives." She continues, "Most helpful, by far, are the public library systems we belong to. Also, we use the Internet and contact other homeschoolers to work out swaps on materials."

An excellent education does not have to be expensive.

Larissa says, "When we were homeschooling on a tight budget, we had to make every penny count. We realized how little it takes to get a good education. Finding good books at bargain prices became a sort of game; we bought classics for pennies!"

Working at Home

A number of homeschooling families have one parent who works from home, in most cases the mother. People ask how I meet writing deadlines with children home all day. I spent a lot of time when the children were younger teaching them how to do chores properly and encouraging them to see our family as a team. We established a schedule that makes sense for us. I get up earlier than they do so I can accomplish some work before they arise. The first few hours they're awake, we spend time together, reading, doing schoolwork,

MONEY SAVER

Many travelers borrow and buy used curriculum, make some of their own learning materials, frequent garage sales for great books, attend free field trips, and rely on the library. Homeschooling mothers say they have become more creative and more particular because of their financial straits. They take more time to research materials before purchasing, because they can't afford to make costly mistakes. They find clever ways of covering subjects, which end up more fun for the children than costly textbooks.

and having a talkative lunch. By early afternoon, they've had their needs taken care of and are ready to pursue their individual interests, and I'm free to write some more.

Many mothers report the same sort of thing. Some worked at home before their children came home to school, some brought a part-time job home, others generated work from their homes to replace income they lost by leaving their jobs. It may not be an ideal solution but it is a workable one.

Esther says, "At times I feel we have done the bare minimum of schoolwork, though I've always made a great effort to provide my daughter with great books. I credit her high test scores to all the reading she does."

Children who live with a home business acquire business savvy and practical knowledge that will serve them well later. Katrina says, "By having a home-based business, we have learned to be creative and stick to a budget. The children have learned the business ropes by being with us."

Nicole homeschools three children in Virginia. She echoes the sentiment, saying, "I run a business from home. It enhances the children's education—they help, they learn, they see me solve problems."

Aside from business know-how, these children learn how to work independently. Christina works at home typesetting books. She says, "Normally, I work about two hours during the day. The children use the other computer or otherwise manage without me. I then spend another two hours working at night, after they have gone to bed."

If you choose to work at home, be prepared for some rough spots. Trudy speaks frankly, "Working at home takes a lot of time and energy out of homeschooling, but I am home to help when needed. Conducting business can be hard—children don't always understand that."

Trudy's right. Children don't always seem to understand the urgency or importance of business phone calls. It helps my children if I let each one know when I'm placing an important call. When I receive a business call, I write a note and carry it around to each child. They know to be quieter than usual so I can concentrate on the phone conversation.

Larissa agrees, "Running our business from home was a challenge. I had to be flexible, and I often had to return from dealing with a call to start pretty much all over because my son had gone on to something else."

You'll need help—but middle years children are capable of helping. Linda's family started a home-based computer business a year ago. She says, "When I am busy with the business, I rely on the children more to help run the household. They have learned to rely upon each other a little more, since I'm not always available. Often, our most interesting learning experiences are those spent in the car. We listen to books on cassettes and to different styles and types of music, and talk about everything under the sun."

Jennie is now a columnist for a large homeschooling magazine. Prior to that, she worked as a freelance editor, but the work became too much to balance with the demands of homeschooling. She says, "When I was working long hours, we couldn't do much running around. We usually passed up field trips, for example. Fortunately, my daughters have never been keen on touring pickle factories and the like, so that part didn't matter too much. What became intolerable," Jennie continues, "was the grueling pace of working until the wee hours of the morning, then getting up early to start schoolwork with the kids. I eventually retired from freelance editing and haven't regretted the decision for a minute."

Jennie offers a gentle warning to those considering working at home, "Obviously, if you're going to homeschool, working at home can be ideal, but keeping both family and business running smoothly takes a tremendous amount of work. I used to think that as the kids grew older, they'd need me less, but I'm finding out that preteens and teens need their parents just as much as they always did."

Middle years children need time to talk and to listen. Carving out the kind of time needed is crucial, and it may need to be scheduled into your life if you find days passing by too quickly without these times to communicate.

Mary Sue acknowledges the challenge as well. "My time and attention is more divided," she says. "I've had to become more structured in order to carve out a time that I can be totally focused on learning. If I don't, I put projects and excursions on the back burner or forget about them completely."

> "I used to think that as the kids grew older, they'd need me less, but I'm finding out that preteens and teens need their parents just as much as they always did."
>
> —JENNIE, HOMESCHOOLING MOTHER OF TWO IN MINNESOTA.

Not all travelers bring work home. Though it may initially seem more taxing, some homeschooling parents work outside the home.

Lynn, homeschooling mother of two in California, says, "I work part-time. It seems like I never get enough sleep. My husband and the children's grandparents help out when I work." She believes homeschooling has been beneficial to her situation, though, and says, "It's brought us closer together as a family."

Doris works two and a half hours outside the home every day. She says, "Generally, I work between 6 A.M. and 8:30 A.M. While this doesn't seem like a lot of hours, it really complicates my life and my husband's, since he is needed to help with the children during the time I am working. He gets to work later than most of his coworkers." She continues, "One of the challenges for me is changing roles. I have no time to wind down after working. I switch hats from professional to homeschool teacher and mom on the drive home. The extra income is nice but I don't think this situation will work long-term. I am hoping to find a part-time job that I can do from home."

Rose faces the particularly challenging task of working full time outside the home. "Our solution has been for me to work second shift," she says. "I am with the kids from 8 or 9 in the morning until 2 P.M. or so. I leave at 2:45 P.M. to go to work and get home around midnight. It has been stressful to be away from the home front that much." She continues, "One consolation is that the kids are generally sleeping the last two or three hours of my shift, so it seems like less time lost. All in all, it really stinks, but it's necessary right now."

As in other areas, support is a key factor in balancing work with homeschooling. Seek out those in similar circumstances for encouragement.

SINGLE PARENTS

SINGLE PARENTS FACE enormous challenges. The thought of trying to single-handedly run a household, provide for the family, and homeschool children appears to be insurmountable. Only one of the travelers who answered the questionnaire is a single parent.

Polly, homeschooling mother of two in Ohio, says, "We lost my husband in an accident when my oldest child was nine. I remember feeling it was so unfair for me to take my son for the start-of-year assessment when we were still reeling from his dad's death. His dad had died in August, just as we were preparing to start school. Eventually everything worked out."

Some homeschooling parents carry extra life insurance on both spouses, so in the event of the unthinkable, the surviving parent is able to stay home and educate the children. Others say by working at home, or having a home business, they would hope to provide for the children while keeping them home for school.

I've met a handful of single mothers educating their children at home. One was on government assistance, believing it to be a sensible short-term answer because her child's formative years were too important to risk putting him in school. Another worked from her home, and another worked full time, second shift, outside the home, finding places for her child to stay. Needless to say, extended family or close friends who can pitch in and help can make or break the single parent's desire to homeschool.

By the middle years, children are ready to take on more independent work, a major asset for the single parent. The Robinson Curriculum was designed by a single homeschooling father who needed a way for his children to accomplish their schoolwork independently. You may want to look into the Robinson Self-Teaching Curriculum or incorporate some ideas from the Robinson method into your homeschooling if you are raising children alone (see "Full Service Curriculum Companies" in Chapter 4's Resources section for information).

> Begin to build your support system as soon as you begin to think about homeschooling.

The odds are definitely stacked against the single parent trying to homeschool, but people have done it. Most say they couldn't do so without the support of others, though, so if this is your situation, begin to build your support system as soon as you begin to think about homeschooling. If you don't know where to begin, ask your local support group for help and search the Internet for those who share your status.

THE GIFTED CHILD

AN INCREASING NUMBER of parents are bringing their gifted children home to school, claiming the mundane schoolwork bores their children and slows down their academic achievement. This is a telling argument, but homeschooling gifted children carries a certain weight of responsibility for travelers.

Carol's son consistently completed his work in one-fourth the time the teacher allotted. She says, "He would joke around with the other children and would end up standing outside the classroom as a punishment." She continues, "I was a little frightened by the fact that my gifted eighth grader knew more than I did when we began homeschooling. All eleven of my children were in the gifted and talented program at the school, although at the last, I refused to allow them to participate because the time there was wasted."

> "Homeschooling is ideal for gifted children. My son is challenged at his ability level, rather than having to slow down to the pace of other kids. He has lots of extra time to develop his strengths."
>
> —Regina, homeschooling mother of two in Siberia, Russia.

Once home, Carol allowed the children to move forward at their own pace and included college classes in their education.

Rebecca homeschools her gifted son in Oklahoma. She believes he is learning plenty on his own. She says, "Because my son tests way beyond his age, I am becoming increasingly comfortable with the idea of unschooling."

Teaching two children at once is easier when they work together. Eileen allowed her gifted son to work on the same level as his older brother. She says, "He can advance as he wishes and they help one another."

Travelers with gifted children believe homeschooling is the best solution for meeting their children's needs. Regina points out, "Homeschooling is ideal for gifted children. My son is challenged at his ability level, rather than having to slow down to the pace of other kids. He has lots of extra time to develop his strengths." Her daughter, she says, "is an outstanding pianist, and wins piano competitions in Russia. Homeschooling is ideal for her, too, because she can devote the time necessary to practicing her music."

THE SPECIAL NEEDS AND PHYSICALLY DISABLED CHILD

IF SCHOOL IS TOUGH on the emotions of your lively and healthy child, it's immeasurably worse for the child with a special need or physical disability. Despite an increase in funding for special needs children, there's only so much an institution geared toward the middle can do to meet them.

A mother whose child has cystic fibrosis contacted me about homeschooling. Her son becomes physically exhausted quicker than other children. The frequent breaks he could take at home would be good for him, both physically and mentally.

Two mothers who filled out the survey have children with diabetes. Both credit homeschooling with improved health and concentration. The timing of insulin shots, the monitoring of meals, the ability to rest on "off" days, all add up to an education more suited to a child with this special need and others. For children whose special needs require an alteration in curriculum and approach, such as blindness or deafness, parents know best which materials will suit their child's learning needs, as well as their special needs.

Homeschooling parents of special needs and physically disabled children have exceptional pressures and seem to be at high risk for burning out. If you're in this category, rally support and find ways to take breaks as you need them. Also, there is a fleet of new Web sites available to help connect you with other parents—support perhaps otherwise unavailable to you.

THE ACADEMICALLY LABELED CHILD

NOTHING HEATS UP a discussion about education as quickly as bringing up the host of labels children in school have doled out to them. Emotions run strong concerning ADD, ADHD, hyperactivity, and dyslexia, and run stronger as the terms are used with higher frequency. Some travelers are dependent upon and comfortable with Ritalin, others search for alternatives. Some believe their children were misdiagnosed with ADD, others believe the diagnosis was proper, still others think the whole notion is overplayed. Some say whole language has messed up their child's reading, others say their child couldn't grasp reading through tedious phonics lessons, still others cite distinct vision problems as the root of late reading.

When you bring an academically labeled child home, you can move as your conscience directs regarding what is right for your child. You will escape the various opinions and control tactics of teachers, administrators, guidance counselors, and social workers, all of whose livelihoods, in part, depend on continuing to sell the notion that these children need specially trained help.

> Homeschooling parents of special needs and physically disabled children have exceptional pressures and seem to be at high risk for burning out. If you're in this category, rally support and find ways to take breaks as you need them.

When I began homeschooling, I had no reason to foresee any learning problems. My firstborn child communicated early and well, displayed strong motor skills, and was very mature for his age. Yet, by six it was clear he was not ready to move beyond learning the basic sounds of the alphabet. At eight, he still couldn't sound out blended consonants. He reversed most of his letters, and said they all looked "jumbled up" on the page in front of him. I was beginning to worry.

After trying to separate the wheat from the chaff in reading theories, I wrote Raymond and Dorothy Moore. The dear grandparents of the homeschooling movement responded and encouraged me to wait a couple more years before seeking out intervention. So I waited. I can't say I gave up worrying, but I waited. I read a lot about dyslexia and various approaches to remedying it. We tried a few, on and off. We had T.J.'s vision checked and researched vision therapy. If he got to ten and still couldn't read, I would be ready with the

When you bring an academically labeled child home, you can move as your conscience directs regarding what is right for your child.

knowledge I'd collected. He got glasses just for reading, but even the ophthalmologist wasn't sure how much help they'd be.

Something began to click when he was halfway between his tenth and eleventh birthdays. Within a few weeks, he went from reading simple readers to chapter books written in fairly large print. By twelve, he read Landmark biographies and Mark Twain and C. S. Lewis. Now, at fourteen, there are no signs that he struggles with reading anymore, though he says he does have to take more time than other children when writing things down. Time was on our side.

Those who would be less comfortable waiting should seek help sooner, but avoid labels where your child can hear them. At home, labeling is unnecessary. Children with learning difficulties need more frequent reminders of their strengths. It's important that parents don't blame themselves, but that they continue to move forward, patiently gathering evidence and finding support.

Emily says she sees even more benefits to homeschooling late-blooming children. She says, "I waited until my child was ready. Instead of frustration and tears, we have jubilation and fun!"

Homeschooling allows these parents to come up with a learning environment which will encourage their children. Sabrina says, "For our LD/ADD child, we bring the most out of him by adjusting his sitting and writing time."

Children with learning difficulties will grow in confidence once home. Anna says, "When I began homeschooling my oldest daughter was convinced she was dumb. By slowing things down to her pace and building her confidence, she's a whole new person full of confidence. She's not afraid to approach the unknown anymore."

A number of travelers comment that their lives are less stressful once they bring their children with learning challenges home. Annie says, "My son was labeled LD and ADHD by a private school. He could barely read when he came home. While he was in school, I spent six to eight hours daily working with him on his homework. Homeschooling is much easier than what we were going through then." She continues, "My nine-year-old boy only attended school for kindergarten. They told me he wasn't reading on his own and would need to be held back. I wasn't going to go through that again! When we came home, I taught the two boys how to read together."

> Children with learning difficulties need more frequent reminders of their strengths.

Like many travelers fighting on behalf of their children, Beth grew weary of battling teachers about her children's problems. She says, "When I took my son off Ritalin, the school threatened to kick him out. I pretended to use it and they could not tell the difference. Also, when my daughter was in the second and third grade they wanted to test her for ADD. I decided to homeschool them instead. A year after we started homeschooling, my daughter was diagnosed with diabetes, which most likely had been the cause of her problems in school."

Labels are handed out much too freely in schools, spurring controversy over the motives and methodology of doing the labeling. At home, children can learn label-free.

Rose was glad her daughter didn't have to be subjected to labels. She says, "There were no negative messages about academic achievement levels. My daughter followed a slower maturation schedule, both academically and emotionally. Now she is more on track, but she's never been aware of 'lags.' I am eternally grateful for this."

Each child is unique and each has personal and particular strengths and weaknesses. Sabrina issues an important reminder, "I don't know that any conditions are the same for anyone. That is the joy of homeschooling—tailoring education to the specific needs and desires of your child."

STAY-AT-HOME DADS

THE DYNAMICS OF FAMILY and homeschooling life do change when Dad is home all day, especially if Mom is there, too. By and large, it seems to make relatively little difference which parent is in charge of the homeschooling while the other is off at work. Most fathers who are primarily responsible for teaching their children simply adopt the homeschooling role. But in homes where both parents are home and either one or both use home as their work base, there are different challenges.

Rose says, "My husband works out of our home. While he spends most of his time working, he visits throughout our school day, and usually handles the girls' math lessons. It also allows me to work outside the home and still have a parent at home. There are some downsides as well, though."

Some travelers say feeling like they're being evaluated as teachers is tough when the other parent works from home. Larissa says, "Oh boy! That year or so when my husband was home was hard. School almost completely flew out the window. It was just too hard to have school in one room with him in the next. The time when he came out to correct my pronunciation of an Indian name (I proved him wrong, by the way), was pretty much 'it.' We began to do the traditional school things when he was off doing something away from home."

Others prefer having both parents home, even if it doesn't last forever. Rebecca values the time her husband was home. "For many years he worked at home, in large part to be an available parent. We are glad Dad can be a part of school."

THE ONLY CHILD

FOR ONLY CHILDREN, homeschooling provides an amazing amount of one-on-one attention. There are no limits to the heights a homeschooled only child can soar, academically speaking. But parents who are homeschooling only children say the children get lonesome for company and that they face special challenges specific to their situation.

Renee says, "I went through times when I was much more interested in getting my son together with other homeschooling children than their moms were. Bigger families didn't feel much need to accommodate get-togethers with outside families."

Betty says the isolation from other children has been wearing at times. "We've made her friends always feel welcomed here," she says, "and we've made an effort to connect with other families and her cousins."

Other travelers agree that only children get lonesome at times, but that the one-on-one time together is an academic advantage, especially if the child is highly motivated. In cases where the child is less motivated, homeschooling parents feel pressure to motivate their only children and seek some outside classes with others to help. The same sorts of classes serve as social opportunities for these children, too—a place where they can make friends or simply be with others for a regular period of time each week.

LARGE FAMILIES

Children from large families learn to compromise and pitch in. Teamwork and selflessness are the order of the day.

EDUCATING MANY children of different ages is a Herculean task. Housework multiplies exponentially, younger siblings need to be occupied (see Chapter 13 for ways families keep little ones busy), and children learning different things at different levels want to have their needs and interests met.

Children from large families learn to compromise and pitch in. Teamwork and selflessness are the order of the day.

Abby, homeschooling mother of eight, says, "We have gone through many different stages of homeschooling our large family.

We have tried different schedules. Some have worked better than others." She continues, "We have found that the best system is to work together as a family. There are times when I take a child into a room and work on advanced math, sewing, art, or some other skill that everyone is not ready for or interested in. During those times, I assign the other children specific jobs to do, such as answering the phone and caring for younger children. They have all grown up to understand that their time will come."

Mothers of large families say they try to address individual needs and interests. They try to schedule individual times with each child, but they also foster an attitude of teamwork—older children helping teach younger ones, younger ones learning to be quiet when older ones need to concentrate, and so on.

Sharon says, "Homeschooling has kept us together as a family. Because the children are many different ages and have many different capabilities, we count on learning through unit studies."

Unit studies are a helpful tool for large families, but if they don't suit you, try encouraging older children to work independently. Also, give older children the responsibility of teaching younger ones. Both are tactics that large homeschooling families use with success.

OTHER CHALLENGES

OF COURSE, because homeschool families are each unique, some face challenges not readily categorized. Here are a handful of other issues that sometimes need to be dealt with, and how families view them.

On-Call Dad

Beckie's husband is a railroad engineer on the extra board. He is on call twenty-four hours a day, every day of the year. She says, "He works, then gets eight hours rest, then they can call him back to work. He has no schedule, no days off other than vacation. Homeschooling allows our family time to do things with him when he's home. Evenings and weekends are his busiest times. Our 'daddy time' often occurs during regular school hours. If our kids went to school, there would be long stretches where they wouldn't see their dad at all."

For parents who work long or unpredictable hours, or for those who are out of town a lot, homeschooling's flexibility allows for much-needed family time together.

Large Age Differences

Some travelers have few children who are separated by a number of years, an aspect that presents the parent with special challenges. Wendy says, "My children are so far apart in age that it was almost like homeschooling one child at a time. We found that our social needs were a little different from those of large families. Sometimes it was lonely for our children."

Instead of focusing on their loneliness, Wendy taught her children to think of others. She says, "We found good friends and opportunities to serve others by babysitting young children, opening our home to others, and so on."

Service takes the focus off of self, fills time productively, and builds a sense of self-worth only available from participating in meaningful work.

The Military Life

Military families never know when they might move or go without Dad (or Mom) for extended periods of time. Kayla says, "It's especially difficult when my husband is gone for long periods. We make a constant effort to get out and be with other homeschoolers. I've found online friends, homeschool groups, our church, and scouts to be helpful," Kayla says. "People are our most valuable resource."

On the other hand, homeschooling military families have one big advantage. Unlike others in the armed services, they spare themselves a major stress of pulling up roots: they don't have to look for a new school each time they move.

Extended Health Problems

Homeschooled children aren't under the same pressure to recover from illness or injury as those in school. Larissa says, "During the six months my son was without the normal use of his eyes, we continued to do bits of school while giving him plenty of time to heal. If he attended school, he would have been held back a year because there was so much he was unable to do."

Larissa finishes by echoing the other respondents' sentiments, "Whatever our situation, homeschooling has been beneficial."

SIMPLE STARTING POINTS

✦ *Take stock of your spending.*

Adjust your budget where possible. Read some of the books on budgeting and money-saving ideas in the Resources section.

✦ *Evaluate your options.*

If you are giving up a paying job to stay home to homeschool your children and need to generate more income, consider working part-time or finding work from home.

✦ *Network with those in similar situations.*

If your children have special needs of any kind (gifted, slow learners, physical disabilities), find support and information. See the Resources section for various groups.

✦ *Assess the challenges you expect to face.*

Whether you have an only child or many children, rally support, and come up with a game plan that makes sense for your family's situation.

RESOURCES

Simplifying Life, Saving Money

Books

Dacyzyn, Amy. *Tightwad Gazette III.* Villard Books, 1997. Also, *Tightwad Gazette, Tightwad Gazette II.*

Hendrickson, Borg. *How to Write a Low-Cost/No-Cost Curriculum for Your Homeschool.* Mountain Meadow Press, 1995.

McCoy, Jonni. *Miserly Moms.* Holly Hall, 1996.

Morgan, Melissa, and Allee, Judith Waite. *Homeschooling on a Shoestring.* Harold Shaw, 1999.

Williams, Jane. *How to Stock a Home Library Inexpensively.* Bluestocking Press. See "Homeschool Catalogs" in Chapter 1's Resources section for contact information.

Periodical

Practical Homeschooling (see "Magazines" in Chapter 1's Resources section). The March/April 1999 issue had a special "homeschooling for pennies" section worth reading through.

Used Books and Curriculum

The homeschool dealers listed in this section will buy or sell curriculum materials, and often do both.

The Back Pack, 252-244-0738, http://www.thebackpack.com.

The Book Cellar, 800-338-4257, e-mail bookcellar@juno.com.

The Book Peddler, 800-928-1760, e-mail TheBookPeddler@juno.com.

The Homeschool Publishing House, 508-892-4307, http://www.bravewc.com/hph.

Home School Used Book and Curriculum Exchange, http://www.homeschoolusedbooks.com.

Laurelwood Publications, 540-554-2670, e-mail Laurelwood@juno.com.

Library Shelf, http://www.libraryshelf.com.

The Swap, http://www.theswap.com.

Twaddle Free Books, 804-749-4859.

Special Needs and Learning Difficulties

Books

Armstrong, Thomas. *The Myth of the A.D.D. Child: Fifty Ways to Improve Your Child's Behavior and Attention Span Without Drugs, Labels, or Coercion.* Plume, 1997.

Crook, William G. *Help for the Hyperactive Child.* Professional Books, 1991.

Davis, Ronald D. *The Gift of Dyslexia.* Perigree, 1997.

Fowler, Mary. *Maybe You Know My Kid!* Birch Lane Press, 1993.

Herzog, Joyce. *Choosing and Using Curriculum for Your Special Child.* Greenleaf Press, 1996. Also, *Help! My Eight-Year-Old Isn't Learning!* and *Learning in Spite of Labels.*

Moore, Raymond and Dorothy. *School Can Wait.* Brigham Young University Press, 1989.

Rapp, Doris. *Impossible Child.* Practical Allergy Research Foundation, 1989.

Reichenburg-Ullman, Judyth. *Ritalin Free Kids.* Prima, 1996.

Rosner, Jerome. *Helping Children Overcome Learning Difficulties.* Walker, 1993.

Seiderman, Arthur S., and Marcus, Steven E. *20/20 Is Not Enough.* Crest, 1991.

Sowell, Thomas. *Late-Talking Children.* HarperCollins, 1997.

Taylor, John, Dr. *Helping Your Hyperactive/ADD Child.* Prima, 1997.

Turecki, Stanley, M.D. *The Difficult Child.* Bantam Doubleday Dell, 1989.

Support

ADD Action Group, providing alternative solutions for ADD, learning difficulties, dyslexia, and autism, 212-769-2457, http://www.addgroup.com.

CHADD (Children and Adults with Attention Deficit Disorder), 301-306-7070 or 800-233-4050, http://www.chadd.org. Publishes *Attention!* magazine.

NATHHAN (National Challenged Homeschoolers Association Network), 206-857-4257.

Parents of hard of hearing or deaf children can find an online support network at http://www.brandysign.com.

PAVE (Parents Active for Vision Education), 800-PAVE988, http://www.pave-eye/~vision.com.

Point of contact for wide range of special needs: http://www.nativetongues.com/websnail.

Gifted Children

Books

Olenchak, Richard. *They Say My Kid's Gifted: Now What?* Available at http://www.nagc.com.

Webb, James T. *Guiding the Gifted Child: A Practical Source for Parents and Teachers.* Gifted Psychology Press, 1989.

Yahnke, Sally. *The Survival Guide for Parenting Gifted Kids.* Free Spirit Publishing, 1991.

Periodicals

Gifted Child Today, 800-998-2208, http://www.prufrock.com.

Gifted Education Review, 303-670-8350.

Support

National Association for Gifted Children, 202-785-4268, http://www.nagc.com. Publishes *Parenting for High Potential.*

Large Families

Book

Pride, Mary. *The Way Home.* Good News Publishing, 1985.

Support

A mother of nine manages a terrific Web site (with lots of great links) geared to large homeschooling families; check it out at http://www.angelfire.com/a12/natural/index.html, then enter MrsMomo f9 in the Search box.

Part Three

KEEPING THE LEARNING JOURNEY FUN AND SUCCESSFUL

10

RESOURCES FOR YOUR LEARNING JOURNEY

In This Chapter

- You already have great resources
- More resources you may find helpful
- Simple starting points
- Resources

HOMESCHOOLING CURRICULUM FAIRS are a shopaholic's dream come true. How easy it is to justify spending money on such a worthy endeavor as educating your children! There are more great resources available for homeschoolers than a family could begin to use in a lifetime. You need only a tiny few. By all means, if money and storage aren't issues for you, purchase away. If, however, you're like most travelers whose shelf space and finances are finite, then stop and look around. Take stock of learning materials you already have and organize those first before purchasing more. Gather materials to make them more readily accessible for your children. Watch which items they frequently reach for and learn from to help you evaluate the kinds of things you'll want to add. Where do you see holes that need to be filled? Fill those first. Take your time and do some research before making any large purchases.

> There are more great resources available for homeschoolers than a family could begin to use in a lifetime. You need only a tiny few.

YOU ALREADY HAVE GREAT RESOURCES

WE ASKED homeschoolers which resources they consider essential to their homeschooling, and also posed the question, "If you had to go homeschool on an island and could only take ten things for this with you, what would they be?"

No one could agree on just ten, so we've expanded the list—see the "Top 15 Items Essential to Successful Homeschooling" sidebar. Two wise homeschool moms said "Dad" was an essential ingredient to their homeschooling. No doubt, a supportive and involved spouse is a great asset! Read on to see more essential items travelers listed. You may be surprised to see how many you own already, and how many more you can easily procure.

Library Card

Chapter 12 will deal with getting the most from your local library, but books and libraries were mentioned enough on the essential items list to warrant a quick mention here. If you and your children don't have library cards, get them, one apiece. (OK, so you couldn't use them on a desert island unless you had the library along, too—but that's a special case!) The more cards you have, the more books per visit you can check out. Avoid late fees by coming up with an organization and tracking system. Some homeschoolers reserve a particular shelf for library books. One family uses color-coded plastic milk crates, one per child, with a list of the books tucked inside. Children can write these lists immediately upon returning home on library days.

KEEPING THE JOURNEY FUN

I'm wary of people who too often talk about how life isn't fun; that education isn't about having a good time. A balanced picture of the work it takes to achieve something worthwhile naturally includes an understanding that life isn't always the proverbial bed of roses. But why anyone would choose to create labor where there is rest, or strife where there is peace, or tedium where there is pleasure is beyond me. Homeschooling parents don't have to be martyrs—with a little foresight, planning, and discipline, taking the road less traveled will lead to surprising adventures and unexpected joy.

Read on to learn how to choose your resources wisely, drawing on things right in front of you. Don't overlook the benefits of living in a technological age. Glean from others' experience with occupying younger siblings and keeping house. If you aren't quite yet ready for the journey but are concerned about gaps in your child's education, find out how to complement school with part-time homeschooling.

It's true that nothing worth having comes without a cost, but the abundant rewards will more than compensate you for your efforts.

Some Good Books to Own

Everyone has their favorite books, those books they want to refer to time and again. Some are worthy of heirloom status, rich and beautiful enough to be cherished and passed down for generations. Use gift-giving times to give good books, or look for ways to buy worthwhile titles at discounted prices. Each chapter's Resources section contains titles you may consider adding to your permanent collection. Also, see the Resources section at the end of this chapter for books on children's literature filled with reviews of time-tested titles. Some homeschoolers keep detailed book-hunting wish lists to carry with them when they shop.

The books that were listed over and again in respondents' essential lists were the Bible (came in at number three on its own) and anthologies of Shakespeare and Greek mythology. I recommend each home have these on its shelves—all have had great impact on our language and culture. Purchase a Bible with good notes and a concordance. See the Resources section for useful Shakespeare and mythology titles.

Everyone appreciates a bargain on an out-of-print title or an otherwise unaffordable book. Remember, however, if you take a vendor's time at a homeschool fair and appreciate the guidance, you should be willing to pay the sales price for those items you asked about. Vendors deserve to be compensated for their time. Otherwise, consider the following for getting great titles at less than retail cost.

TOP 15 ITEMS ESSENTIAL TO SUCCESSFUL HOMESCHOOLING

In order of times listed, homeschoolers would want the following close at hand:

1. Pens, pencils (regular and colored), markers, crayons
2. Paper (for writing and drawing)
3. Bible
4. Computer with Internet connection and software
5. A good home library
6. World map, atlas, globe
7. Math texts
8. Encyclopedia
9. Dictionary
10. Musical instruments
11. Art and craft supplies
12. Radio with CD player, music
13. Sports equipment (bat, balls, Frisbee, and so on)
14. Microscope
15. Field guides

✦ **amazon.com:** An online bookstore that offers discounted prices, reasonable shipping rates, and excellent service.

✦ **Barnes and Noble:** Ask for the educator's discount card, which gives you a percentage off any titles you purchase for your homeschool. Also, visit barnesandnoble.com for discounted titles as well.

✦ **Books-A-Million:** Pay $5 for a Books-A-Million discount card if you have this bookstore chain near you. You'll pay yourself back on your first shopping spree.

✦ **Scholastic:** Remember those Scholastic flyers you brought home from elementary school? They're available to homeschoolers too. Get on Scholastic's mailing list and gather a few homeschoolers to meet the minimum orders. You'll save bundles, and there's no shipping charge. See "Homeschool Catalogs" in Chapter 1's Resources section for information on Scholastic.

✦ **Used bookstores:** Check your Yellow Pages in both your home town and when you travel. Scour the shelves at used bookstores. I've found some terrific out-of-print titles and some more contemporary ones for a fraction of the current price. See "Used Books and Curriculum" in Chapter 9's Resources section for homeschooling book dealers who carry used books.

✦ **Used curriculum sales:** Many homeschool fairs include used curriculum areas. Take time to pick through the offerings. Some people have made selling used books and curriculum a family business, or at least pay for a good portion of the next year's curriculum by selling last year's. Expect to save approximately 50 percent. Also, check the Resources section in Chapter 9 for homeschool used curriculum companies. Many are on the Internet.

✦ **Library book sales:** Most libraries have book sales to clear out books that are either slightly worn or not being checked out enough to warrant keeping them. My local library has a room devoted to the ongoing sale of used books. Other libraries designate special days for huge sales, usually once or twice a year. I've paid a quarter for some wonderful out-of-print and classic titles at these sales. Check with your Friends of the Library for information.

✦ **Garage sales and rummage sales:** You may have to wade through boxes and boxes of books before you find one gem, but books sell for next to nothing at garage and rummage sales. To get good titles at rummage sales, you need to show up the first day, but books don't move as quickly at garage sales. If you wait until the last day of the sale, you can often haul away the books as a service, getting them for the labor of carrying them. Look for sales being held by families with college age children.

✦ **Flea markets and antique stores:** Book prices are slightly higher at flea markets and antique stores, but they're still inexpensive and they've usually been somewhat culled through for you, because the salespeople know which titles are worthwhile.

✦ **Grandparents' basements:** When my parents sold the home I'd grown up in, my siblings and I were all asked to go through things to find which had been ours. The basement was covered with boxes upon boxes of books, which with few exceptions held very little interest to the others. I found a box full of Landmark history titles, two large dictionaries and other reference books, and a falling-apart bird guide my grandfather had signed and given to me as a child. My husband had similar good fortune when his mother sent him things from his childhood. Our favorite is an old copy of *The American Boys Handy Book* (see "Project Ideas for the Middle Years Child" under "Books" in Chapter 2's Resources section) which his father had signed and given to him. He immediately took the book, signed and dated it, and gave it to our son. Though the title is still in print, the older, hardcover version signed by two generations of his family is a precious treasure to my son.

Think of your backyard as a great science and nature schoolroom.

Your Backyard

My children spend hours in the backyard. They turn over rocks to look for insects and snakes, take turns on the rope swing, and squeal with delight if they see a bunny. They build makeshift forts and traps to catch animals, and gingerly pick up fallen birds' nests.

> The more comfortable kids are, the longer they read. I'm thankful they don't have to identify reading with sitting at a desk under fluorescent lighting!

Learning flourishes in backyards, planned and unplanned. We purchased inexpensive rubber boots so even rain doesn't prevent us from climbing the hill to watch the water flow during huge storms. We take pictures for our scrapbooks. T.J. and his friends will go through his copy of *The American Boy's Handy Book* to find the just-right thing to build, and then use, outside.

Think of your backyard as a great science and nature schoolroom. If you don't have a backyard or nearby neighborhood woods or park, schedule picnics at city and state parks and incorporate some of these ideas into your homeschooling. Keep disposable cameras and your nature notebooks nearby, to either photograph or draw things you want to remember. Check nature books geared for getting kids to explore the outdoors (see "Books" in Chapter 6's Resources section for some titles). Here are some other ideas to get you started:

- Keep a rotting log to observe throughout the years.
- Watch for birds' nests in the spring. Don't go near them but find a clear vantage point from which to observe the eggs, then the hatchlings, then the baby birds' first flights. Build a birdhouse.
- Experiment with kites and paper airplanes. Which days do they fly the farthest? How do they compare with the birds?
- Gather old sheets and blankets for outdoor forts. Hope the neighbors don't mind!
- Plant a garden. Put children in charge of a section or allow them to plant their own individual gardens. Plant vegetables, flowers, and herbs. Which are the easiest to grow?
- Identify types of trees and plants. Which bloom when?
- Identify various insects and bugs. When are you most likely to see a bumblebee? A worm? A snail? A firefly?

Your Kitchen

My kitchen is a close second to the backyard as a learning resource. The children go through the cupboards to find things to throw together for experiments. We keep a number of kitchen science books on hand, though the children manage to come up with plenty of ideas on their own.

From a young age, they would save clear film containers and begin freezing various substances in them. They learned that toothpaste freezes suspended in water and alcohol won't freeze at all. They clocked the amount of time it takes for frozen items to melt, in direct sunlight and in the shade. They've made charts and graphs to tally their results. All because of their own curiosity and because I said yes.

Reference Materials

You may already have a good dictionary, encyclopedia (on CD or on your shelves), world map, globe, and atlas. If not, you can add these items for pennies at garage sales. If you don't have a map, globe, and atlas, choose one to get you started and add the others later. World maps are the most inexpensive. Get a new one and laminate it to prolong its life. Then keep an eye out for maps at garage sales and whatnot—the map of the world has changed several times in the last fifty years, and tracking the differences can lead into some very interesting discussions. There are a number of other resource items you may find useful over the years (world history books, time-line books, a thesaurus, a good book of quotes, and so on).

Good Writing Surface and Lighting; a Comfortable Place to Sit

One traveler listed a rocking chair "for healing broken hearts" on her Top 10 list. My children still love to sit and rock while reading. They also love to sprawl out on the couch or curl up in their favorite chair. The more comfortable they are, the longer they read. I'm thankful they don't have to identify reading with sitting at a desk under fluorescent lighting!

We've invested in $7 clip-on lamps to hang over their desks and beds. Also, we placed school desks near big windows, so the children work near natural light and with trees and skies in clear view as much as possible. Instead of traditional school desks, we purchased (or inherited) art and drafting tables and stools, so the children sit higher with a better view of the out of doors while doing schoolwork.

Any decent writing surface will do. We, like most homeschoolers, also do a great amount of work at the kitchen table.

They need lined paper for writing, plain paper for drawing, graph paper for math, construction paper and poster board for projects, specialty paper for art, and copy paper for computer-generated reports.

Radio, Tape Deck, CD Player

As I've discussed in Chapter 8, in my family we try to play classical music as much as possible. We listen to a variety of music and have each added favorite CDs to our collection over the years. Music lightens the mood of the home.

Radios are a great source of information too, and a lot less graphic than television.

Paper and Writing Utensils

Homeschooled children go through a lot of paper! They need lined paper for writing, plain paper for drawing, graph paper for math, construction paper and poster board for projects, specialty paper for artistic endeavors (good drawing paper, watercolor paper, and so on), and copy paper for computer-generated reports.

Also, middle years children need writing pencils and pens, colored pencils, and markers. They tend to use crayons less than they did when younger.

Gather all paper and writing utensils in one area. Stack paper according to its kind. Separate markers from colored pencils, pencils, and pens. We use stackable clear, rectangular Rubbermaid containers, purchased on sale at the local super store. All pencils (including colored) go in one box, markers in another, and crayons in yet another. Favorite writing or art pencils stay in jars on each child's desk.

I keep a box of used paper, stacked upside down (blank sides upward) for children to use for sketches and rough drafts. I buy large boxes of copy paper (for the computer and drawing) at the local warehouse store or on sale at the office supply store (ask for case discounts). All other paper (lined, graph, notebook, and specialty), I

HOW WE DID IT

We like Berol Prismacolor colored pencils best. They are smooth and soft and leave beautiful watercolor-like hues on the paper. However, they are expensive. After making our initial investment in a large set, we try to keep close tabs on the individual colors we need and replace only those, a few at a time. (They're sold individually at most art and craft stores.) Each pencil has a color name and color number stamped on it. Have children sharpen from the opposite end of this name and number, so when it's time to replace the color, you will be able to figure out which you need. Also, we keep a chart of colored squares, with names and numbers next to each color smudge. In the event that we sharpen the pencils too far, we have a record of the color on file. I try to buy the pencils only when they are on sale, and put them aside for gifts—they make good tie-ons, stocking stuffers, Easter basket fillers, Hanukkah prizes, party favors, and so on. I do the same with decorative writing pencils.

purchase on sale only. Watch for specials in Back-to-School flyers, and stock up then. Also, stores like Hobby Lobby and Michael's have frequent sales, special purchase days, and coupons in their sale flyers. Buy good art paper at these stores on sale.

MORE RESOURCES YOU MAY FIND HELPFUL

Although the following resources aren't necessary for homeschooling, they are used often enough by homeschoolers to warrant mentioning them here.

Broken Appliances

Resist throwing away broken appliances, electronic equipment, bicycles, and whatnot. The middle years child loves to tinker and learns a great deal about electronics and physics by poking around broken items—sometimes nurturing them back to life in the process. We know one young homeschooled gentleman who purchases broken lawn mowers at garage sales, repairs them at home, then resells them.

Computers

Although computers may not be as necessary as some people think they are, this is an electronic age and an increasing amount of information is available, either through software or the Internet. See Chapter 12 for the many ways you can get the most from your computer's learning potential. If you don't have one, you may want to begin saving for this major purchase. And you won't need to save as long as you might think—new systems adequate for family use are selling for under $1,000, and if you're willing to settle for older equipment, you can probably find the latest-and-greatest from three or four years ago for $500 or less!

Art and Craft Supplies

Aside from colored pencils, markers, and good paper, look for watercolors, charcoal, and other artistic media. Browse through craft and sewing catalogs to see which items may interest your children. Making piñatas is fun and easy, and you only need balloons, flour, water, and newspaper for the shells. Paint with tempera paints.

I don't think crafts need to be dumbed down or junky to appeal to children, and I don't have room to store or display such things in my house.

My children like making and using homemade play dough and slime, and have dabbled with various clays, their most favorite being Sculpy. We also use a lot of modeling beeswax, for sculpting and to decorate candles.

It's worth the money to invest in good art supplies. The better the materials, the better the quality of artwork produced. Fiskars scissors, for example, cut better than others. Cheaper scissors frustrate small hands and leave paper edges more ragged. The same principle holds for other items.

I have an aversion to many craft items marketed toward children. I don't think crafts need to be dumbed down or junky to appeal to children, and I don't have room to store or display such things in my house. If you haven't already done so, order the Hearthsong catalog (see "Catalogs" in Chapter 2's Resources section) for high-quality craft kits and ideas for children.

Musical Instruments

Every child should be exposed to at least a little music instruction. Even if you don't look to private music lessons, consider adding a harmonica, recorder, or keyboard to your home. Children can learn the basics independently if you don't feel you have the ability to teach them.

Bicycles and Sports Equipment

Family bike rides are a great way to spend time together, exercise, and explore. Keeping bikes in top shape teaches children responsibility as well as some maintenance skills. Also, a good bat and some balls, a Frisbee, and a few kites all make for fun and active family times.

Electric Pencil Sharpener

Plug the pencil sharpener in at a central location. It will save time and frustration whether a tip breaks in the middle of a test or another wears down in the middle of a great drawing.

Animals

Dogs, cats, gerbils, hamsters, fish, guinea pigs, frogs—these animals and a host of others help children learn to take care of others and also provide an extensive range of learning experiences. Sensitive issues like breeding and reproduction are approached more easily when animals are around to serve as object lessons. The wider the variety of animals, the greater the learning. There's nothing like a furry cat or a loyal dog to add to the warmth of your home. For years, our two labs served as the children's pillows while they were reading. Now we're working hard to train two puppies to serve the same purpose. We realize that such mellowness comes with age, so we practice patience while we train.

Sundry Items

Other items homeschoolers often use include magnets, marbles, calculator, dominoes, board games, deck of cards, binoculars, microscope, telescope, building and connecting blocks, and television. Each of these items, if chosen carefully, can add hours of fun and learning to your children's education.

SIMPLE STARTING POINTS

More and more, people decide to homeschool midyear and need to gather resources to begin immediately. If you find yourself in a position where it seems urgent to remove your child from school but don't have the time or finances to obtain large amounts of curriculum and materials, get a copy of your state law, find your local support group, and use the following ideas as an emergency starter kit. These steps will take you far into your learning excursion and will give you time to research before adding to your homeschooling supplies.

✦ *Locate materials around your home.*

Gather all reference items, good books, paper, and pencils. Clear off a shelf you already own, or build or purchase a new one specifically for the homeschooling items. Decide where your children will most likely be doing their schoolwork (remember, the kitchen table and the couch count!), and keep the shelf nearby for easy access.

✦ *Check out high-quality literature from the library.*

The books can serve as your children's reading. Include historical novels or biographies so you can be covering history too. Have children write reports on the books for writing and assessment.

✦ *Buy each child a journal.*

A simple spiral notebook will do. Have the children write journal entries three to five times per week. Between journaling and book reports, you should be satisfying any legal requirements for writing.

✦ *Purchase a math text.*

If you're not sure which one to buy, or if you don't have time to wait on mail order, visit a local teaching supply store and buy a paperback edition geared toward your child's age and ability.

✦ *Look for easy-to-use science materials.*

While at the library, check out some good field guides or kitchen experiment books (see Resources section at the end of this chapter).

Use your backyard or kitchen with these books and you're covering science. Have children keep a written, drawn, or photographic record of their experiments—that will cover art as well as science.

✦ *If you haven't done so, call National Public Radio and your nearest public television station for their schedules.*

Mark your calendar with special documentaries and other educational programming (see "Armchair Voyages" in Chapter 11 for more ideas on using television in your homeschool). You'll cover the arts, history, science, and other subjects with these two stations, free of charge.

✦ *Begin to exercise together.*

Take walks, go on hikes, or ride bikes with your children if you don't have other activities that count for physical education.

RESOURCES

Homeschooling Resource Guides

Bell, Debra. *The Ultimate Guide to Homeschooling.* Word Books, 1997.

Duffy, Cathy. *Christian Home Educators' Curriculum Manual: Junior and Senior High, 1997–1998.* Grove Publishing, 1997. Also available for elementary grades.

Pride, Mary. *The Big Book of Home Learning: Preschool and Elementary.* Crossway Books, 1999. Also, *The Big Book of Home Learning: Teen and Adult.*

Reed, Donn. *The Home School Source Book.* Brook Farm Books, 1994.

Rupp, Rebecca. The *Complete Home Learning Source Book.* Three Rivers Press, 1998. Also *Good Stuff.*

Wade, Theodore. *The Home School Manual.* Gazelle, 1995.

Books with Great Literature Recommendations

Bluedorn, Nathaniel. *Hand That Rocks the Cradle.* Nathaniel Bluedorn, 1998, contact Trivium Pursuit.

Glaspey, Terry. *Great Books of the Christian Tradition.* Harvest House, 1996.

Hirsch, E. D. *Books to Build On: A Grade-By-Grade Resource Guide for Parents and Teachers.* Delta, 1996.

Hunt, Gladys. *Honey for Your Child's Heart: The Imaginative Use of Books in Family Life.* Zondervan, 1989.

Trelease, Jim. *The Read-Aloud Handbook.* Penguin, 1995.

Wilson, Elizabeth. *Books Children Love: A Guide to the Best Children's Literature.* Crossway, 1987.

And see "Simplifying Life, Saving Money," Chapter 9's Resources section for penny-pinching resource ideas.

Middle Years Children's Books: Shakespeare and Mythology

Here is my one recommendation for using abridged books. Both Charles and Mary Lamb's and E. Nesbit's Shakespearean tales are woven perfectly for middle years children to understand without losing the beauty of the original text. The three Workman titles listed are complete and unabridged, but are presented in comic book form, again, much more approachable for middle years students.

Aliki. *William Shakespeare and the Globe.* HarperCollins, 1999. Also, *The Gods and Goddesses of Olympus.*

D'Aulaire, Ingri, and Edgar Parin. *D'Aulaire's Books of Greek Myths.* Dell Picture Yearling, 1992. Also, *Trolls and Norse Gods.*

Lamb, Charles and Mary. *Tales from Shakespeare.* Book-of-the-Month Club, 1995.

Macrone, Michael. *Brush Up Your Shakespeare!* HarperCollins, 1994. Also, *By Jove! Brush Up Your Mythology* and *It's Greek to Me: Brush Up Your Classics.*

Morley, Jacqueline, and James, John. *Inside Story: Inside Shakespeare's Theater.* Bedrick Books, 1997.

Nesbit, E. *The Best of Shakespeare.* Oxford University Press, 1997.

Shakespeare, William, illustrated by Ian Pollock. *King Lear.* Workman, 1984. Also *Othello* and *Macbeth.*

Stanley, Diane, and Vennema, Peter. *Bard of Avon: The Story of William Shakespeare.* Morrow Junior Books, 1992.

Audiotapes

A storyteller's version of Greek myths and a storyteller's version of Shakespeare for children, both by Jim Weiss (see "Audio" in Chapter 5's Resources section for information).

Science Titles

Diehm, Gwen, and Krautwurst, Terry. *Nature Crafts for Kids.* Discovery Toys, 1992.

Heddle, Rebecca. *Science in the Kitchen.* Usborne, 1992.

Herbert, Don. *Mr. Wizard's Supermarket Science.* Random House, 1980.

Hoyt, Mary. *Kitchen Chemistry and Front Porch Physics.* Educational Services, 1983.

Landry, Sarah B. *Peterson First Guides: Urban Wildlife.* Houghton Mifflin, 1994. Also, *Field Guide to the Birds,* and many more.

Various authors. *Golden Nature Guides* (from Golden Books). Subject matter of the various books includes birds, moths, fishes, flowers, insects, and many more.

11

THE LEARNING JOURNEY MERGES ONTO THE INFORMATION SUPERHIGHWAY

In This Chapter

- The computer, your vehicle on the information superhighway
- Armchair voyages: Africa via PBS and Other Great Trips
- Educational videotapes
- Simple starting points
- Resources

The majority of respondents say they now include more technology in their homeschooling than when they began their journey. There has been a proliferation of educational videos and software over the past ten years, much of it marketed toward homeschoolers. New cable networks produce educational television and offer helpful teacher resources. Today, television networks maintain Internet sites that complement their programming. Many of these sites offer kids' areas and teachers' resources. Each year more curriculum companies offer online options, so check with yours if you're interested in schooling online. (See "Full Service Curriculum Companies" in Chapter 4's Resources section for an extensive list.) Corporations and nonprofit organizations also maintain

Corporations and nonprofit organizations also maintain Web sites that are virtual gold mines of information, all free of charge.

Web sites that are virtual gold mines of information, all free of charge.

Researching this chapter I was astounded at the learning opportunities available on the Internet—my children stayed close by, noted favorite sites, and visited them as soon as I was away from the computer.

This is a technological age. While you can learn most of the basics you need without technological support (though computer knowledge is now a basic!), there's no denying modern-day technology makes your job easier, and the children's learning more fun. Whether you use television, videos, and computers to enrich studies or as a fundamental core to your children's education, your middle years homeschoolers will profit from including some technology in their learning environment.

THE COMPUTER: YOUR VEHICLE ON THE INFORMATION HIGHWAY

FIFTY-FIVE RESPONDENTS have computers in their homes and most say their children started using them as preschoolers. Travelers were almost evenly split between being unconcerned about the amount of computer use and cautious about it, though all see computers as both the wave of the future and a present contribution to their children's schooling. All but one of the middle years respondents say they especially enjoy learning on the computer and use it with ease. Whatever you want to explore, software or an Internet site can help.

Well over half the respondents' children use the computer daily. Homeschooling parents who limit computer time do so because they worry about children's becoming too dependent on the computer for learning, not interacting enough with others, accessing unsavory sites on the Internet, suffering eye strain, and lacking creative stimulation.

An equal number of respondents say they don't worry about computer use. They see computers as a legitimate educational tool, part of the children's lives both now and when they grow to adulthood. These homeschoolers say their computers are in central locations in the house—they realize the dangers of unrestricted Internet access, but they keep a handle on its potential for bad. In most homes, parents set computer time limits, many by using a timer. In a handful of homes, parents hope to teach self-discipline by allowing their children to limit themselves, and only interfere if they feel an inordinate amount of time is being spent in front of the screen. Sixteen travelers say they don't set limits at all, saying computer time is well spent and that children will eventually tire of the computer on their own.

Soaring into Educational Cyberspace

Homeschool Internet learning continues to increase with the rise of online classes and educational opportunities coupled with the steady influx of new homeschoolers.

If you need a tutor for a subject, chances are you can find one over the Internet, even if your child doesn't take a formal class. I have enjoyed mentoring child writers at times. A scientist named Robert

HOW WE DID IT

Most respondents have more children than computers. To divide computer time fairly, they recommend setting a timer. The timer's buzz signifies when it's time for one child to finish and another to begin.

Krampf maintains a Web site and extensive e-mail list of interested children to whom he sends his "experiment of the week." He is available to answer questions (see Resources section for information).

Homeschooling parents and children participate in live interactive chats and workshops. Many are for fun; others for informational purposes. *Home Education Magazine, Homeschooling Today,* and *Practical Homeschooling* (see "Magazines" in Chapter 1's Resources section) all host various chats, and often invite guest speakers to talk on a variety of topics.

Full-service curriculum companies offer online classes, with teachers available. Other curriculum providers monitor e-mail support groups to answer questions and to help those new to the curriculum draw on the experience of those who have been using it awhile.

If you prefer a solo flight, you can find various learning opportunities throughout the online world to navigate on your own. Visit the finest art museums in the world, and keep up on new exhibits. Explore science, history, and cultural museums. Most have teacher's resource areas that provide useful information and ideas for further learning.

PBS, Discovery Channel, and CSPAN are among travelers' favorite learning sites. You can check upcoming television scheduling and incorporate worthwhile programming into your homeschool days. Each of these sites offers an eager learner an immense amount of information. If you're short on ideas, they have special classroom ideas that can be altered for homeschoolers. My three children enjoy trying to figure out *Kratt's Creatures'* Creature of the Week. PBS online features various topics, such as a tour of Vietnam, Frank Lloyd Wright's architecture, and how plants react to light. The search engine will take any specific day in history and tell you what important events happened then.

PBS, Discovery Channel, and CSPAN are among travelers' favorite learning sites.

The History Channel's Web site also takes browsers back in time on specific days in history, or lets them choose an entire decade to study online and hear speeches by famous historical figures. Take history quizzes if you like. Sign up to receive the History Channel's special programming via e-mail.

Let your ideas and needs lead you in your worldwide travels. There's so much more, all at the click of your mouse.

The Discovery Channel offers Mind Games and Expeditions among a host of other interesting things, and also has direct links to the Learning Channel, Animal Planet, and the Travel Channel. The Travel Channel online features various locales, changing them periodically.

CSPAN is especially useful during election times, but always has plenty of information worth checking out, and offers extensive teachers' resources. Children can search CSPAN for a U.S. president, and retrieve his picture, brief biographical information, an important quote, and some trivia.

Let your ideas and needs lead you in your worldwide travels. There's so much more, all at the click of your mouse.

Staying Grounded with Software

Although many middle years homeschoolers soar the Internet, most of their computer time is spent right at home with educational and games software. On average, homeschool travelers spend 70 percent or more of their computer time with software they've carefully chosen to supplement their learning, as a primary tool for learning, or just for fun.

A walk down the aisle of a large computer or office supply store throws the more susceptible shopper into sensory overload—the brightly colored boxes with catchy titles and cartoon characters beckon the eager homeschooling parent. Not all, of course, are worth anything more than the box they come in. As with books and

FAVORITE WEB SITES

Crayola: http://www.crayola.com

Discovery Channel: http://www.discovery.com

Legos: http://www.lego.com

Nickelodeon: http://www.nick.com

Nintendo: http://www.nintendoland.com

Public Television: http://www.pbs.org

See Resources section for more great Web sites.

other learning materials, if software doesn't get used, it's money wasted.

An online company called Learningware Reviews posts hundreds of software reviews geared toward home educators. The company also has chat rooms, archives of relevant articles, and online help. See the Resources section for more information.

The upcoming paragraphs go through the various subject areas (plus a few) that I've discussed so far in the book. I'll take a look at programs travelers mention frequently as the most helpful. Hopefully, their experience will help you cull through the glut of choices. Like most learning materials, computer software goes on sale frequently. Watch your local store flyers, and also stay in touch with homeschooling Dorling Kindersley and Discovery Toys representatives. Often, these companies offer buy-one-get-one-free sales. You'll be saving money and supporting another homeschool family.

Keyboarding

Children will enjoy the computer more if they are able to use the computer easily, including finding the keys they need to type information. The hunt-and-peck method works for many people, but eventually tops out at a speed much slower than touch typists can reach. Three favorite typing titles are *Mavis Beacon Teaches Typing, Typing Tutor 7,* and *Mario Teaches Typing 2.* By incorporating lots of practice through games, these programs take the dullness out of the drill work in learning to type.

While the vast majority of respondents say their children enjoy learning to type via one of these programs, my oldest child preferred the more old-fashioned method of going through a simple typing book called *Type It,* published by Educators Publishing Service (see the entry for Explode the Code in the "Spelling, Grammar, and Writing" section of "Learning Materials" in Chapter 5's Resources section for ordering information). The book cost $12 and took my son from being cautious about computer and Internet use to comfortably navigating his way in less than a year. He liked *Type-It*'s no-nonsense approach.

Once children learn to type well, they can easily navigate the Internet, write letters to friends, and type reports for their schoolwork. Using computers proficiently carries certain risks however, especially for children. Sitting at a keyboard staring at a screen for hours on end wreaks havoc with developing eye muscles and still-

TEN FAVORITES—EDUCATIONAL SOFTWARE

- Carmen Sandiego
- Gizmos and Gadgets
- Incredible Machine
- The Lost Mind of Dr. Brain
- Magic School Bus
- Math Blaster
- Oregon Trail II
- SimCity 2000
- Storybook Weaver Deluxe
- Strategy Games of the World
- See Resources section for more great software titles.

growing wrist joints. While limiting time is one obvious solution, you can take other precautionary steps as well. Be sure to adjust the height of the seat (adjustable seats are perfect for families made up of children ranging in ages) or a desk that allows children to sit comfortably while typing. Consider purchasing an ergonomic keyboard, designed to protect your child's wrist. Frequent breaks will protect eyes from strain. Don't wait until your children remark on pain in their wrists, headaches, or tired eyes before you act. Rehabilitation is much more difficult than prevention.

QUICK & EASY

With a good search engine, it doesn't take long to find a Web site of interest. However, by maintaining a set of bookmarks or favorites for Web sites with useful links, you can cut down your search time considerably. The following Web sites should link you with almost any science, history, art, or cultural museum in the world. Many have activities, quizzes, and teacher's resources available.

http://www.art.net/
http://www.lam.mus.ca.us/webmuseums
http://curry.edschool.Virginia.EDU/~lha5w/museum/
http://www.icom.org/vlmp/

Encyclopedias

Most major encyclopedia publishers also create software CD-ROM versions. My family has been content with the Grolier CD, which came free with the purchase of our computer. Most homeschool respondents say they prefer the World Book CD. Dorling Kindersley offers an Eyewitness encyclopedia, which is very easy to use and kid-friendly, also popular with homeschoolers.

Language Arts

Sixteen respondents use software to supplement their language arts studies, including creative writing, spelling, vocabulary, and grammar. My older daughter will spend much more time with a computer spelling program than she will with a spelling book, so we are planning on using a combination of Spelling Jungle and Dorling Kindersley's I Love Spelling! to carry her to the seventh or eighth grade. Other travelers report the same kind of success with spelling programs, especially for kinesthetic learners.

Most middle years children will spend longer with a creative writing program that incorporates artwork than they will with an adult word processing program. Hands down, travelers' favorite creative writing software is Storybook Weaver Deluxe. I must echo the praise—not a day goes by that Storybook Weaver isn't part of my daughters' learning adventures.

Math, Science, Thinking Skills

Math drills take on new life with the brightly colored animated figures available on most math software. Children participate in all sorts of adventures while honing their math skills. Their frustration is kept to a minimum because they can click on answers if need be. If the answers are incorrect the software lets the child know, which removes the homeschooling parents from the role of bad guy. For full math curriculum, check out the Quarter Mile Math Programs (see Resources section). Math Blaster is ranked number one on homeschool surveys but travelers say its contents aren't enough to serve as a full math curriculum.

The Magic School Bus software series holds a great deal of appeal for children in the early part of their middle years. If your children like the television series, books, and videos, this software is sure to be a hit. Dorling Kindersley came up with another winner with the I Love Science! CD. It introduces children to physics, chemistry, and biology basics.

Perhaps most popular among homeschoolers are the various thinking skills programs, including The Incredible Machine, The Lost Mind of Dr. Brain, Strategy Challenges, and Thinkin' Things. Thinkin' Things III is considerably more difficult than the first two. All four of these titles are challenging for middle years children, as they are for most adults. They make fun family projects, and it may well take more than one family member to figure out some of the problems posed.

> Perhaps most popular among homeschoolers are the various thinking skills programs, including The Incredible Machine, The Lost Mind of Dr. Brain, Strategy Challenges, and Thinkin' Things.

History, Geography, Social Studies

The various Trail software packages (Africa Trail, Amazon Trail, and Oregon Trail) and the various Sims (SimTown, SimAnt, SimCity 2000, and so on) are used with regularity in travelers' homes. With the popular SimCity, children act as city planners, balancing city, environmental, and individuals' interests to produce thriving—or failing—places for people to live.

The most popular in the Trail series continues to be Oregon Trail II. As with some of the thinking skills games, families enjoy playing Oregon Trail II together, helping one another reach the end of the trail incurring as few illnesses, disasters, and family deaths as possible. Children learn history and geography as they trek across the United States.

Foreign Languages and the Arts

More than any other area of study, homeschoolers seem to be using foreign language software as the main teaching tool for that subject. See "Languages" in Chapter 8's Resources section for recommendations for foreign language software.

The Opening Night CD puts children into the role of writer, director, and performer of their own production. With Opening Night: Behind the Scenes, they tour backstage and interview various professionals with The Children's Theatre Company of Minneapolis, one of the most successful children's theater companies in the nation.

Keep your eyes open for various children's books on the arts—many include CDs to accompany the text. See this chapter's Resources section for three great titles.

ARMCHAIR VOYAGES: AFRICA VIA PBS AND OTHER GREAT TRIPS

Thirteen homeschoolers say they don't use television or videos in their homeschooling—or for recreation—saying it's too hard to separate the good from the bad, and that television viewing is passive, mindless, and addictive. Some of these same parents say they prefer computer use, because children have to participate on some level. Homeschoolers who do use television and videos (and some use videos only) say that children tend to remember what they've seen on television, that interesting programming combines auditory and visual appeals to grab children's attention and reinforce what is being conveyed. The flip side of this, of course, is that bad programming can have an equally strong but negative impact on young minds.

Check television stations' Web sites, make note of interesting programming, and tune in. The world will be at your fingertips.

Just as cable television brings more junk to the television screen, so it brings more wonderful educational programming. Cable stations' names clue viewers in to their specialty, be it history, gardening, biographies, arts, science, or others. These stations provide a great service to homeschoolers. You can enrich an area already of interest to your child or find programming that makes learning in a less desirable subject area more palatable. Few children have trouble absorbing that which is rendered through the television screen. New cable stations appear almost monthly, so stay abreast of what your cable provider offers, and never hesitate to call with your request for something they don't yet carry. Here's a quick look at a handful of homeschoolers' favorite educational stations.

Public Television

Time-tested PBS ranks number one with respondents. PBS is a delightful alternative to most of what is now on network television. Many middle years children continue to enjoy PBS children's programming, specifically *Kratt's Creatures, Wishbone,* and *Adventures of the Book of Virtues.* However, middle years homeschoolers also enjoy and learn from much of the adult programming. PBS is noted for fine programming in history, science, arts, technology, and news. Its slower-paced documentaries and news shows leave the viewer time to absorb what is being presented, and often include guests more intelligent than the average celebrity-of-the-week on other news talk shows. Fine and performing arts thrive on PBS, especially during fundraising weeks. Travelers' favorite PBS shows include *Great Performances, NOVA, Masterpiece Theater,* and *National Geographic.*

Discovery Channel

The Discovery Channel runs a close second to PBS for homeschooling viewers. Spanish-speaking viewers, or those who want to immerse themselves in the language, can check into receiving Discovery en Español. Aside from neat kids' programming such as *Real Kids, Real Adventures,* and *Sci Squad,* middle years children can also learn from and enjoy the channel's many specials on animals, tornadoes, roller coasters, and other science-related topics.

History Channel

Being history buffs, my family was thrilled when our cable company began carrying the History Channel. Many other travelers share our delight in the station's programming. To get in-depth knowledge on wars, ships, trains, and many major events and figures in world history, get the schedule from the History Channel and plan to tune in. We use this channel as a complement to many of the Landmark history books our children read, or vice versa. Mike Wallace's *20th Century* and Peter Jennings' *The Century* are history survey courses at their finest, and available by tuning in to the History Channel.

Other Good Television Stations

My family travels around the world via the Travel Channel's *Lonely Planet* and *Amazing Destination.* Occasionally, the hosts of these programs will visit a seedier part of a town, so some parental guidance and control of the remote is in order. However, with some moderation, these programs expose children to how people in other nations really live, what they eat, how they make a living, and so on.

A&E (Arts and Entertainment) is not a fluff entertainment channel. Rather, the station offers sophisticated, in-depth biographies on the regular *Biography* and an equally in-depth look at the arts with *Breakfast with the Arts.* Watch for the new Biography channel as a spin-off. Middle years children also watch and learn from home repair shows, cooking and gardening shows, and special documentaries.

Don't limit yourself to the stations or shows mentioned here. Check television stations' Web sites (see "Favorite Web Sites" sidebar and Resources section), make note of interesting programming, and tune in. The world will be at your fingertips.

Educational Videotapes

Five travelers say they use educational videotapes such as Math-U-See and Saxon math videos in lieu of texts to cover a subject area. Other homeschoolers list the Moody Science videos as important contributors to their children's science studies. Most homeschoolers who use videotapes say they use them more as enrichment, but with the continued production and marketing of video tutorials, a growing number of homeschoolers are beginning to look toward video learning, especially in areas they feel less competent to teach.

Aside from math and science, sign language is a topic well adapted to video presentation (see "Sign Language" in Chapter 8's Resources section). To learn to sign, one must see the motions, so videos are the perfect way for children to learn this skill.

There are many wonderful videos available to enhance learning. If you're doing a unit on Shakespeare, check out one of the many versions of his plays to help explain the text before reading. Watching old movies is a great way to look back at our nation's history and enjoy a family evening. National Geographic produces videos that drive home science lessons, and the Magic School Bus videos are a good starting place.

When the School House Rock videos were released, I ran out and bought each of them. I couldn't wait to share the goofy cartoon lessons with my children, and I (and they) were surprised to see how many of the songs I still remembered from the ABC Saturday morning programming of my childhood. All three of my children learned the Preamble to the Constitution, thanks to the History Rock video. With the help of a few children's books on the Constitution, they each have had a decent grasp of its meaning years before most of their schooled peers.

If possible, rent and watch videos before purchasing them. Some are worth shelf space, others aren't. We pull the Moody science and School House Rock videos off the shelf frequently; others we check out from the library only occasionally.

As life becomes more technological, it only makes sense to incorporate a degree of technology into your homeschooling. The time you allow it to take and the priority you give it is up to you, but by using technology as a tool, you will give yourself a world's worth of resources and find help teaching in those subjects that might otherwise intimidate you.

SIMPLE STARTING POINTS

✦ *Find a keyboarding program that suits your child.*

Encourage practice sessions three to five times per week, for thirty minutes each time—that's enough to produce great progress within weeks.

✦ *Evaluate the usefulness of computers and television in your homeschool.*

Which areas do you feel you'd rather not teach? Which areas are especially difficult for your children to learn by more traditional methods? Consider computer, television, and videos for these subjects.

✦ *Soar through cyberspace with your children.*

Check out some of the sites listed, and veer off to others as they present themselves (via links and recommendations on other sites). Jot down or bookmark those you find useful or interesting, so you can easily visit them again.

✦ *Read software reviews.*

Check out Learningware Reviews and other companies that review software, including the various homeschool magazines, most of which have regular computer software review columns. After going through various titles, pick your favorite for each subject area. Keep your eyes open for suitable software that comes onto the market.

✦ *Make television a useful tool.*

If you decide television and videos have a place in your homeschool, obtain scheduling from various educational networks and look into accumulating videos to use. Note worthwhile programs, then schedule times to watch shows and videos that complement what you're studying.

RESOURCES

Educational Software

Language Arts

I Love Spelling, Dorling Kindersley
Reader Rabbit III, The Learning Company
Sierra's Schoolhouse English, Sierra
Spelling Jungle, Sierra
Storybook Weaver Deluxe, MECC
SuperSolver Spellbound! The Learning Company

Math, Science, Thinking Skills

The Incredible Machine, Sierra
The Lost Mind of Dr. Brain, Sierra
I Love Math, Dorling Kindersley
I Love Science, Dorling Kindersley
Leonardo the Inventor, Interactive Publishing Corporation
The Magic School Bus (various), Microsoft
Quarter Mile Math Programs (800-541-6078 or 800-843-5576 for info)
Stars and Stories (check http://www.wildridge.com for info)
Strategy Challenges, Edmark
Thinkin' Things (I, II, III), Edmark

History, Geography, and Social Studies

Africa Trail
Amazon Trail
Oregon Trail II
SimCity 2000
SimTown
Foreign Languages and Arts
Art Gallery: The Collection of the National Gallery, London, Microsoft

Opening Night, MECC
Opening Night: Behind the Scenes, MECC

See "Languages" in Chapter 8's Resources section for recommendations for foreign language software titles.

Books with Accompanying CD-ROMs

Dewhirst, Carin and Joan, narrated by Leonard Bernstein. *Peter and the Wolf.* Friedman/Fairfax, 1997.

Ganeri, Anita. *The Young Person's Guide to the Orchestra* and *The Young Person's Guide to the Ballet* (from Harcourt Brace). *Orchestra* CD is narrated by Ben Kingsley.

Educational Web Sites

Art

A&E (Arts and Entertainment Channel): http://www.A&E.com
Cartoon Mania: http://www.worldchat.com/public/jhish/cartoon.html
Cyberkids Gallery: http://www.cyberkids.com/Gallery/Art.html

Current Events and News

CNN: http://www.cnn.com
CSPAN: http://www.cspan.org
MSNBC: http://www.msnbc.com
The History Channel: http://www.historychannel.com

General

The Learning Channel: http://tlc.com
Phoenix Special Programs and Academies: 800-426-4952, http://www.online.phoenix.academies.org

Movie Reviews

Screen It! Entertainment Reviews for Parents: http://www.screenit.com

Science

Chemistry for Kids: http://www.chem4kids.com
NASA: http://www.nasa.org
Robert Krampf's Science Education Company: http://members.aol.com/krampf/home.html
The Weather Channel: http://www.weather.com

For the Sports-Minded

ESPN: http://www.espn.com

(See Chapter 4's Resources section for full curriculum companies with online academies. See Chapter 8's Resources section and various sidebars in this chapter for more educational Web sites.)

Educational Videotapes

The American Testimony (history), 281-565-7711
Chalk Dust Math Videos, 800-588-7564, http://www.chalkdust.com
Magic School Bus Videos
National Geographic Videos
Saxon Algebra on Videotape, 800-284-7019, http://www.saxonpub.com
Schoolhouse Rock Videos, ABC Videos
School of Tomorrow, upper level science videos, 800-976-7226, http://www.schooloftomorrow.com
The Wonders of God's Creation series (*Planet Earth, Animal Kingdom, Human Life*) and *The Amazing Forces of God's Creation,* Moody Videos

Books

Coleman. *Homeschooling and the Internet* (self-published). Lifetime Books and Gifts, 941-676-6311, http://www.lifetimeonline.com.

Dinsmore, Mark and Wendy. *Homeschool Guide to the Internet.* Homeschool Press, 1996. Available from Lifetime Books and Gifts, 941-676-6311, http://www.lifetimeonline.com.

Winn, Marie. *The Plug In Drug: Television, Children, and the Family.* Penguin, 1985.

Catalogs

Edusoft, 619-562-6812, http://www.edusoftonline.com.

Lawrence Productions, 800-421-4157, http://www.lpi.com.

National School Products, 800-627-9393.

S&S Software, 520-384-3844, http://www.sssoftware.com.

Soleil, 800-501-0110, http://www.soleil.com.

LearningWare Reviews (online catalog): http://www.learningwarereviews.com.

12

HOMESCHOOLERS' TOP THREE DESTINATIONS

In This Chapter

- Support groups
- Your local library
- Your community: a microcosm of the great wide world
- Simple starting points
- Resources

HOMESCHOOL TRAVELERS list support groups, libraries, and communities as vital to their successful journeys. The vast majority of homeschoolers belong to at least one support group, most often a local one. Many also belong to state, national, and online support groups. The sight of children in the library in the middle of a school day is now commonplace, because libraries are a popular hangout for homeschoolers. And, in growing numbers, homeschoolers are using other resources their communities have to offer, from touring small businesses to volunteering at the local food shelf. Perhaps homeschooling is becoming a misnomer. While their base is home, it's clear that homeschoolers use the world around them for their education, unlimited by the constraints of conventional schooling.

SUPPORT GROUPS

AS I NOTED earlier, most homeschoolers belong to their local support groups, and many also belong to state and national groups. A growing number of homeschoolers are using the Internet to stay on top of legislative alerts or find others who face the same challenges. Over fifty respondents say they now draw support from the Internet, either in place of local groups, or in addition to them. People belong to various groups for various reasons and no two groups are alike.

Perhaps homeschooling is becoming a misnomer. While their base is home, it's clear that homeschoolers use the world around them for their education, unlimited by the constraints of conventional schooling.

Local Groups

I've belonged to local groups that centered on gathering children together for casual park days, and others that held highly structured field trips and classes. Some local groups offer resource centers, filled with curriculum, books, science kits, and other learning materials.

Larissa says, "I belong to the homeschool co-op because it gives my sons a chance to take classes one day a week that I would not have taught them, for whatever reason. For example, I would rather not dissect a cow's eyeball!"

In states that require membership in umbrella or covering schools, homeschoolers gain their local support through them. "We chose our covering school because it is, in our opinion, the best organized and largest of the groups in the area," Catherine says. "They offer a wide variety of activities and fellowship opportunities for students and moms."

Some support comes through more informational gatherings. Gail says, "I run a monthly informational meeting, not exactly a support group, but we invite speakers and provide information for newcomers. Also, my husband and daughters run a teen night."

Missy looks back on the importance of support groups. "The local group provided social opportunities for me and my children. Also, they offered activities that lent themselves to group involvement. I also appreciated hearing how different curriculum worked for different people."

Many homeschoolers who can't find a local group that meets their needs have advertised in local parenting publications and on the radio, or posted notes at the libraries, to find others of like mind.

Many homeschoolers especially enjoy the field trip opportunities, much like Missy. However, others find ways to access many of the same places with just their families or with one or two other families.

Jennie says, "We were once involved in a homeschool co-op, but there were personality and philosophy clashes. I find that my children and I do much better if we find things we love to do and happen to discover other homeschoolers there. We've found homeschoolers and support in a many places, including Tae Kwon Do and dance."

Rose says, "We no longer belong to a support group due to time and an actual preference not to be influenced by what others are doing. It's all wonderful, but I'm too easily tempted to drop one thing midstream for another. We're at a point where we can't afford to do that anymore."

Rose has put together hand-picked activities for a small group of homeschoolers, such as lining up a teacher at a local nature center for a small group.

Many homeschoolers who can't find a local group that meets their needs have advertised in local parenting publications and on the radio, or posted notes at the libraries, to find others of like mind. If group interaction is important to you but you can't find a support group to suit you, think about starting your own.

State Groups

Homeschooling has grown to the point where most states have more than one statewide support or networking group to choose from. Send off for information on each, see what kind of support and activities it provides, and consider joining. State groups are wonderful for keeping homeschoolers abreast of any pending legislative threats to homeschooling, as well as for networking and providing conferences and other large events. Even without membership, you can usually attend conferences, curriculum sales, and special workshops. Other times, membership is required.

Rose writes, "We have belonged on and off to the two state groups here. We now belong to another one designed for teens so my daughter is eligible for certain activities, such as a teen spring cruise."

One state group has worked to provide various homeschool days at large museums along the lines of the privileges public schools find. Homeschool Day at the U.S. Space and Rocket Center saw over 300 homeschoolers come through and enjoy discounted rates on regular exhibits and movies, and special hands-on activities for the children. Thanks to the efforts of other state groups, theme parks such as Six Flags Over Georgia host homeschool days. If you'd like to see more of this sort of thing and working on a larger scale to benefit homeschoolers appeals to you, get involved with your state organization.

National Groups

There are a handful of national groups, each with different purposes. The National Homeschool Association networks with inclusive state groups to help people find local support and have occasional nationwide conferences or gatherings. The National Center for Home Education exists primarily to stay on top of homeschooling research and provide information to the media and other interested parties. The American Homeschool Association began to serve homeschooling businesses and support group leaders but has spun out on the Internet to serve as the major source of support for many homeschoolers. The Home School Legal Defense Association provides legal insurance and information for those who desire it. There are a number of national groups designed specifically to provide information and networking for people of the same faith or who face similar challenges.

You may find the need or desire for none, all, or one or two of the national groups. All are interested in promoting a positive image of homeschooling to the nation at large, and are often contacted when major newspapers or magazines cover homeschooling. See "Support Groups" in Chapter 1's Resources section for a list of the largest national groups and an e-mail list that should point to ones with more narrow scopes.

E-mail and Internet Groups

Larissa says, "I belong to a small e-mail group of homeschoolers which provides my greatest support."

Larissa shares the experience of many online homeschoolers. She spent time on various Internet homeschooling boards and e-mail lists, then connected with a much smaller group of people. An e-mail 'loop' was born and has been active for over four years. The group of six women recently gathered in Atlanta, Georgia, for their first-ever group get-together. I was one of the group, as were a few of the other survey respondents. I know of other e-mail groups who have had the same sort of reunions.

I've participated in a number of online boards and e-mail lists as well. There's no better way to get a wide range of information quickly than to participate regularly in such groups. When my son struggled with reading, when I was interested in exploring the ideas of Charlotte Mason and the Robinson method, when I was looking for like-minded people who shared my faith, and when I needed people willing to fill out the lengthy questionnaire for this book, I had an international group of homeschoolers to draw from. As my children move toward the high school years, I'll begin to hook up

MONEY SAVER

Field trip costs can add up. You can control costs somewhat if you volunteer to organize a few field trips each year. Look for free tours of such places as restaurants, factories, or television stations. Most of these have minimum age requirements and are perfectly suited for the middle years child.

with Internet homeschooling parents of high schoolers. And my son wants to be part of a group with others who will be using his curriculum of choice (Sonlight).

About a half dozen times, I've been part of smaller spin-off e-mail loops, people who find each other and share anything from religious beliefs to methodology to sense of humor. Each time, it's been wonderful to glean from the more intense support of a smaller group. For those who have trouble finding like-minded support locally, the Internet provides a great answer.

Rachel says, "A few people I know started a Jewish homeschool group on the Internet because we didn't have Jewish resources available."

Catholic homeschoolers, conservative Christian homeschoolers, Muslim homeschoolers, New Age homeschoolers, Unitarian homeschoolers, and many others, provide e-mail lists and Web sites to interact with other homeschoolers of similar faiths. The same holds with methods and curriculum—whatever you use, whatever your approach, you can find something, or start a group, to hook up with others who share your ideas.

Lifetime friends are being made on the Internet. I've hosted a number of homeschooling families I met on the Net as they come through my town. Catherine is among a number of homeschoolers who shared the same experience.

She says, "I am active on a Web site called The Swap (http://www.theswap.com). I receive good advice and have bought and sold curriculum there. I met one of the participants who came to town to go to Space Camp here."

Beckie says, "My online groups are my lifeline. I talk to these people daily; they help me get my adult fix."

YOUR LOCAL LIBRARY

LIBRARIES ARE A homeschooler's best friend. The shelves are loaded with useful titles, and those you can't find you can order through interlibrary loan. Libraries now have computers with both software and Internet access for you to use, and also have audio- and videotapes available. It takes a little more planning and foresight to use the library than to purchase your literature all at once for the year, but the time is worth the money you would otherwise spend, and you won't need the same amount of storage space to accommodate the collection. Many homeschoolers teach their children using only paper, pencils, a good math workbook, and resources from their library.

I recently attended a homeschooling day at a library in a large southern city. The library staff laid out refreshments and provided two rooms for the homeschoolers: one for home business and used curriculum sales, the other for ongoing workshops. What a service! Many homeschoolers across the country use rooms at their libraries for similar events. Librarians are on call to answer questions and help out when needed.

If you'd like to encourage literature discussion groups and can't find a homeschooling parent to facilitate the gatherings, ask your local librarian to lead one. Parents can meet with the librarian to come up with a mutually agreeable title, then each can assign the book to their children. This kind of gathering is perfect for the middle years child.

Many homeschoolers teach their children using only paper, pencils, a good math workbook, and resources from their library.

If a number of homeschoolers are unfamiliar with how best to use the library, schedule a day for the library staff to take homeschooling families on tour. Most libraries are willing to stock homeschooling information on their shelves, and many will post notices and keep local information on file for those who come in and ask. Librarians continually report a large number of questions regarding homeschooling.

If you want to see your library carry a particular title or magazine, place a formal request. Get your friends to do so as well. Most of the time, if libraries get enough requests to justify the expense, they will carry an item.

My children and I have put our librarians on our Christmas list and bring them trays of cookies at random. We appreciate their work on our behalf and want to continue on good terms.

If you're concerned that your children will be too isolated when they begin to homeschool, know that most homeschoolers are out and about in the real world far more than their schooled peers.

YOUR COMMUNITY: A MICROCOSM OF THE GREAT WIDE WORLD

IF YOU'RE CONCERNED that your children will be too isolated when they begin to homeschool, know that most homeschoolers are out and about in the real world far more than their schooled peers. Homeschoolers don't take their communities for granted—they tend to look for every nook and cranny that can be used as a learning opportunity for their children. Educational field trips, volunteering and service, and participating in scouts, athletics, and the arts all help create more well-rounded adults, and all are available for the homeschooler who seeks them out.

Field Trips

There are abundant field trip opportunities for homeschoolers; in fact, most of us get to a point where we have to pare down the amount we're attending. Some field trips are better suited to groups, others can be appreciated much more with your family only. A lot depends on your reasons for attending—some homeschoolers seek the socialization of field trips, others find it overstimulating and distracting from the bigger picture. There are some field trips such as tours of large factories or television stations that may not be possible for a family to attend on its own.

With the growth of homeschooling, there seems to be a newer trend for museums to treat homeschool groups in more school-type ways. Twice this past year, those of us arranging field trips had long chats with the museum personnel to explain that our children didn't want to be divided by age groups; they wanted to stay with their families. Always call to get the details of a field trip before deciding to go. Nothing is more frustrating for me or my children than to waste four or five hours stuck somewhere we'd rather not be, because a field trip sounded better on paper than what it was in reality.

Middle years children are a perfect fit for field trips, and are able to handle those that offer detailed and technical information. Many car factories, television stations, and other similar places only offer tours to children age ten or older, so check and see if your children are old enough, then enjoy the tour. Middle years children are full of questions, and often those guiding a tour will comment on the interest level of homeschooled children. It's this same age that is ripe for an extended study, an offshoot in their learning adventure, based on a field trip that piques an interest. Consider anything or anywhere as a potential field trip. Pay attention to your paper's weekly events calendar and travel section for ideas. Browse the library or bookstore

HOW WE DID IT

Our favorite thing to do is to go to the local nursing home and perform using puppets, choir, and drama. We have built wonderful relationships with the residents, and the children have learned an appreciation for the elderly. This would not have been possible with a regular public school schedule.

—KATRINA

shelves for interesting travel, museum, or parks guides and magazines. Small town heritage festivals can be a fun way to spend a Saturday afternoon, and are ripe with learning potential. We have attended local Scottish festivals, fiddlers' conventions, and other such out-of-the-ordinary (for us) events. Each time, we have come away with smiles on our faces and tons of new knowledge.

How much work you want to make field trips is entirely up to you. For most field trips, we show up, enjoy, and move on after the fact. Others have sparked an interest in my children and they want to study the subject further. Many museums and historical sites have museum stores with learning materials available for purchase. Because it was a legal requirement to study our state's history, we kept photographic journals with accompanying reports. Some homeschoolers give their children worksheets to fill out; others have them write a brief story about what they learned.

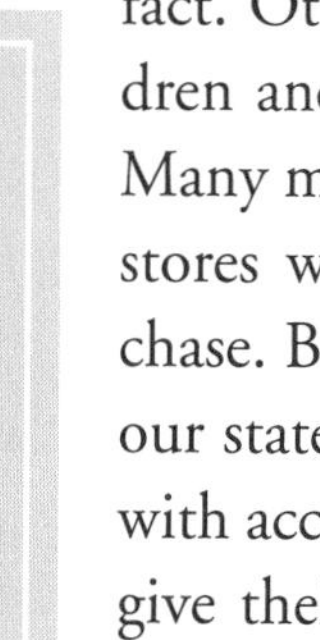

QUICK & EASY

Get the Internet address of your local library, and keep it posted in an obvious place. Check titles needed or wanted before you make the trip!

On occasion, a field trip calls for some preparation so children will get the most from it. Prior to visiting Helen Keller's home, we rented *The Miracle Worker* and watched it together. Each child read a biography of Helen Keller suited to their age level. When we arrived at the house, they were already interested, and were more able to listen and ask intelligent questions. Putting their hands on the well pump where Helen spelled W-A-T-E-R in the movie (and in real life) took on larger significance.

Before we visited a Russian Treasures art exhibit, we looked up the time period in our *Timetables of History* book. Since the tour was running around the holiday season, it was easy to tie in our attendance of *The Nutcracker*. Tchaikovsky wrote the ballet during the same period in Russia's history in which much of the art was produced.

Children are able to place knowledge in a larger context and to get the most out of field trips with a little preparation. While we rarely prepare ahead of time, we are always glad when we do.

Volunteering

As children progress through their middle years, they often find extra time on their hands. Time they once spent playing with dolls and action figures they now want to fill, at least in part, with more adult activities. Service teaches children to think outside themselves and consider the needs of others. Cultivating a habit of service early on puts service in its place: not something to make a big deal of or to seek recognition for—just part of living responsibly. At first glance, it seems that many opportunities aren't open to middle years children, but with a little digging and a lot of promotional work, middle years homeschoolers should be able to find areas for volunteer service.

Cultivating a habit of service early on puts service in its place: not something to make a big deal of or to seek recognition for—just part of living responsibly.

If parents are involved with any volunteer work on their own, the children are most often welcomed along. When my husband or I are asked to serve in any capacity, we often ask if our children can help. Children can make sandwiches and box lunches to serve workers on Habitat for Humanity homes, for example. My children helped me guide a tour group through our area's annual arts festival. Libraries are sometimes open to homeschooling volunteers, as are soup kitchens and thrift stores geared toward serving those with lower incomes.

The smaller the organization, the more likely it is to be open to help from middle years children. Larger, more established groups are often caught up in red tape that prohibits them from using help prior to a child's sixteenth birthday.

If you're involved with your church, start there. Children can serve within the church community (kitchen, cleaning, nursery,

SERVICE IDEAS

- Mow an elderly neighbor's lawn.
- Help make a meal for a new mother.
- Baby-sit for a younger mother—without pay.
- Volunteer for Habitat for Humanity.
- Work at a local soup kitchen, food shelf, or other similar outreach program.
- Volunteer at your local library.
- Work in your church nursery, volunteer to help with Vacation Bible School, or help in the church kitchen.

Bible and Sunday school, and so on) or help with church outreach activities. Get to know the people who are in charge and have them get to know your child. My son has twice helped out at a local neighborhood store geared to serving those on government assistance. He's helped as part of his youth group, but hopes to return as an individual volunteer.

If groups near you are closed to middle years children, then find ways for your family to serve others without an organized group. Mothers of babies welcome someone scrubbing their toilets and mopping their floors. When my children were younger, I was deeply grateful for a homeschooling family who consistently offered to watch my children if I had an appointment. Check out the "Service Ideas" sidebar for a list of ideas to get you started.

Mentorships and Apprenticeships

As with service, it may take a bit more looking to find mentoring and apprenticing opportunities for the middle years child than it will when they grow older, but it's not impossible. Getting to know individuals in organizations and offices can make all the difference in having a door opened to a middle years child.

Bea's daughter began to apprentice for a dog groomer at the age of twelve. She swept floors and helped with filing. She watched how grooming was done. By the time she was fourteen, she'd gained enough experience to groom pets on her own. After that, she began working for pay. Homeschoolers have assisted in photography studios, dental offices, and a number of other situations. Develop relationships with people in businesses that interest your child, and ask for the opportunity.

Look for people who work from their homes. They often need help and will be more open to the idea of having a middle years child around than some larger businesses are. If your child has an intense interest, such as writing or science, seek out a writer or a scientist to act as a mentor. Your child could meet with the professional at regularly scheduled intervals to ask questions and watch the work in progress.

Though the idea of mentoring and apprenticing may be unfamiliar, it's like homeschooling—more and more people are participating all the time.

Community Activities

As noted in Chapter 8, homeschoolers participate in community activities through scouts, sports, and the various arts. Many take lessons run by privately owned companies, others choose those funded through their community arts councils or city agencies, still others find adults to teach similar classes to homeschooling groups. If you're looking for a particular activity, be sure to check out your options before signing up. Find what best suits your child and your family. For example, in our town, children take swimming lessons through the city, privately, or at the local YMCA. Homeschoolers gather for swim days at the local city pools. There are also a number of privately owned neighborhood pools where children swim during the summer months and compete with other neighborhood pools on swim teams if they wish. And there are four United States swimming programs that work out year round.

While the choices may not be as great in some areas, you'll find similar smorgasbords in most sports, dance, music, the martial arts, scouting, and 4H. If you aren't content with what's being offered, look for a qualified person to teach a small group of homeschoolers. The group will most likely grow. It's sometimes difficult to land a part in local children's theater productions, for example, and many people aren't able to make the sort of commitment required. More and more, homeschoolers are performing their own plays with their homeschooling groups. Children get exposure to theater without the commitment they would have to make to a larger company. Other children, of course, want to make that commitment and the local theater company suits their needs perfectly.

Ask around, check out the different options, and don't be afraid to be part of starting something new.

Alternative Education Programs

Though not an option for most homeschoolers, in some states, the public school system opens its doors to homeschoolers for a variety of classes. Some middle years children also take advantage of extended education programs of local community colleges and universities.

For lab sciences, upper mathematics courses, and all sorts of specialty classes (interior design, computer programming, cake decorating, and so on), having the option of school classes with paid-for materials is a bonus for many homeschoolers.

About half the respondents say they are philosophically opposed to using public school programs and wouldn't use them even if they were available in their states. The other half say they're open to using any program they think might add to their child's overall education.

Those who are philosophically opposed to participating in government-funded homeschooling programs argue that accepting government funding and help goes hand in hand with accepting government regulations and control. Though government programs for homeschoolers differ in the states where they are available, they all include various measures of control, such as assessment and oversight by school officials. Some school districts have created specific upper administrative positions or departments to oversee and "help" homeschoolers. Based on the historical success of the homeschooling movement, it is natural to have doubts about their motives. It's wise to assume that, once in place, those whose livelihood depends on such administrative jobs would actively pursue increasing their workload to justify the existence of the positions. Most homeschoolers prefer not to help school officials in this pursuit.

The programs may look convenient, or even necessary to some homeschoolers, but it's worth thoughtful consideration before deciding whether to participate. There is no way around the fact that, on some level, you'll be exchanging personal freedom for convenience and cost, and setting a precedent that may eventually affect homeschoolers.

Rebecca's son takes two classes at the local community college, one of which is computer repair.

Deb says, "We never rule out using any resource in the future, including public schools. We like to keep any options open that would benefit our children."

> "We consider ourselves 'educational consumers.' We look where we can get the product we want at the best value."
>
> —JANICE

Gail's two daughters took drama and advanced chemistry at the local public high school. She says, "It gave them a taste, without complete immersion, of public school life, and no desire to be there full time." The two girls returned home full time the following year.

Janice says, "We use these programs for subjects I can't do easily at home, or don't want to do at home because it would be too demanding for me. We consider ourselves 'educational consumers.' We look where we can get the product we want at the best value. Sometimes that means we pay someone else to teach the kids.

Sometimes we send them to the public school for a class or two. Sometimes we join with other families to pool our efforts in some area, and sometimes we stay home and do it ourselves."

SIMPLE STARTING POINTS

✦ *Try to locate more than one local support group.*

Attend meetings of each. Listen closely, ask questions. If there isn't a group that fits your needs, don't get discouraged. Spread the word and try to find some like-minded homeschoolers to hook up with. Check out Internet homeschooling support.

✦ *Consider joining your state homeschooling organization.*

In addition—or as well—try finding a state Internet group to stay on top of legislative issues that may affect homeschooling, and to get information regarding upcoming conferences and workshops.

✦ *Visit the library often.*

Schedule frequent trips to your library and introduce yourself and your children to the staff. They will be a great help to you, and can help fill you in on available resources and how to access them.

✦ *Find out if your local support groups offer field trips.*

If interested, join and get on the mailing list so you will be notified of upcoming events. Also, contact the groups listed in the Resources section and begin planning some field trips of your own.

✦ *Think about ways your child can volunteer in the community.*

Nurture relationships with people who can help find a way for your child to serve.

✦ *Don't rule out the unusual.*

Look into the various options available for activities and special interests, whether mentoring, apprenticing, or taking classes either privately or through a local public school or community college. Be sure to find out what, if any, strings are attached to public school options for homeschoolers.

RESOURCES

Travel Guides

Bookstores and libraries are loaded with good travel guides. Check the regional section if you want to plan local field trips, then find a title as specific as you need. The two most popular names in travel guides are Fodor's and Frommer's. Fodor's offers City Packs for most large cities. They are purse size, have a plastic cover, and are easy to use.

Helpful Places

Open your Yellow Pages, call the following places, and request their standard information packets. You'll find all sorts of lesser known sights worth seeing.

Chamber of commerce
Tourist bureau
Historical society
Art league, art museum, arts council
Any other museums, botanical gardens, societies, or similar organizations.

Book

Purtell, April, Gaunt, Elizabeth and John, and Harris, Gregg. *The A-Z Guide to Educational Field Trips.* Christian Life Workshops, 1997.

13

ACCOMMODATING YOUNGER TRAVELERS

In This Chapter

- Curious younger siblings who want to hop on board
- Balancing inclusion with encouraging independent learning
- Same family, different journey: observations on birth order
- Simple starting points
- Resources

RIGHT AFTER, "Am I capable of teaching my child at home?" comes the second most asked question, "How will I teach the older child with younger children who already take up my time?"

A good question it is. To pretend that homeschooling days always flow smoothly with younger children contentedly occupying themselves while you work with older children is not realistic. When you first bring your middle years child home, younger siblings will need some time to adjust to sharing their mother. Little children get sick, don't always understand "wait," are sometimes noisy even while playing independently, and are masters at messing up entire rooms in milliseconds when they are, at last, quiet. But, every day, homeschooling parents across the country manage to help their older children learn while caring for younger siblings. It takes some compromise on all fronts, but it is possible.

CURIOUS YOUNGER SIBLINGS WHO WANT TO HOP ON BOARD

YOUNGER CHILDREN LEARN by observing, listening, and participating in their older siblings' homeschooling adventure. They hear the older siblings ask questions and get answers. They want to be part of the action, so they listen—and learn.

"My younger child has learned so much by osmosis, simply by being around when I was teaching the older child a new concept," says Corinne.

Margie agrees. "Our second son surprises me with what he knows from hearing everything that his older brother is learning."

Older children learn from younger ones as well. Teaching younger children new concepts with older siblings close by is a great way to cement knowledge they have already been exposed to. As Christy says, "The oldest learns from things the younger children and I talk about, too."

> To pretend that homeschooling days always flow smoothly with younger children contentedly occupying themselves while you work with older children is not realistic.

Younger children want to be a part of things. They want to be treated equally to their older siblings, and that's a trait homeschoolers can capitalize upon. Use this natural desire to expose younger children to all sorts of knowledge. Because it's important to them to be included, they will usually listen with care and remember what they've learned.

Older children eventually outgrow field trips geared to younger children (fire stations, playgrounds, and so on) and sometimes would rather stay home to conquer schoolwork. On the other hand, some field trips geared to older children won't allow younger siblings to participate. Try to find a family with a similar age spread that you can swap field trips with, so the older children can learn from the technical field trips closed to younger ones, and younger children can fully enjoy the simpler ones without the homeschooling parent worrying about giving up the older child's study time.

Most field trips, however, are suited for wide age ranges. If the tour guides lecture, it may be difficult to keep little ones quiet and still, but most guides are sensitive to the younger children. Many living history farms, hands-on museums, and other excursions easily accommodate younger children. Like Corinne, Margie, and Christy, I've often been surprised by my daughters' knowledge they have picked up around the house, but even more so, from field trips. Also, when they see their older brother learning something, they tend to

HOW WE DID IT

I found having a box with special things available only for schooltime with the older children helps a lot. Fill this box with learning games, puzzles, art materials, videos, computer programs, and so on. I wonder if my daughter sometimes used to encourage my son to need my one-on-one attention just so she could pull out her "special box"!

—PHYLLIS

The thing that works best for us is to have a special box for the younger children. In the box is "school" for the younger ones, including scissors, glue stick, crayons, paper, coloring books, etc. They can only use these items when the older ones are doing their school work.

—KATRINA

assume it must be important, and they want in on the knowledge. T.J. and his youngest sister spend hours placing pennies on a large world map spread out on the floor talking about all the places they want to travel. This sort of interaction is common in homeschooling families.

Laura says, "We read aloud a lot, even on topics the youngest isn't particularly interested in, but at least he feels included. We attend field trips and events that are geared to a broad range of interests and keep age-appropriate materials on hand, offering alternatives suited to his needs."

Often, older children help teach their littler siblings, a great way for the homeschooling parent to delegate and teach responsibility, and to informally assess older children's grasp of knowledge.

Corrie, homeschooling mother of three in South Carolina, says, "My daughter loves to teach her younger brothers. If my two-year-old starts counting or identifying colors, she may stop her work and teach him a new color, shape, or number. He enjoys the attention from her."

Carol's children work with one another too. She says, "The older children work with their younger siblings. I take some time each day to work with the youngest, but the bulk of her day is spent playing or doing her work with one of the older children."

Deb says, "Usually, when one child is doing something interesting, the others gather around. The easiest way to motivate any of the children is to be interested in something yourself and it's as though you've instantly become a magnet. They can't stay away!"

Many travelers teach various children together, especially when they are close in age.

Ruth, homeschooling mother of two in Pennsylvania, says, "The second child learns by listening to the older child's lessons. Because my two children are so close in age, we study all subjects except math and language together on the same level."

Like Ruth, many travelers with multiple children point to the usefulness of unit studies when teaching to many levels. Sharon says,

"We cover the same topics, just at an easier level for the younger ones."

Lynn, who homeschools two children in California, agrees. "I teach all subjects to both children at the same time. I gear them to each child's level."

Younger children are offended if they're not allowed to participate, and why shouldn't they be, if they're capable? Phyllis says, "My daughter learned to read at age four. She was insulted if she wasn't allowed to do school with her brother."

Phyllis works as a covering school administrator and says that she sees the same thing with most families. She says, "Many younger siblings want to do school the same as their older siblings. It's best to let them."

Some small children demand workbooks and a learning space to call their own, a shock to many of us who approached learning a little later with older siblings. My youngest was intensely interested in curriculum I was bringing home for her older sister and brother and began to ask for 'real' school books too. This year, I purchased a number of age-appropriate workbooks and set up a school area she could claim. After breakfast every morning, she'd get settled and begin to work through her books. She'd remind me if I was supposed to help with a particular lesson. She helped with the older children's science experiments. By early February, she had completed a year's worth of curriculum and I was ordering more! The older two get a kick out of watching her sail through work.

> Younger children are offended if they're not allowed to participate, and why shouldn't they be, if they're capable?

Anna says, "Our two-year-old has a desk just like her sister. She has some bins next to her desk, filled with puzzles, blocks, Legos, paper, crayons, and so on. We rotate these as she tires of them. We also include her in our oral lessons and any book reading. These things make her feel like she's 'doing school' too. When we do math, we give her blocks, and she feels as if she's doing her math."

In fact, Anna's little girl *is* doing her math!

It's delightful when youngest children see learning as so natural and so much fun that they eagerly want to hop on board. How much more wonderful that the enthusiasm nurtured early on continues through their learning journey, an enthusiasm lost to most schoolchildren by around the fourth grade.

BALANCING INCLUSION WITH ENCOURAGING INDEPENDENT LEARNING

HOMESCHOOLERS AGREE the best way to handle younger siblings is to include them. After all, families learning together—all the siblings learning with and from one another—is the very essence of homeschooling. However, there are times when younger siblings either can't or won't be able to participate with older siblings. Some science experiments are too dangerous for eager hands that may not understand, "don't touch," for example. Furthermore, working through an intricate writing project or difficult math problem requires a certain level of quiet. At times like these, younger siblings need to be otherwise occupied, and be led toward independent learning. Younger children can learn, over time, to be quiet observers when need be.

> After all, families learning together—all the siblings learning with and from one another—is the very essence of homeschooling.

Christina says, "It's important to enforce manageable rules such as, 'You must not disturb your brother and me for the next twenty minutes.' We try to keep lessons short."

By teaching young children to sit and play quietly for periods of time, parents can focus better on the older children who will finish their work quicker. Rewarding younger children often, at least at first, encourages them to work independently. Allow them to choose a favorite picture book to read together as a reward, for example. They will come to see the give and take of their actions, and will look forward to their quiet, focused attention from you too.

Katrina says that by learning to "sit with us during reading times and drill work, they are getting an early exposure to things they will later learn on their own, even if they don't understand everything now." She continues, "I have noticed the younger children seem to have an advantage later because they are usually in the room while we work with the older ones. They pick up the material quicker, because they were exposed to it over a longer period of time."

With time, younger siblings learn to proudly and happily work independently on projects of their own.

Keeping younger siblings close by encourages them to participate in learning and is a tangible reminder that they are an important part of the family unit.

Wendy takes advantage of nap times but also says, "When he's awake I keep my son close by. It keeps him out of trouble and he likes working with us and feeling like a part of what we're doing."

Janice says her youngest stays nearby too, "She always is there with us as we read aloud, and sits alongside coloring or playing in her own workbooks."

The youngest of children sometimes are the ones getting the most from certain lessons, like sponges absorbing every new piece of knowledge around them.

Many travelers say the most obvious time of day to conquer projects without little ones around is nap time. However, parents and older siblings are tired in late afternoons too, and nap times are seldom long enough to provide ample time to work with older children. While nap time provides a workable solution, it's only a partial one. With time, younger siblings learn to proudly and happily work independently on projects of their own.

Abby says she gives each of her children schoolwork or chores of their own. With seven to homeschool, it's important to foster an

KID-TESTED SCHOOLTIME OCCUPATIONS FOR YOUNGER SIBLINGS

Here are the many ways travelers recommend occupying younger children while they work with older ones:

- Coloring books, drawing, age-appropriate workbooks
- Other children to play with
- Television and videos
- Computer games
- Music for listening to and dancing
- Water games
- Special things that only come out during schooltime
- Blocks, Legos, manipulatives
- Another place to play
- A desk of their own to work at
- Puzzles
- Play-Doh—or the homemade variety
- Books to look at
- Chores around the house

atmosphere of cooperation. Gretchen also gives her younger children their own work to do, and has the older ones teach the younger ones if necessary.

Esther says, "My five-year-old often joins us in current events discussions and looks at the map with us if we are trying to figure out where a particular country is. He comes on field trips designed for his ten-year-old sister and asks lots of good questions."

Many of the travelers say they sometimes use television shows or videos to keep younger siblings out of harm's way while the older ones are working. Laura says, "He likes fun computer games, manipulatives, and limited use of the VCR." Anna's daughter will watch "an occasional Barney video or another we've checked out from the library. She also likes a few computer programs."

Some mothers use options available for preschoolers outside the home. Sabrina's youngest attends preschool three days a week. Other travelers make similar choices.

More important than academics, younger children learn some of life's important lessons by being around older ones. Kayla's young daughter learns from her big brother, but not just academics. Kayla says, "My daughter learns a lot from her older brother. He allows her to be more grown up, more sure of herself, because he can tell her what to expect and what is appropriate, in his opinion." She continues, "She is highly motivated and busy all the time. She sometimes challenges him to work harder or do better."

These homeschool siblings are learning to balance interdependence with independence and give with take.

SAME FAMILY, DIFFERENT JOURNEY: OBSERVATIONS ON BIRTH ORDER

IT'S ALMOST A cliché to hear about the poor oldest children, the parental guinea pigs, and homeschool travelers are not exceptions to the rule. When asked to talk about how their homeschooling has changed from the oldest to the youngest children, parents share the belief that they made their mistakes with their oldest ones, and that the younger children are the beneficiaries of the experience. Don't be discouraged. These same parents also tell tales of oldest children who are high achievers. Typical of birth order in general, firstborn homeschoolers are organized, intelligent leaders. With the benefit of homeschooling to top it off, who can stop them? At the same time, younger children enjoy the benefits of parents who are eager to learn and become better over time, and also of having their older siblings around to set examples and offer help.

Lila says, "The advantage of being first is the undivided attention that the child gets. But the younger ones benefit from having heard the material taught to the older ones. My fourth child is ahead of his older siblings when they were his age. He'll probably learn to read sooner than they did."

Parents say they learn the most about parenting and homeschooling with their firstborn children. Deb says, "The firstborn bears the brunt of having first-time homeschooling parents. The second and third children in our family benefit from his being our guinea pig."

When asked to talk about how their homeschooling has changed from the oldest to the youngest children, parents shared the belief that they made their mistakes with their oldest ones, and that the younger children are the beneficiaries of the experience.

Jennie agrees. "The victim of an overanxious new homeschooling mother, my first child was often the unfortunate guinea pig. She had the dubious pleasure of experiencing a long parade of unsuccessful reading and math programs. I must have learned from my mistakes, though, because I was much more relaxed with my second child, who learned to read simply by looking over my shoulder while I read aloud."

Most travelers do relax over time, but they also become clearer about their goals and how to reach them. Esther says, "The younger children definitely benefit from what I learned with the oldest. When we got three-quarters of the way through our reading curriculum and my son began complaining about being bored, I knew it was not imperative that we finish the book." She continues, "At the same time, because it took me until she reached about ten to realize my oldest daughter had a phonics 'deficit' which was adversely affecting her ability to spell, I'm more certain to work on phonics with the younger ones."

As in any vocation, experience pays off. Travelers become better homeschooling parents with time.

Carol says, "I cried with my oldest when we tried to understand algebra. Then came twins. They got a wonderful education. The baby was taught by the twins and her older sister. While I missed teaching her myself, the twins were perfectly capable and I was very busy because I was teaching Latin to other homeschoolers. As most parents," she continues, "we have become more relaxed in our parenting so their approaches to learning are influenced by that. We have noticed our two oldest have vastly different learning styles and we try to encourage them to the best of their abilities in their own ways."

It's hard to know which comes first, whether the parents' becoming more relaxed passes that to the children or if children's individuality and needs direct the parents toward relaxing.

Laura says, "Somehow I do spend more effort on the oldest, but her interests and abilities are in a more traditional area. She likes more structure while the younger ones prefer free exploration. Birth order may be informing my homeschooling methods from the bottom up more than from the top down."

Judy's firstborn is similar in learning, but takes less of her time. "He is an independent learner," she says. "The younger siblings are not as quick to work along and have required far more one-on-one time."

Like most parents, homeschooling travelers worry about their middle children being forgotten. Sharon says, "The middle children sometimes get less attention, because of the urgency of the older children's studies and the physical and emotional needs of the little ones. Also, the little ones have less mommy time because of the school time with the older ones."

Bea's first two children attended school for a while. The second two have been homeschooled their whole lives. She's approached learning differently, allowing the younger two more years to play before becoming serious about academics. She says, "The older two got a more formal, traditional education. The younger two are behind the place they might be in the public schools, but they'll catch up."

Many travelers comment on their becoming more relaxed in homeschooling as they develop more confidence. Sometimes this relaxing is directly related to their methodology, other times it is more about letting go of worry. They gain confidence as they journey along the road of homeschooling. By learning from the first, parents learn which things are important to foster early on and which things are better left for later. They know that because each child is unique, learning opportunities will present themselves at different times and in different ways, but that they will come.

QUICK & EASY

Small children love water play. Gretchen puts her toddler in a high chair with water and toys. Others say they keep all their plastic kitchenware in low cupboards so toddlers can get to it and play with it freely.

Laura says, "I'm a lot less likely to force something on the younger children; rather I wait for an opportune time, knowing the right time will come."

Sally agrees. "I have relaxed a bit and don't get so uptight."

Parents become less concerned about the schools' timetables and more inclined to adapt to their children's. Some grow into unschooling.

"My poor firstborn didn't get the benefit of a mother and father committed to unschooling. We were much more nervous and concerned that he learn things on a particular timetable similar to the public school," says Suzi.

Some families move toward more organization and structure, especially as children get older and can handle it. Other families notice that structured learning isn't going to work for them. Larissa says, "The one advantage the younger ones did have is that I had already realized that highly structured learning was not the ideal for this household."

By necessity, children in large families learn patience. They also benefit from the vast amount of experience their parents gain by parenting a number of unique individuals.

Abby says, "The second through seventh children didn't have to wait for us to learn to be more relaxed, but so many children produce a time crunch! They have to learn that some things have to wait. The younger children have benefited from having more available to them in the way of group activities, though I should say this has its downside as well."

Abby points to what many homeschooling parents notice over time. While homeschooled children, in general, are a well-behaved bunch, en masse, parents notice negative peer pressure at work. As homeschooling grows and support groups become larger, there will inevitably be more group-induced behavior challenges facing homeschooling parents who want to participate often. At home, peer pressure from siblings is more positive.

Christy says, "My oldest child has been challenged by his younger sisters. He always wants to be the one knowing the most. As they have gotten older, this isn't always the case."

I've seen similar things in my home. My middle child began reading prolifically very early. It motivated my son years ago to work harder at his reading, and now as his sister works her way through Shakespeare, it motivates him further. The same child who loves to read, however, struggles with math. She moves along a little more consistently than she might, however, because she's not oblivious to the fact that her younger sister is coming along right behind her, tearing through math workbooks.

Mary Sue says, "It's easier for my second and third children because learning is more integrated into our lives. The second two learn from the first, the youngest learns a lot from the two oldest."

> "We tell our oldest that he is teaching us, that we don't know anything about raising a twelve-year-old. That helps him understand why it always seems easier for his younger brother and inevitably for his younger sister."
>
> —SABRINA

As confident as homeschooling parents are, they are equally humble about their own learning journeys. As with any vocation, it becomes easier to follow with experience.

"We tell our oldest that he is teaching us, that we don't know anything about raising a twelve-year-old," says Sabrina. She continues, "That helps him understand why it always seems easier for his younger brother and inevitably for his younger sister. Our third child is a piece of cake because we don't have to work hard to get her to do things; she sees her brothers doing them and has since birth so it is natural to her."

Homeschool families are each unique in the way they incorporate younger children into their learning environments and the way birth order seems to affect the parents' teaching. Yet there are many common experiences from which to glean wisdom. Younger children will learn from older ones, older ones will be motivated by younger ones, and parents will become more confident and less worrisome over time. Those are things you can count on as you begin your journey.

SIMPLE STARTING POINTS

✦ *Prepare younger children for the older child's homecoming.*

Talk with younger children a lot about how their older sibling will be coming home to school. Encourage an attitude of excitement and anticipation, but be honest about forthcoming changes.

✦ *Develop a game plan for occupying and including younger siblings.*

Gather appropriate learning materials and toys. Consider boxing some up in a special area to save for concentrated learning times.

✦ *Include younger siblings.*

Get the youngest siblings their own library cards if they don't already have them. Look for field trips suited for all ages.

✦ *Consider using a fun prepared curriculum or unit studies for youngest children.*

Try something like Five in a Row (see the Resources section) or activities mentioned in homeschooling magazines. Knowing that Mom or Dad will be setting aside time for them will thrill them as well as motivate them to learn.

✦ *Find out how observations about birth order can help you prepare.*

Talk to other homeschoolers about how they see birth order affecting their homeschooling. What have they learned over time?

RESOURCES

Books

Beechik, Ruth. *Teaching Preschoolers.* Accent Books, 1979.

Dobson, Linda. *Homeschooling: The Early Years.* Prima, 1999.

Gee, Robin. *Entertaining and Educating Your Preschool Child.* EDC Publishing, 1987.

Herzog, Joyce. *Including Very Young Children in Your Homeschool.* Joyce Herzog, 1998. Also, *Multilevel Teaching.* Simplified Learning Products, 800-745-8212.

Leman, Kevin. *The New Birth Order Book.* Fleming H. Revell, 1998.

Oberlander, June R. *Slow and Steady, Get Me Ready.* Bio Alpha, 1992.

Soyke, Jean. *Early Education at Home.* At Home Publications, 1991.

Wilson, Bradford. *First Child, Second Child: Your Birth Order Profile.* Kensington, 1983.

Periodicals

See Chapter 1's Resources section for information on the major homeschooling magazines. Here's what they offer that may be of interest to travelers with young children:

Growing Without Schooling: Because of its unschooling focus, this magazine consistently includes letters from homeschoolers and articles that present a realistic—and encouraging—picture of how the unschooling lifestyle naturally incorporates little ones.

Home Education Magazine: Becky Rupp's Good Stuff column is great for all ages, and frequently offers reviews of fun learning ideas and materials appropriate for a wide age range, including very young children.

Homeschooling Today: This magazine includes three regular columns geared toward younger children: Preschool Page, Preschool Unit Studies, and Lessons for Younger Children.

Practical Homeschooling: PHS offers extensive reviews of homeschooling products, both old and new, many of which are geared toward younger children.

The Teaching Home: Those from large families and those with little children underfoot will find ideas and support from articles geared toward them (especially the large section where readers write in).

Unit Studies Geared Toward Younger Travelers

Five in a Row, by Jane Lambert. This series of unit studies is based on reading a picture book to a young child (between the ages of four and eight), five days in a row, then doing activities across the curriculum using the book as the base. Phone 816-331-5769, or check out http://www.fiveinarow.com.

14

KEEPING HOUSE (AND SANITY) WHILE YOU HOMESCHOOL

In This Chapter

- ✦ Housework: a family affair
- ✦ Finding time with your spouse
- ✦ Simple starting points
- ✦ Resources

OUT OF THE thousands of homeschoolers I've met over the years, hundreds of whom I've visited at home, five or six keep impeccably clean houses. It's not that housework doesn't matter to homeschoolers or that homeschooling appeals to those who find housework unimportant. Rather, having children home all day every day learning in a creative environment is not conducive to round-the-clock spic and span floors and ever-dusted furniture. Respondents are evenly split between thinking it's more difficult to keep house with middle years children home all day and believing housekeeping is easier with more hands to pitch in. Whichever the case, almost every homeschooler freely admits to struggling in this area.

The few homeschoolers I know who have spotless houses do so because they make cleaning a priority, not over spending time with their children, but over things such as hobbies, cooking elaborate meals, gardening, and so on.

Out of the thousands of homeschoolers I've met over the years, hundreds of whom I've visited at home, five or six keep impeccably clean houses.

While most homeschoolers may not have homes fit for *House Beautiful,* they strive to maintain a certain level of neatness, primarily because a neat home is a more efficient one. It's frustrating for anyone to have to stop a project midway because no one can find the roll of tape or bottle of glue. It's hard enough to get out the door to make a field trip on time without having to launch a search mission to locate the hairbrush and ponytail holders.

Healthy eating is generally important to homeschoolers, as are making holidays special and entertaining guests. It takes time to plan and prepare meals, even more for holidays or when guests are invited. So, as in everything else, homeschoolers make choices. They find ways to maintain a semblance of order that meets their needs without taking away too much precious time from learning together with their children. While it may be an ongoing challenge for most homeschoolers, it's one they meet with flexibility and creativity.

HOUSEWORK: A FAMILY AFFAIR

ALL BUT ONE respondent say their children help with housework, and cite the importance of teaching responsibility as well as needing their help to keep the household running. Housework is a tag team effort for most families. Rather than structured lists, most families say they all pitch in as the need arises. Eighteen respondents, however, say they prefer a less hit-and-miss method, and use charts to delineate children's duties and keep the home running smoothly.

> All but one respondent say their children help with housework, and cite the importance of teaching responsibility as well as needing their help to keep the household running.

By their middle years, homeschooled children take care of their own spaces and things related to their activities. They clean their own rooms, keep their learning areas tidy, and pack their own equipment and snacks for outside activities. Homeschooled children by age thirteen are most often capable of running their households, a trait remarked on by many respondents and certainly something I see in my own home. No longer does the house fall apart when I'm sick or have a deadline to meet. Rather, the oldest child steps in and, with the help of the younger two, divides and conquers household chores. I don't think my children are unusual; I think they're typical of middle years homeschoolers. The rest of us do the same when one of the three is meeting special demands, such as sports tournament weekends or extra dance rehearsals.

It's one thing to hang a sweet plaque on the wall reminding you of the importance of rocking babies, reading to young children, or listening to older ones; it's quite another to balance teaching algebra and editing science reports with the day-to-day demands of housekeeping. And while all the precious sentiments might make you feel better, they don't keep underwear clean or bathrooms germ-free. And they don't help you find that roll of tape when you need it.

Homeschooling will change your life for the better—but make no mistake about it, it will change your life a lot. The house will get messier quicker with a number of children home all day, but with some planning and help, you can manage to keep the house neat enough, provide reasonably nutritious meals, and still give your children lots of free rein to explore the world around them. Check out the various sidebars to see how other homeschooling families schedule their time.

Dust or Read?

To maintain a reasonably tidy home takes forming good habits that fit your homeschooling lifestyle. Assigning the late-sleeping child the chore of unloading the dishwasher doesn't make sense if you run your dishwasher overnight and need it unloaded first thing in the morning. The majority of travelers say they do most chores right after breakfast, before getting to schoolwork. Vacuuming, mopping, dusting, laundry, and pet care are all, like dishes, things that need to be addressed the most frequently.

HOW WE DID IT

4–5 A.M.: I get up. I am able to get work completed for my bookselling business, as well as have a little solitude.

8 A.M.: I wake up the kids. Two or three mornings a week, we have a Mom-cooked breakfast, the other mornings it's cold cereal.

9 A.M. to around noon: Academic work, setting goals, planning schedules. The general plan is about an hour and a half being together, a daily meditation and prayer to start the day, a bit of reading aloud and then science. After that, I have some one-on-one time with each child, to review the independent work they are doing and help with any problems.

Afternoons: We usually have some outside lesson or activity scheduled (piano, dance, homeschooling group activities). Other than that, the kids are pretty much responsible for managing their own time in the afternoons and evenings. They use it to get together with friends, watch television or play video games, read, work on assignments, crafts, and so on.

One day a week I work in the used book shop I helped start, and the kids come with me. They bring work to do, and there's a VCR there, so I try to find

Dishes

There's no way around the fact that dishes need to be washed every single day. A number of travelers use paper products for lunch, claiming it saves them valuable cleanup time in the middle of already busy days.

For those whose ecological standards won't allow them to use paper products daily, simple lunches can help with cleanup. We run the dishwasher overnight, and a child unloads it first thing each morning. If we limit lunches to simple sandwiches and fruit, only

videos that relate to their studies. Usually, my son and I spend time having history or civics discussions. He has a lot of questions in his curriculum to think about and answer, and our talks help him get his thoughts organized.

Evenings: My son always works on his math with his dad. My daughter usually practices dance.

8–9 P.M.: I'm exhausted and often head to bed, letting my husband (a night owl) have the pleasure of the children's company.

The children also structure their own time on weekends. We usually have a Sunday afternoon one-on-one time together when they turn in their work and we plan the next week's assignments and activities.

We continue academic work year round. We tend to get a lot accomplished and be most highly structured in the late spring through fall, and have a very relaxed time through the Christmas season and winter.

—GLORIA, MOTHER OF FOUR
WITH TWO STILL AT HOME.

luncheon plates and glasses are needed. A quick rinse and then loading into the dishwasher takes care of the plates. My children are supposed to save glasses to use throughout the day, rinsing as needed. They somehow have a hard time remembering this maxim (as evidenced by the number of glasses on the top rack of our dishwasher every evening), but it's a maxim just the same. Having them responsible for loading their own dirty dishes serves as a reminder.

Most homeschoolers rotate meal cleanup. Others have all the children responsible for their own dinnerware and rotate cleaning the pots and pans only. However you decide to divide kitchen cleanup, teach those who do dishes to clear and wipe down counters and table tops as well. Then an occasional deep cleaning of the refrigerator, stove top, oven, and appliances is all that is necessary to add to your weekly or monthly chore list.

Picking Up

Keeping the floor clear of toys is a time-consuming feat. Children of all ages can be taught to stop a few times a day for pickup time. Fifteen to twenty minutes of group effort spent before lunch, afternoon activities, and bedtime can keep most of the day's mess cleared off the floor and table tops. The number one enemy of keeping the house picked up is the lack of storage space. Try to avoid purchasing items before you have cleared out others, either by sending them off to Goodwill, putting them away for a garage sale, or boxing them for permanent storage. Lots of shelves and containers (baskets, Rubbermaid tubs, and so on) are necessities for homeschooling families—not luxuries.

Pushing Vacuums, Mops, and Brooms

Once the pickup is done, it's amazing to see just how much dust, dog hair, and sticky stuff waits underneath. Some travelers find it easier to mop up frequently, little spaces at a time, or on an as-needed basis only. Others say that regularly scheduled cleaning keeps carpets, hardwoods, and tile floors in tip-top shape and prevents gradual grimy buildup.

More than any other area, floors require good cleaning tools to stay at their best. In my family, we tend to avoid using the broom, preferring the special attachment on our vacuum to go over the noncarpeted areas of our house. We vacuum the carpeted areas the same days. Others prefer frequent sweepings of their hardwood and kitchen floors. Regardless, if you have pets, you may want to schedule this activity each day. Any middle years child can be taught to take care of the floors. Mopping needs to be done less often, perhaps once a week (or, as many travelers note, when company is coming). Our family is split—half of us prefer the run-of-the-mill O-Cedar sponge mop; the other half like a Sh-Mop we bought from the Clean Team (see the Resources section). It comes with terry cloth covers we remove and replace after mopping each room of the house, tossing the dirtied one into the laundry as we go.

> Fifteen to twenty minutes of group effort spent before lunch, afternoon activities, and bedtime can keep most of the day's mess cleared off the floor and table tops.

Dusting

Like many homeschool families, we tend to notice the house needs to be dusted when we can barely read the computer screen or the youngest child begins to draw designs with her finger on the television. And like many homeschooling families, we find the same dust artist is the child who loves to wield the feather duster when the time comes. Young children usually like dusting, so let them do it! We use old cloth diapers and soft rags for most dusting, all of which are kept right next to the feather duster. We rarely apply any solution to our wood, for the oils in most products attract more dust quite rapidly.

WHAT HOMESCHOOLED CHILDREN CONTRIBUTE TO HOUSEHOLD CHORES

Listed in order of those things they do most.

- Sweep, vacuum
- Clean kitchen, wash dishes
- Laundry
- Take out garbage, recycling, compost
- Clean bathrooms
- Take care of pets
- Set and clear tables
- Yard work (raking, mowing, and so on)
- Cook
- Help grocery shop
- Pick up living areas
- Care for younger siblings
- Wash windows

Instead, we occasionally use the new squeezable Murphy's wood soap on woods and an all-purpose cleaner for appliances and electronic equipment.

Bathrooms

Bathrooms are best manhandled once a week by the unfortunate soul whose turn it is. The bathtub may pose a problem, but with the right tools even that shouldn't be too difficult for most middle years children to clean. Most bathrooms are too small for families to clean together, so rotating is the fairest way to approach the chore.

Young children usually like dusting, so let them do it!

The fewer cleansers you own, the easier bathroom duty is, so look for a good all-surface cleanser and some abrasive cleanser for the toilet and tub. Throw all loose items within sight into a plastic bucket (brushes, decorative items, and so on), then spray down everything else. Wipe away. We keep a bottle of Comet behind each toilet, along with a toilet brush. If company shows up unexpectedly, it's no big deal for one of us to dart off and give the toilet a quick, cleansing swish.

Pet Care

Depending on how many pets you have, divide the care for them one per person, or rotate days or weeks. If children bicker over whose turn it is to feed an animal, a chart on the refrigerator can be a great help. Other, more demanding animal-related tasks (daily walks, scooping up their messes in the yard, keeping baby animals from chewing up furniture) are best approached by a rotating system as children become old enough to handle the tasks.

Laundry

Many homeschoolers say they set aside a day or two per week for laundry, but I can't imagine a day without doing laundry. If you choose to do laundry less often, divide and conquer it by giving everyone a step in the laundry process: someone can sort and wash, someone can fold, and someone else can put away. In many homes, Mom handles the wash, but separates clean clothes into various colored baskets for children to fold and put away their own stuff.

Many homeschoolers say they set aside a day or two per week for laundry, but I can't imagine a day without doing laundry.

We handle laundry a load at a time, one each day. The washing machine gets started right after all morning showers are taken. The items washed the day earlier are placed in the dryer, anything that may have been left in the dryer is folded and put away. The children all put away their own clothes. I handle everything else. If we get backed up, then we have a folding party, but those are never quite as much fun as the name implies.

Preparing Meals or Slinging Hash?

When my family first began homeschooling, it seemed the entire homeschooling community was interested in natural foods. The other homeschoolers we knew baked their bread, ate very little (if any) meat, and shopped at small health food co-ops or through natural foods buying clubs. After several moves, we've gotten to know more of the homeschooling world—and we've met homeschool families who live on comfort food, those who are gourmet cooks, and those who rely on fish sticks, frozen pizza, and Ragu. We also

HOW WE DID IT

8 A.M.: I wake my daughter up. We eat breakfast and do a few chores.

9:30–10:15 A.M.: We work through Greenleaf history or world geography together.

10:15–10:45 A.M.: Begin writing or typing. Either I assign a lesson or she has a class on the Internet.

10:45–11:30 A.M.: Get dressed for chapel and algebra class at a local private school.

12–12:30 P.M.: Chapel.

12:35–1:35: Algebra.

1:40 P.M.: I pick her up from school.

2:00–2:20 P.M.: Lunch

2:30–3 P.M.: Finish any writing assignments and begin literature assignment, which she has the rest of the day to complete as she wants to.

—LEIGH, MOTHER OF TWO WITH ONE STILL HOME.

know many who frequent drive-through windows of fast food chains.

As with cleaning, if you want the best foods available prepared carefully and served in a relaxed atmosphere each evening, you are going to have to make meal planning and preparation a high priority. If you're happy to grab a few prepared items from the cupboard or freezer and toss them together for a quick snack, then you'll spend less time on meals but you'll most likely be giving up something in the way of nutrition and taste. Few homeschoolers are purists; in fact, most find a balance between cooking meals from scratch and using prepared items (or take-out) as well.

Decide the best approach for meal planning for your family. Do you want to cook once a month and pull from the freezer? Are whole foods and fresh vegetables important components of your diet? Realistically, do you have time to bake bread? Your shopping schedule and preparation time will be directly affected by your priorities.

Cooking Once a Month

Many travelers couldn't live without large freezers because they cook ahead in bulk, divvy up the portions, and draw from the food for a month at a time. If this idea appeals to you, read *Once-a-Month Cooking* to get started, then stock up on the cookware and plastic ware the book recommends. You'll do the bulk of your grocery shopping once a month, too, so bring lots of helpers. Preparation will be a snap, as you get on a schedule of knowing what to eat when and learning to rotate foods through your freezer. Adding a fresh salad or some fruit is all that will be needed for dinner.

Whole and Fresh Foods

If you're interested in eating natural foods or enjoy gourmet cooking, you're going to need to do more frequent planning and daily preparation. Working with dried beans, for example, requires you to think about the next day's meal the evening before, so you can put them on to soak. Keeping fresh fruits and vegetables in the house requires more frequent trips to the grocery store or farmer's market. These sorts of activities will become habit, but can be easily forgotten in a busy homeschooling environment. *Moosewood Restaurant Cooks at Home* is probably the best whole foods, gourmet cookbook available. The recipes take thirty minutes or less to prepare.

Convenience Foods and Take-Out

With the vast array of convenience foods on the market (including natural food name brands), it's no wonder people are consuming them in record numbers. Why spend hours watching over a pot of spaghetti sauce when you can purchase a large enough jar to feed an average family for less than $1 on sale? Or, better yet, why not drive through a fast-food Italian chain and get a large bucket of spaghetti with bread sticks enough to feed the same family for under $10, complete with dinnerware?

Convenience foods and take-out foods are not as expensive as they used to be, though most aren't as nutritious, economical, or tasty as homemade. But if you don't like to cook or don't have time for it, planning meals around convenience foods may be for you.

Fitting It In

You may want to set aside a specific time to plan meals and to shop. I tend to plan meals for two weeks at a time, because that's how often my husband gets paid. I pull out cookbooks, magazine clippings, and my personal recipe file and spread out on the large table, with pen, paper, calculator, sale flyers, and coupons. Though I shop mostly at one store, I can easily fit in others en route to activities, so I take note of particular sales. My meal planning takes approximately one to two hours. I write my grocery lists in the order I will come across those items in the store, cutting down my shopping time.

I never grocery shop during school hours, because we're too busy doing other things. Instead, unless a particular child wants to come along, I use the hours they spend at various activities to make my grocery store runs. I know homeschoolers who rise early in the morning and shop at twenty-four-hour groceries before most of the world is awake. Others shop with their children midday, others on weekends or evenings. There's no one best way for everyone, only the way that makes sense for you.

> I pull out cookbooks, magazine clippings, and my personal recipe file and spread out on the large table, with pen, paper, calculator, sale flyers, and coupons.

My family is probably typical of most homeschooling families in that we use a combination of foods and preparation ideas to survive. The key is to keep the big picture of the month's activities in the back of our minds, then plan more carefully week to week. Here are some basics that help make the household run smoothly.

✦ At the beginning of each month, I poll the children on any food items they'd particularly like. My ten-year-old plans and prepares a few meals each month. She chooses the menu and writes up separate grocery lists for me for each. When the week comes, I take her list and add it to my own. We keep all recipe books handy, and my personal recipe file is organized and easy to access.

✦ My children are primarily responsible for getting their own breakfast. More than any other meal, we rely on convenience type meals for our first meal of the day. I stock the refrigerator, freezer, and pantry with frozen waffles (sometimes leftover from homemade on the weekends), cereal, yogurt, breakfast bars, fruit, and juice. We keep lunches as simple as possible, and rotate preparing them.

✦ Regardless of which kind of food we plan to eat, we pull things out of the freezer and make the bulk of the meal in the mornings. Everyone has more energy then than later in the day.

✦ I use the crock pot until we can't stand the sight of one more stew, soup, or sauce.

✦ Whenever I use the crock pot or other large cooking pot, I fill it to the brim, then freeze the leftovers. I sometimes do the same with baked items, such as cooking two chickens at once or doubling cookie or muffin recipes.

✦ When deadlines aren't looming and children's activities aren't at their height, we bake enough bread on Tuesday mornings to last the week.

✦ I have noticed, over the years, that we use certain items over and over, such as garlic, lemons, butter, olive oil, and taco seasoning. Also, there are certain convenience items I like to have on hand, such as jarred spaghetti sauce and flour tortillas. Whatever your necessary items, keep them on a permanent grocery list and be sure to keep them on hand. Keep a shopping list posted in the kitchen, and make it a rule that whoever opens a new box (jar, bag . . .) of something from the storage cabinet adds whatever-it-is to the list. That way, you never get to the bottom of the box while you're cooking, then discover you only have half as much as you need in the house.

Whatever your necessary items, keep them on a permanent grocery list and be sure to keep them on hand.

Yard Work and Home Maintenance

Yet another wonderful thing about homeschooling is that yard work and home maintenance do not have to be put off until weekends. Most travelers don't schedule yard work but address it as the need arises. The same is true of home maintenance. In the winter, the yard will need to be mowed less than in the spring or summer. (In the northern states, you get the winter off! But there's snow or mud to deal with. . . .) After large storms, we pick up the yard upon rising in the morning and we paint when the house needs painting.

The two major household and yard chores that need to be addressed regularly, and thus are chores you may want to rotate among your children, are mowing the lawn and emptying garbage and recycling cans (and getting those items to the curb on appropriate days).

HOW WE DID IT

Average day? We're supposed to have average days? The most "average" days we have are co-op days. On those days I wake the boys up around 8 A.M., which is no small feat. We're at co-op by 9 A.M. and they take classes while I teach or assist.

Other days are less predictable. My oldest son usually gets up early to play a favorite online game. His spelling and typing have improved phenomenally since he's been doing this. When I kick him off the computer he'll choose one subject he wants to focus on that day and work on that.

My younger son wakes up later. He also tends to find one or two areas to zero in on each day. We learned he works better when he works more like college students—concentrating on one or two subjects a day instead of trying to fit little bits of each subject into every single day. The only exception is piano. Daily piano practice is a must.

—LARISSA

Paper Everywhere!

Entire books have been written on controlling the paperwork required in running a household, and the work increases with each child you educate at home. There are a number of methods, from specially designed notebooks or expensive planners to elaborate filing systems. If you don't already have a filing cabinet, you may want to purchase one. You don't need to spend a fortune—begin with the plastic milk crate type files that come with their own accessories. Then, take stock of your needs and figure out a plan to conquer, or at least somewhat control, the paper in your home. A good calendar system is a must for any family, so decide whether a notebook style or large block calendar works best for you and get into the habit of writing down everything.

Household Bills and Correspondence

Do you pay bills once a month or more often? Mark those days on your calendar and keep bills filed. When the time comes, pull out the bills and write the checks. If you want to keep receipts, create a file specifically for those.

Keeping on top of other correspondence is a more elusive task. Personal letters that need to be answered, catalogs, informational letters regarding the children's activities, and more, all add up to one big mess for most homeschooling parents. If you're at a complete loss on how to deal with all this paper, read one of the books written on the subject. Otherwise, create files with names you'll remember, and file papers as they come in. Nothing can set a home on edge quicker than having an important paper or form buried in that one area where everything gets dumped. A few minutes each day, as mail is opened, is all it takes to keep household bills and correspondence organized, once you find the system that works for you. Look for quiet moments to answer letters and fill out forms, or schedule a time for doing so.

Controlling Your Child's Creations

The best way to control middle years travelers' work—that is, to make sure you save what needs saving and organize it in a way that will let you demonstrate the effectiveness of your homeschool when you need to do so—is to encourage the children to figure out how to do it themselves. It will teach them responsibility and lighten your load. Some children need more help with this than others. Some won't be ready at all. If children can find a method that works for them (various clearly labeled notebooks or larger notebooks with separate files are wonderful!), they can keep up with their work throughout the year, then you can help file and store that which needs to be kept at year's end. Refer to the "Record Keeping" section in Chapter 4 for more ideas.

Holidays

Regardless of whether or not they school year-round, many homeschooling families take large chunks of time off from their regular school routine during various holiday seasons. Rather than accept the status quo stress that comes with adding holiday planning, many travelers shut down school from Thanksgiving to New Years so they can enjoy the shopping, gift wrapping, card sending, extra parties, and baking that come with the season.

> Entertaining does not have to be elaborate nor should it be about impressing others. It's not a race. It's an act of friendship, of hospitality.

Non-Christian homeschoolers appreciate being able to recognize their feasts, festivals, and special remembrances as well and schedule them naturally into their school-year calendars. This is something often not easy to do with public school systems geared to the Christian holidays and celebrations.

Use the freedom of your homeschooling life to build upon the traditions you started with the birth of your child. In my family, we have made Ukrainian eggs at Easter, rolled candles for Valentine's Day, come up with every imaginable combination of red, white, and blue desserts for July 4, and so on. We've incorporated holidays from other cultures on occasion as a window into that nation and people. You may think you're taking school off during holidays, but you'll more likely find learning all around you. If you're uneasy releasing yourself completely from all conventional schoolwork for large periods of time, then use holiday times to create mini unit studies and direct children's learning accordingly.

Entertaining

Not every homeschooling family enjoys throwing big parties. Mine doesn't. But we do enjoy inviting individual families or small groups over for meals and encouraging and stimulating conversation. We also want our children's friends to feel welcome here.

Entertaining does not have to be elaborate nor should it be about impressing others. It's not a race. It's an act of friendship, of hospitality. Children who grow up in a home that is consistently open to others learn to entertain, but they also learn to be real friends to real people. Make it a habit to have people over for meals, cook-outs, or even a dessert after other social affairs. Don't feel as if you have to make everything from scratch—bakery bread is easy to come by (most groceries have great bakeries now), and prewashed and torn lettuce goes a long way to cutting down salad preparation time.

FINDING TIME WITH YOUR SPOUSE

AS CHILDREN REACH their middle years, finding time with your spouse should come more easily than when the children were little and babysitters were a must. Most twelve- and thirteen-year-old homeschoolers are perfectly capable of babysitting younger siblings for short periods of time, though a few states may have laws mandating higher minimum ages. Check. Even so, middle years children are busy with their own interests and activities, leaving you time on occasion. If need be, you can swap sleepovers with others.

A number of homeschoolers joke about going out on dates with their husbands at Wal-Mart. For my husband and me, it's more often the grocery stores. Homeschoolers come up with other ways to catch up and keep the relationship with their spouse alive too, such as putting on a kid-friendly movie and popping popcorn for the children in one room, and going to another room to talk. Some travelers give a high priority to finding regular time together with their spouses, believing that strong families are built on strong marriages.

They schedule regular date nights and have regular babysitters on call. Others feel equally strongly that families are about families and that children will grow and be gone all too soon, so they rarely seek out special activities to do with their spouse alone.

It's important to discuss this issue with your spouse. Come to an agreement on how much of a priority you give to spending time away from the children, then set realistic goals for doing so. Do what's right for you and your spouse and your children—a good lesson to carry with you in all your homeschooling decisions.

SIMPLE STARTING POINTS

✦ *Evaluate your standards.*

How clean is your house now? How important is it to you to maintain similar standards when you bring your children home? Think about what you can live with and what you can't.

✦ *Make a master plan.*

Look through the various chores and decide how often you'd like to see each one done. Decide if you prefer approaching chores on an as-needed basis and enlisting help as it comes up or if you'd rather have a more structured system in place. Look through the Resources section for help on organization and cleaning tips.

✦ *What, when, and how do you eat?*

Assess the importance you give to the types of food you want to prepare and eat, and the kinds of mealtimes you want to have. Schedule time for planning, shopping, and preparation.

✦ *File away!*

If you don't have one already, come up with a reasonable filing system to handle the paperwork in your house. Factor in the need for more space and time to accommodate children's schoolwork.

- *Don't forget your spouse!*

Decide how you are going to find time together in the midst of a homeschooling lifestyle.

RESOURCES

Books

Aslett, Don. *Clutter's Last Stand.* Writer's Digest Books, 1984. Also *The Cleaning Encyclopedia, Make Your Home Do the Housework,* and others.

Bond, Jill. *Dinner's in the Freezer.* Holly Hall, 1996.

Campbell, Jeff. *Talking Dirt: America's Speed Cleaning Expert Answers the 157 Most Asked Cleaning Questions.* DTP, 1997.

Dadd, Debra Lynn. *Nontoxic, Natural, and Earthwise.* Tarcher, 1984.

Eisenberg, Ronnie. *Organize Your Family!* Hyperion, 1993.

Griffith, Elise. *Busy Mom's Low Fat Cookbook.* Prima, 1997.

Harris, Gregg. *The Home School Organizer.* Noble, 1995.

Haughton, Natalie. *Best Slow Cooker Cookbook Ever.* HarperCollins, 1995.

Moosewood Collective. *Moosewood Restaurant Cooks at Home.* Fireside, 1994.

Schofield, Deniece. *Confessions of an Organized Homemaker.* Betterway, 1994.

Wilson, Marilyn S. *Once-a-Month Cooking.* Focus on the Family, 1986.

Catalogs

The Baker's Catalog, 800-827-6836, http://www.kingarthurflour.com.

Jeff Campbell's The Clean Team, 800-717-2532, http://www.thecleanteam.com.

The Urban Homemaker, 303-750-7230.

Organizational Tools

See homeschool catalogs and vendors for a variety of record keeping tools, such as *Homeschooler's Journal, Homeschooler's High School Journal,* and *Relaxed Record Keeping.*

Steward, Jennifer and Harris, Gregg. *Choreganizers: The Visual Way to Organize Household Chores.* Noble Books, 1995.

15

PART-TIME HOMESCHOOLING: COMPLEMENTING PUBLIC AND PRIVATE SCHOOLING

In This Chapter

- You don't have much time— where do you most want to go?
- Teachers turning home see the difference
- Simple starting points
- Resources

An interesting shift has taken place in the years I've been homeschooling. I once had to find polite ways to refuse the help of well-meaning friends with children in schools who would persistently offer a peek at their children's textbooks and other curriculum. I heard a lot about how much those kids were learning, as if to suggest I might want to be sure I was keeping up. Now, friends corner me at the ballet studio or swimming pool to ask about materials my children are using. Particularly as school years wind down, people approach me about homeschooling their children during the summer months. They see gaps in their children's education, want to fill them in, and know homeschoolers find useful and creative ways of teaching.

Each year, an increasing number of parents of schoolchildren attend homeschooling conferences and curriculum fairs. They know they will find sound educational tips and innovative learning materials to supplement their children's schooling.

If you find yourself in this position—if, for whatever reason, homeschooling full time isn't a realistic goal for you but you see gaps in your child's learning—then read on. Find some useful tools and ideas to help smooth out the rough edges of your child's schooling. While politicos and administrators argue over whose job it is to educate your children and how to fix the schools, you have little choice but to take some sort of action—what else can you do? Your children's education is your responsibility no matter where they attend school. The buck stops with you. You're perfectly capable of supplementing your children's education; in fact, you're most likely spending hours a week helping with homework already! Think of part-time homeschooling as a more interesting offshoot of doing just that, and enjoy.

YOU DON'T HAVE MUCH TIME—WHERE DO YOU MOST WANT TO GO?

YOU MUST MAKE important decisions about how to use the time you have with your child in the few hours available. Part time is just that—part time. Don't set unrealistic goals for yourself or your child. Assess the areas you see as the weakest, or as being largely ignored by school. Think about your child's favorite subjects and interests. How might you capitalize on those for fun and rewarding enrichment activities that will help across the curriculum? What are your motives for part-time homeschooling? Does your child need specific remedial help to get up to speed or do you want to spark a love for learning that isn't being nurtured by the schools? Are you part-time homeschooling more for remediation, acceleration, or enrichment?

Take your time to think through what you hope to accomplish, then ascertain how you will fit in the extra work. The time won't magically appear. You may need to drop an outside activity or two from your schedule, or you may just have to limit television and computer game time.

Be sure to factor in "kid time"—frequent breaks where your child doesn't have to be producing something for anyone.

While middle years children are capable of handling more challenging and focused work, remember your child is in school already six or more hours a day. Middle years children still need time to be children. Be sure to factor in "kid time"—frequent breaks where your child doesn't have to be producing something for anyone. For one thing, you don't want to send the message that your child's self-worth depends on being able to perform tasks day after day. Second, we all need down time to renew ourselves and to nurture our creativity. Impromptu play or drawing are as productive and as important to your child's development as being able to multiply speedily. Set high goals and expectations—children will generally rise to the level expected of them—but don't burn your child out. Be sensitive to the nuances of childhood and strive to maintain a healthy balance as you decide which supplemental materials and activities to incorporate into your part-time homeschooling.

Supplementing Academics

It's a rare child who can progress through school achieving equally high marks for each subject area according to the preordained timetable. Just as babies who walk at anywhere from eight to fifteen months are considered within the normal range, all teachers know there are perfectly normal—and equally widespread—ranges for learning to read, write, and calculate. Yet their hands are tied. They must keep thirty students progressing at relatively similar rates to cover the dictated amount of material by year's end. Parents of most children find themselves frustrated with this reality. Gifted children are slowed down, slower learners are left behind, and the regular kids are virtually ignored because they don't have any special interest group lobbying for more attention to be given them. If you have a gifted child, you may want to use your time at home helping develop that extra potential. Slower learners will need patience and help repeating certain material so they don't continue to be frustrated by the methodical pace of classes moving on without them. You'll find their areas of giftedness. Capitalize on those, building confidence as well as skill. And average children, of course, aren't really average at all. They have particular interests and needs and desires. Part-time homeschooling will give you the chance to nurture their unique gifts, giving them a sense of greater accomplishment than they might otherwise get from school.

Obviously, one-on-one attention helps tremendously, so if you begin to feel overwhelmed by your choices, relax. While materials and curriculum can make a difference, they're not everything. At the same time, homeschooling is so successful, in part, because parents tend to treat all children as gifted. That is, just as gifted and talented children often get the best and most interesting learning materials and activities in school, so do almost all children who are schooled at home. Parents don't skimp. They want to spark love for learning as well as teach material, the latter working much better with the former helping it along.

> The best thing a struggling reader can do is to read more. . . . The same rule of thumb applies to writing: the more a struggling writer writes, the better the writing will become.

Aside from seeking advice from homeschoolers, if your child's school has a respected gifted program ask the gifted teachers at school for the kinds of activities they do and materials they use. Take notes. Most schools will allow you to check books out for periods of time, and teachers can make specific recommendations for what they've seen work and what will help your child the most with regular and enriched schoolwork.

The next sections take a look at various subject areas and how you might best approach part-time homeschooling with them. Also, be sure to go through the Resources section for commentary on materials you might find useful.

Language Arts

The best thing a struggling reader can do is to read more. Read through books with your child, taking turns reading aloud every other page. Stop to discuss difficult parts to be sure your child understands the material. Consider using books on tape and having your child read along. If your child doesn't understand how to identify the plot, climax, main characters, and themes of books, print out a simple worksheet on the computer and fill it in together the first few times, then encourage your child to identify the parts of a story independently and discuss it with you.

The same rule of thumb applies to writing: the more a struggling writer writes, the better the writing becomes. Have children write as often as possible. Buy them a cloth-covered journal and encourage them to record their activities, thoughts, daily schedules, or anything else they think about. If your child writes well in some areas but not others, concentrate on the genre that needs work. Some children, for example, are great creative writers but can't seem to convey factual information. Other children shine when writing book reports but freeze up when they try to incorporate dialog into fanciful stories.

Math

Assess whether your child needs more drill work or a better grasp of mathematical concepts. It's easier to be creative when working to build conceptual understanding than it is with adding drill work to a child's schedule. However, if it's drill work that's needed, then by all means, add it.

Choose from flash cards, timed drill sheets, or math games for drill work. Children can improve their speed working with mathematical equations by spending fifteen to thirty minutes a day on them. Concepts can be built by incorporating math manipulatives, cooking, building, and games into your child's time out of school. Much of what you do every day can be turned into mathematical learning adventures, rather than having to carve out extra time from other areas. See "Consumer and Practical Mathematics" in Chapter 6 for more ideas on how to use everyday activities to build math concepts.

A friend of mine checked out her daughter's math book from school, wanting to ensure readiness for advanced middle school math the following year. The math book is creative, colorful, and complete. The mother is working with her daughter on the first page of each two-page spread, taking time to explain and go through the problems. The daughter enjoys the time and attention. Then, on the second page, the child works every other problem (choosing odds or evens), limiting the time she spends on the drudgery while at the same time giving her plenty of practice. The mother offers rewards for work completed, adding to the pot of learning joy.

Science

Most elementary and middle school science classes aren't especially challenging, and the methodical and superficial treatment of the subject matter condescends to children. Look at the kinds of questions your child misses and at the shortcomings of the science fair projects your child builds. When you identify the areas of weakness, look at teacher's supply stores, homeschool vendors, or homeschooling catalogs (via mail or on the Web) for helpful materials. Putting together a model of a skeleton or playing Aristoplay's Some Body game drives home the names of various body parts and how the body works. Nature hikes with field guides and gardening expose children to botany. Check into computer software, Internet sites, and science shows (PBS, Discovery, and other stations are great resources) for more help. Be sure to read the various recommendations on science experiments and resources in Chapter 6 for ideas.

History, Social Studies, and Geography

While many children need help with understanding the world around them, more often, parents see these subjects as being poorly taught or taught from skewed perspectives. If your children are taught historical facts or viewpoints that you believe contradict your own, you can remediate best throughout the course of the year by keeping up with what your child is being taught and discussing it at home, providing materials that support your point of view.

To nurture a love of history, incorporate historical fiction and lots of biographies into your children's supplemental reading lists. Play history games, visit living history farms and other history-related museums and parks, and attend reenactments. Watch suitable documentaries, and visit appropriate Web sites. Read Chapter 7 for more ideas, but it probably won't take much to make your children enjoy history at home. Their newfound enjoyment of the subject will probably spill over into their schoolwork.

For social studies, take an interest in civic activities and local events. Participate more fully in the area around you. Many events will lend themselves to certain reading materials or projects. Be flexible and use your library's staff for help. Again, use television and the Internet as much as possible. Children can gain vast amounts of knowledge from the screen without feeling like they're doing more school.

If memorization of facts is a problem, whether historically significant dates, names of the branches of government, or nations of the world, look for good educational board or card games that include this sort of information. Put

QUICK & EASY

Simple flash cards are easy to make. Have children make them—they'll retain more of the information. For one example, they can write the name of a state on one side and the name of the state capital on the other. Allow children to decorate the state side with the state flag, flower, bird, and an outline of the state.

up a timeline and begin to track certain dates in history. Games don't have to be elaborate to be fun. Laminate a world map and spread it out on the floor. Have one person call out a place, then the others hurry to locate it first.

Foreign Language and the Arts

Chances are, middle years children aren't learning a foreign language in school yet. If it's important to you that yours do so, or if they need help, check out the "Languages" section in Chapter 8's Resources section for a number of good programs, and jump in! It may be more fun if the whole family commits to learning the language together. Like Esther, promise a meal out at a fancy international restaurant for finishing sections or chapters. If the restaurant is authentic, the food and atmosphere will spur more discussion and research, and that will increase learning.

Middle years children hardly get any arts teaching at all anymore, as school funding for those subjects decreases. Again, refer to Chapter 8's sidebars and Resources section for ideas for good materials and how to obtain them. Set up an arts and crafts area in your house—a place the child can go anytime and easily access materials. As with foreign languages, if others in the family want to join in, the learning will be more fun. I try to draw with my children as often as possible. It helps them to see how inept I am, for one thing, but they also think it's just plain fun to have Mom sitting and working with them. For dance, theater, and music, enlist outside help if you aren't capable of teaching the art forms yourself. Attend arts events as much as possible. Expose your children to a wide variety of styles and genres. The memories will be as great as the learning.

Extra Time for Your Child's Interests

Your time is limited—there are only so many hours in a day. Children learn intangibles and often experience their greatest successes (confidence builders) from outside activities. But adding any extracurricular activities to school days and part-time homeschooling will be impossible unless you somehow combine interests or use them as springboards for academics. You will need to take advantage of learning opportunities in everyday activities all around you. For any intense interest, look for a unit study (or design a simple one on your own) to use as your base, especially if your child's weak area is language arts, science, history, social studies, or geography. Use the Internet to explore areas of interest. Go through Chapters 5 through 8, and Chapter 10, for lots of fun learning ideas. Here are a few additional ideas to get you started thinking about how to use activities your children are already involved in or those that you could incorporate easily as catalysts for academic enrichment.

Baseball

Do you have a baseball fanatic? You can use this sport to improve academics across the board. Have children read biographies of baseball players or great historical fiction about the sport. Matt Christopher's books are easy to read and popular with middle years boys. The *Childhood of Famous Americans* series includes biographies on Lou Gehrig and Babe Ruth, and legendary Americana author Zane Grey has written two great titles on the sport as well (*The Shortstop* and *The Young Pitcher*).

Boys will likely be more enthusiastic about reading books tied to their interests, and with authors like Zane Grey on their reading list, you're exposing them to great literature. Most children enjoy reading *Sports Illustrated for Kids.* Have them send in drawings and letters to the editor, or vote and comment on many of the polls. There's nothing like getting published to encourage writing and art skills!

Baseball is a natural for improving math skills. Have children keep statistics at a game, figure

Adding any extracurricular activities to school days and part-time homeschooling will be impossible unless you somehow combine interests or use them as springboards for academics.

batting averages, or graph a particular athlete or team's stats throughout a year. The March/April 1999 issue of *Homeschooling Today* magazine includes a unit study on baseball titled "Baseball and Study Skills" you may find helpful (see "Magazines" in Chapter 1's Resources section for ordering information).

Any of these kinds of things can be done with most any sport, so if baseball isn't your child's interest, go with whatever interest is strongest.

Cooking

We all cook nearly every day. Include an interested child in helping you plan and prepare meals. Assign writing the grocery lists to the children, and be sure they know to go through the cupboards to eliminate items from the list you already have on hand. Have them help look for and clip coupons from the Sunday paper's inserts. When you shop, have the child calculate savings on those brands compared with other items to find the best buy. Give them a budget to stick to.

When cooking, improvisation is usually in order. If you don't have all the right ingredients, which make good substitutes? Why? Have children figure amounts needed for your family, and double or half recipes accordingly, honing math skills.

Assign a research paper for a particular food item. Have children find out where the food comes from, who produces it, and how much is harvested every year. What is the general history of the food? Where is it eaten the most (in which region or nation)? Children will be getting practice in writing and research, as well as history, geography, and social studies.

Butterfly Kit

Is your child interested in nature? Purchase a butterfly kit. Have the child set up the kit and keep a journal, along with artwork, on the changes in the cocoon. Buy or check out from the library a few field guides on moths and butterflies. Have the child graph which species live where, and then map their migration patterns, noting the numbers of species in various parts of the region, country, and world. The child can write a report on the findings.

Children will be using math skills, reading, writing and research, and learning about geography as they study butterflies.

It's becoming harder all the time to delineate who exactly qualifies as a homeschooler.

These ideas are a fraction of things you can do and the ways you can begin to think of how to include the world already around your children's busy life to enrich their academics. Don't be afraid to come up with your own ideas, and to take off on your own path. The library staff can help, or you can stay home and navigate the Internet to find ideas and appropriate learning materials.

Part Time Can Lead to Full Time

It's becoming harder all the time to delineate who exactly qualifies as a homeschooler. As you've seen in the pages of this book, parents homeschool for many different reasons, in many different ways, using many different materials and methods, and under many different circumstances. Many, many people were in a similar situation to you when they started. They helped their children enrich schoolwork or spent extra time filling in gaps, believing they couldn't afford to homeschool or didn't have whatever mystical connection it takes to do so. Some continue to help their children when they are out of school. These parents are often the most proactive in schools. As they become aware of the kinds of learning materials available and what makes up a good education, they encourage (or push) their school's teachers and administrators to new heights.

Many times, however, parents tire of fighting an uphill battle with the schools and realize through part-time homeschooling how capable they are. They figure out ways to afford homeschooling, and take the plunge to do so full time. If you can homeschool part time and see success, chances are, you'll only see more if you decide to join the ranks of full-time homeschoolers.

TEACHERS TURNING HOME SEE THE DIFFERENCE

SCHOOLTEACHERS ARE well represented among the ranks of homeschooling parents. Among those whose children attended school for a few years before coming home, many say they never suspected that school would be hard on their children, even though they saw school as being hard on most students. Also, because of their training, homeschooling didn't readily occur to them as an option. Others, however, say they decided to homeschool their children precisely because of what they saw in schools.

Thirteen of the respondents are former schoolteachers. None see any similarities between their experience in the classroom and their experience homeschooling their children. All see a plethora of differences. At home, travelers enjoy flexible schedules. Many homeschool through the hottest summer days, for example, and take longer breaks midyear or when the weather is pleasurable. Homeschoolers enjoy off-season travel rates too.

Hands-on learning, one-on-one tutoring, and less lecturing all help children learn better, and are all things former schoolteachers say are easy to implement at home, not so easy at school. They don't miss the burdensome administrative requirements (which take precious time away from actual teaching), constant interruptions, or discipline problems inherent at school. Here are some other important advantages of homeschooling former schoolteachers see:

- Homeschooled children are self-learners and take responsibility for what they learn as opposed to being spoon-fed information that has to be presented to them according to school's arbitrary timetable.

✦ Homeschooled children learn without peer competition and comparisons; instead, they learn because they are self-motivated. Self-esteem is preserved at home. Parents of schoolchildren have to work much harder, particularly during the middle years, to help their children maintain a sense of self-worth.

✦ Academics are not dumbed down or geared to the middle for homeschooled children, but are fitted to the capability and interests of the individual. Homeschooled children have time to complete projects in the way they want to complete them. They have time to read as much as they want.

✦ Homeschooled children interact with different age groups as their norm, a much better model of adult life than spending the majority of one's days with multitudes of people the same age.

✦ Homeschooled children attend far more field trips than those in school, with more time to explore and ask questions. No school buses wait to carry them away at a predesignated time.

This is not an exhaustive list. The advantages of homeschooling are too many to count. You'll begin to see some as you start your part-time journey. Don't be surprised if it whets your appetite for more.

SIMPLE STARTING POINTS

✦ *Set reasonable goals.*

Take stock of what you want to accomplish through part-time homeschooling. Drop other activities if necessary.

✦ *Try to hook up with other homeschoolers.*

Attend a homeschooling conference or curriculum fair. Ask questions and find appropriate learning materials that meet your standards and that your child will enjoy.

✦ *Schedule time to work with your child.*

Expect that your child will be tired, and not too keen on anything that looks like more schoolwork. Nonetheless, your company will mean a lot, especially if the work is for remedial purposes.

✦ *Use extracurricular interests to spur learning.*

Think about which everyday or extracurricular activities your child enjoys the most or excels in. Use these activities as a starting point for further learning.

✦ *Consider homeschooling full time.*

As you experience success with part-time homeschooling, go over your reasons for not doing it full time. Have they been relieved by your part-time success or are there some areas you still need to address? Be honest, but don't let fear keep you from homeschooling full time. You'll find lots of help and support.

RESOURCES

SPEND TIME going over the Resources sections in the previous chapters. They all include creative learning materials perfect for part-time homeschooling. Look for the following products at homeschooling fairs or in various homeschooling catalogs throughout the resource sections. This is not an exhaustive list, but only a reminder of some of the products you may find most helpful for your part-time journey.

Aristoplay: I can't think of a company that offers more in the way of learning games in every subject area imaginable. Combine learning time with family time and no one will miss the television! See "Other Learning Materials" in Chapter 7's Resources section for information on this company.

Calculadders and Wrap-Ups: These two products are great for math drill work. Calculadders are timed math drill sheets. Wrap-Ups are hand-held plastic math tools—each with a different number and function. To work with them, a child adds, subtracts, multiplies, and divides as needed for each problem, wrapping a string across to the correct solution. The pattern the wrapped string makes indicates whether the problems have been worked correctly.

Dover Publications: See Chapter 1's Resources section for information. Dover products are often carried by major bookstores, high-quality toy stores, and many homeschool vendors, as well as from their company directly. The kits, paper dolls, and coloring books are full of learning potential, yet children won't feel as if they are doing additional schoolwork.

Learning Language Arts Through Literature: Order the appropriate level for your children and watch them fall in love with reading and writing. Learning Language Arts Through Literature offers a full reading comprehension and writing curriculum around some of the best children's literature available. See "Spelling, Grammar, and Writing" in the "Learning Materials" section of Chapter 5's Resources section for information.

16

ENJOYING THE ROAD LESS TRAVELED

In This Chapter

- Not everyone will say bon voyage
- Challenges as learning experiences
- Aha! Who's teaching whom?
- A look back at the middle years

EVEN AS HOMESCHOOLING grows year by year, it continues to be the least traveled road of the educational journey. People aren't likely to ask you if it's legal to homeschool anymore, but you won't be immune from raised eyebrows, either. Don't let people sap you of your homeschooling joy. Come up with a plan. Collect short phrases to put people at ease while avoiding lengthy explanations. I often remind my children of an old sports maxim: The best defense is a good offense.

Learn to play good offense. Teach your children polite answers to nosy questions and practice them. For example, I have taught my children to answer those who ask, "Your Mom makes you homeschool? with, "She doesn't make me homeschool—she lets me!" You

Don't let people sap you of your homeschooling joy.

have nothing to apologize for. We all know homeschooling works regardless of your motives, philosophy, educational tools and methodology, and lifestyle.

Simple one-liners come in handy because they give you possession of the conversational ball and turn a discussion around in a matter of seconds. You'll soon figure out your own, and if you come up short, ask other homeschoolers for suggestions. Use the responses that feel right to you.

Casual acquaintances, however, aren't the only ones who will ask questions. Many of your friends and family will not be thrilled with your decision to homeschool. You may have some rough days where you question the decision yourself. Other homeschoolers have handled disapproving relatives and friends, faced inevitable challenges that come up at home, and learned unexpected things as they journeyed onward. So will you. Finally, gain encouragement from those who have raised children well beyond their middle years. Read their memoirs and tuck them away safely in your heart. Draw upon them if you begin to question yourself. Homeschooling should be among the most rewarding excursions you will ever take. Read on to find out how to keep it that way.

NOT EVERYONE WILL SAY BON VOYAGE

TWO-THIRDS OF THE respondents say what most homeschoolers know to be true: nearly always, the decision to homeschool your children will upset some of those closest to you. Almost always, a grandparent or two, an aunt or uncle, or a close friend will disapprove of your decision. Don't expect school personnel to applaud you when you withdraw your children, either. In most cases, it won't happen.

How much people outwardly question and criticize you is out of your control. How you decide to handle the questions and criticism isn't. The support of other homeschoolers in this one area will mean more than anywhere else. Listen to their experiences. Many homeschooled before it was legal, many others began before it was as accepted as it is today. The criticism was stronger, and homeschoolers had far fewer statistical studies to point to for proof that their decision was a legitimate one. They forged ahead on their journeys anyway because they knew it was right for their families. We can be grateful for their courage, and can learn from how they faced the critical eyes of others.

If you live far away from disapproving friends and relatives, you can more easily avoid confrontations over your educational choice. Aside from an occasional phone call or visit, you won't have to deal with the topic. However, if your critics live close and are persistent, you need more resolve and more support.

Well-meaning criticisms are sometimes nothing more than sincere concern born out of a lack of knowledge about homeschooling. If this is the case, count yourself among the fortunate, answer the questions politely, and expect to be respected, even if closely watched, as you move forward. Time is on your side, and so long as the skepticism is mostly quiet and subtle, you can live with it. Usually people who are genuinely interested and concerned can have their fears allayed with a good homeschooling book recommendation, a magazine or newspaper clipping, or a reference to a study on children educated at home.

Most often, critical fires burn themselves out after a few years of homeschooling. Grandparents, aunts, uncles, and friends see that your children are learning and are socially well adjusted and well mannered. Often, as they see your successes as well as those of your homeschooling friends, those who are initially critical become supporters of homeschooling over time.

Most often, critical fires burn themselves out after a few years of homeschooling.

Generally speaking, homeschoolers who report successfully dealing with the harshest and most persistent critics say they explain their decision once. Then they quit explaining and refuse to discuss it further. As much as you love your well-meaning friends and relatives, your decision to homeschool is none of their business, and their criticism is unfounded and draining. If it persists, it's not well meaning either. Some critics may never become proponents of homeschooling. Hopefully, their disapproval won't interfere with your relationship to a degree that causes discomfort for everyone. If nothing else, in time, most learn to keep their thoughts to themselves and at least respect you enough to acknowledge that it's your decision to make.

Judy says, "Basically, everyone even remotely related to us was (and still is) upset with our decision to homeschool. In the beginning we handled it by saying that we were just 'trying' it. Now we just don't discuss it."

Judy has been homeschooling for eight years. Her children's test scores are impressive, they participate in a number of outside activities, and are coveted friends of all who come in contact with them. If Judy's children don't prove the goodness of homeschooling to her family, it's not because of anything Judy or her husband have said or done. It truly is the family's blindness and insistence on holding on to their ignorant position. Not discussing it is really her only option.

Judy handled the conflict wisely from the start. Many travelers embark on the homeschooling journey not sure how long they might stay on the road. Even if you are sure you're homeschooling for the long haul, telling others you're "just trying it a year at a time" may be a good way to put their fears to rest. They will eventually see the years-at-a-time add up, but at least they only have to worry in one-year increments.

While it's most upsetting to have family and close friends who disapprove of your homeschooling venture, you can expect a number of more casual friends to express their disdain as well. These sorts of relationships carry less weight, and therefore may be dealt with on a different level. Choose between offering safe answers or completely truthful ones, depending on your comfort zone. For example, quite often, when people ask me about my children's socialization, I think it's safer to talk about all the activities they're involved in—it's the answer people want and it's truthful enough. However, the whole truth is that I think school socialization is a terrible thing and I'm thankful my children aren't exposed to it. I also think my children's socialization is a much better model on which to build healthy and kind adults. However, statements like these can become fighting words very easily. It simply isn't worth my time or emotional energy on most occasions to enter this sort of conversation. Nor does it ever really convince anyone.

There's an art to deciding how best to handle the questions, but it's an art you can, and will, learn.

Investing time in convincing people of the legitimacy of homeschooling is probably better spent, at least for a while, with family than it will ever be with casual acquaintances. With each conversation, assess the situation and decide how much you want to share with people. There's an art to deciding how best to handle the questions, but it's an art you can, and will, learn.

CHALLENGES AS LEARNING EXPERIENCES

YOU WILL FACE a number of challenges aside from dealing with unsupportive people. Some will be closer to home, right under your roof. Children need an adjustment period when they come home from school, and often the parents are quicker to want to jump in and set a schedule than the children are. Children may be used to following the instructions of the teacher, but that's quite different from seeing you in the teacher's role. Habits that come naturally to children who have always been homeschooled will take some time for those coming home from school to develop.

Many travelers bring their children home to school because of disturbing attitudes they see their children developing in school. Undoing those disturbing attitudes doesn't happen over night. And, hard as it is to admit, some children are more difficult than others. School tends to pigeonhole these kids and make them even more difficult over time. Again, undoing the patterns set, especially if the tendency was already there, takes time. Even for the best of kids, keeping them motivated and happy can sometimes challenge parents.

Lynn says, "Getting the kids to focus and learn things at the time I want them to can be a challenge. Many times I have to change my schedule to meet their needs. Once in a while, it's frustrating for me."

While many homeschoolers forge ahead unquestioningly, others reevaluate constantly. Parents who feel up to teaching an eight- to thirteen-year-old aren't always sure how or if they will be able to continue as their children get older.

Rebecca says, "It's a challenge for me to trust that homeschooling will be the right educational choice as my son gets older, assuming he still wants to homeschool."

Other homeschoolers share Rebecca's concerns. The future is full of unknowns for everyone. No one can predict what will happen, the kinds of interests children will develop, how their goals might shift, or what kinds of resources will be available in years to come. Although you can prepare for what's ahead the best way you know how, you can't foresee the future. Nonetheless, even though you can't be sure where the homeschooling road will lead, you can be sure that you will see rewards down the road. Enjoy homeschooling today.

It's unrealistic to think that various individuals in the same family are always going to be ready to do the same projects at the same time. Parents carry the authority to make final decisions, and the decisions they make and how they implement them can make a world of difference in the tone of the homeschooling environment. Lynn is generous and wise to take note of the children's needs and alter her schedule, but this isn't always possible. Sometimes schedules can't be altered or a number of other needy children put the parent in the position of making difficult choices. Children need to learn cooperation—a skill that will serve them well throughout life. At the same time, respecting their needs and teaching to their interests as much as possible makes for an environment more conducive to learning—and a more peaceful home. Only you know your individual children. You can seek advice and encouragement from other people, but thoughtful consideration about how best to achieve a sensible balance between parental authority and meeting children's needs (the two don't have to be mutually exclusive!) is in order.

Homeschooling is no guarantee of a slower lifestyle. Bringing home highly motivated children who are accustomed to participating in a wide variety of activities and the social stimulation of school can be a shock to the new homeschooling parent.

Doris says, "It's a challenge to keep up with all their activities and lessons, maintain a household, nurture a marriage, and find time for myself. I am trying to do a good job at making sure my children are experiencing all they need to experience."

Doris's sentiments are common, which is why homeschool burnout is a popular topic for homeschool workshops and magazine articles. Parents need to be sensible about how much is too much. We all want what's best for our children and we all want to say yes as much as possible, but if the homeschooling parent is burning out, or if the marriage is suffering as a result of one parent being overly involved with the children, then chances are the homeschooling won't continue for long anyway.

> Lynn is generous and wise to take note of the children's needs and alter her schedule, but this isn't always possible. Sometimes schedules can't be altered or a number of other needy children put you in the position of making difficult choices.

Deciding which things are worth your time is crucial. How many experiences do children need to be well rounded? Which experiences are worth investing time in?

Doris continues, "I believe there is a difference between what they really need and what some of their schooled friends are experiencing. I don't believe they have to experience dances at the age of twelve or thirteen, for example."

Dances may be easier to let go of than other activities. As much as homeschooling is about fulfilling the potential of children, mothers and fathers must have their basic needs met too, in order to be able to continue giving. Each person's capacity for giving is somewhat different. What drives one person to burnout is something another person perceives as a motivational hurdle to jump. Assess how best to balance the kind of lifestyle you want for your children with the kind of lifestyle you can handle for yourself.

While there are plenty of homeschoolers in plenty of support groups, there is no guarantee that your child will make homeschooled friends quickly. Some do, others take longer. It's great to find other children who homeschool, but it may not be enough to build friendships.

Linda says, "My greatest challenge has been finding like-minded friends for my children. Thanks to the Internet we have been able to do this. We drive longer distances than I like, but at least they all have one or two good friends now."

Helen agrees that finding like-minded friends is difficult. She says, "Homeschooling does not guarantee that kids have a lot in common, however, the girls became that much closer because they counted on each other as friends."

Many families see the same thing. As children grow and develop friendships outside the family, their bonds with siblings continue to strengthen because of the extra years they had to form them.

AHA! WHO'S TEACHING WHOM?

AS I'VE MENTIONED BEFORE, it's a well-kept secret that homeschooling parents learn as much as the children through the family's homeschooling journey. Parents meet their doubts and fears head on and use them as tools for personal growth. They sometimes face great financial difficulties, disapproving family members, or a host of other challenges, but they proceed, knowing homeschooling is right for their child. They become content with a simpler life, better at dealing with confrontation, and more able to find peace in all sorts of circumstances.

Homeschoolers learn to think outside the box, adjusting and readjusting their lifestyles. Homeschooling parents begin to see learning all around them, regardless of whether or not they take a freeform or highly structured approach to the school day. If children can learn to love to learn, then adults can as well, regardless of what kind of education their childhoods held. They enjoy filling in their own educational gaps, sometimes after years of not seeing themselves as bright or creative. One of my greatest pleasures is developing friendships with homeschooling parents who either didn't finish or barely got through high school. As they homeschool their own children, they add volumes to their own education and confidence levels. As they see their children learn according to their learning styles and motivated by their own interests, parents identify their own learning styles and find time to capitalize on their own interests, too. Children learn a lot from their parents, but homeschooling parents learn a lot from their children. The homeschooling learning journey is a family affair, with everyone playing important, and shifting, roles.

A LOOK BACK AT THE MIDDLE YEARS

AS THEIR CHILDREN head to college or the workforce, homeschooling parents remember the learning and are thankful that the children were able to have a wholesome, well-rounded, and excellent education. They remember other, more important things most of all, however.

"I'll always have fond memories of his interest in science experiments and magic tricks," says Renee. She continues, "It kept him busy exploring different books and finding new tricks. He even went to advanced magician's classes!"

Like many homeschoolers, Renee misses reading aloud to her son perhaps most of all. She says, "I miss all the reading I did for him during the early years. Those were wonderful hours."

She issues a warning to homeschooling parents of middle years children, "I'm amazed how anxious parents often are to get their kids reading on their own. They don't know how much they're missing! The time spent reading together is so precious. There's nothing else that provides the same bond and shared imaginative journeys."

Phyllis misses the reading aloud too. She says, "Of course, I wanted them to be leading their own educational pursuits and being responsible for their own life by now, but just to read aloud to them once more would be nice—that snuggling up to read a good book together is hard to beat."

Right up there with reading aloud, parents look back and remember the freedom to spend days according to their family's unique timetable and passions.

Missy says she remembers "the closeness we shared as a family, the freedom of movement to come and go as we pleased, the chances to change what didn't work and try new things, the immediateness of not letting disagreements go on forever, and having the opportunity to iron them out without waiting for a school bell to ring."

She continues, "I loved watching *I Love Lucy* reruns every morning, piling on the bed and laughing together, and reading good history books every day after lunch."

Do homeschooling parents look back with regrets? Who doesn't?

Do they see things they'd do differently if they had the chance over again? Of course. You will too. But none say they would choose not to homeschool their children. They are pleased with the academic and social successes their children accomplished through homeschooling. More important, they are pleased with the memories. I hear a lot of aging people say they wish they had spent more time with their children, less time on work or outside interests. We all would want more, no matter how much time we have had, because time with our children matters more than work or any outside interest.

Count on the fact that when you reach the end of your homeschooling journey, you will most likely have some regrets. Also count on the fact that you will know you spent precious years with your children, an important part of accepting the depths of your responsibility as a parent. Your homeschooling model will teach your children about balancing personal responsibility with freedom, a lesson absent from most young people's lives today.

No one ever looks back on life and says, "I wish I'd spent less time with my children." Everyone knows there's never enough time to spend with those they love, but homeschoolers also know they claimed the most time possible. The benefits, and the memories, will last a lifetime.

INDEX

D

E

F

G

H

M

T

Every Homeschooler's Complete Resource

Today, millions of parents just like you are discovering the unique rewards of homeschooling. *Homeschooling Almanac, 2000–2001* is your indispensable guide for homeschooling success. Inside, you'll discover a world of homeschooling resources, such as:

- **More than 900 educational products, ranging from books, software, and videos to games, crafts, and science kits**
- **A state-by-state breakdown of legal requirements, support groups, and homeschooling organizations and conferences**
- **Detailed descriptions of various homeschooling approaches**
- **And much more!**

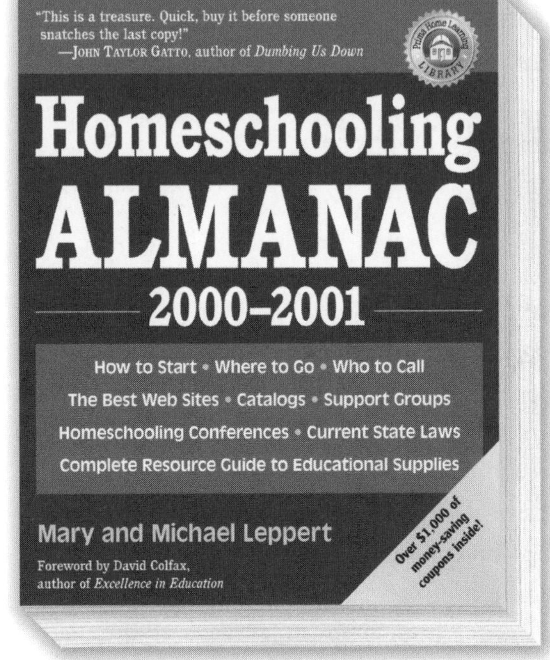

ISBN 0-7615-2014-7 / Paperback
688 pages / U.S. $24.95 / Can. $36.50

To order, call (800) 632-8676 or visit us online at www.primalifestyles.com